COLONIALISM TO
CABINET CRISIS

Published by
Kachere Series
P.O. Box 1037, Zomba, Malawi
Kachere@globemw.net
Kachere Books no. 44

ISBN: 978-99908-87-75-4

The Kachere Series is represented outside Africa by
African Books Collective, Oxford (orders@africanbookscollective.com)
Michigan State University Press, East Lansing, MI (msupress@msu.edu)

Cover Design: Josephine Kawejere
Graphic Design: Patrick Lichakala

Printed in Malawi by Assemblies of God Press, P.O. Box 5749, Limbe

Colonialism to Cabinet Crisis

A Political History of Malawi

Andrew C. Ross

Edited and with an Introduction
by T. Jack Thompson

Kachere Books no. 44

Kachere Series
Zomba
2009

Kachere Series
P.O. Box 1037, Zomba, Malawi
Kachere@globemw.net
www.kachereseries.org

This book is part of the Kachere Series, a range of books on religion, culture and society from Malawi. Related Kachere books:

Andrew. C. Ross, *Blantyre Mission and the Making of Modern Malawi* Kachere Monograph no. 1

Shepperson and Price, *Independent African: John Chilembwe and the Nyasaland Rising of 1915* Kachere Monograph no. 13

Robert I. Rotberg, *Hero of the Nation: Chipembere of Malawi: Autobography* Kachere Books no. 12

Colin Baker, *Chipembere: The Missing Years* Kachere Books no. 25

Patrick Makondesa, *The Church History of Providence Industrial Mission* Kachere Theses no. 5

Jack Thompson, *Ngoni, Xhosa and Scot* Kachere Books no 22

Klaus Fiedler, *The Making of a Maverick Missionary: Joseph Booth in Autralasia* Kachere Monograph no. 26

John McCracken, *Politics &Christianity in Malawi 1875-1940: The Impact of the Livingstonia Mission in the Northern Province* Kachere Monograph no. 8

John Lloyd Chipembere Lwanda, *Politics, Culture and Medicine in Malawi.* Kachere Theses no. 6

John Lloyd Chipembere Lwanda, *Music, Culture and Orature: Reading the Malawi Public Sphere 1949-2006* Kachere Books no. 35

T.S.E. Katsulukuta, *Kutchona: Buried in the Debris of Independence* Kachere Texts no. 30

James Tengatenga, *Church, State and Society in Malawi: The Anglican Case* Kachere Theses no. 12

Austin Cheyeka, *Church, State and Political Ethics in a Post-Colonial State: The Case of Zambia* Kachere Theses no. 13

Series Editors: Raymond Likupe, Klaus Fielder, P.A. Kalilombe, F.L. Chingota, J.C. Chakanza Martin Ott, Shareef Mohammad, Chimwemwe Katumbi François Nsenguyumva

Dedication

This book is dedicated firstly to the Patriots of Malawi who struggled against racism, colonial rule and dictatorship to achieve modern Malawi – especially J.F. Sangala, Dunduzu Chisiza and the 1964 Cabinet.

Secondly it is a tribute to the historians of Malawi, who have worked arduously that the true story of Malawi be recorded for future generations. In particular it recognises the scholarship and encouragement of Professor George Shepperson which has inspired so many others.

Finally, it is dedicated to Malawi and Scotland, the two most beautiful lands on Earth, and to their historic ideals of freedom and equality

Contents

Foreword

by Professor George Shepperson

The Rev Andrew C. Ross (or Andrew Christian Ross, to give him his characteristic full name) who died at the age of 77 on 26th July 2008 in Scotland's capital, Edinburgh, was an author well-known to readers of Kachere publications. In 1996 a slightly revised version of his Edinburgh University doctoral thesis was published as the first 'Kachere Monograph' under the title of *Blantyre Mission and the Making of Modern Malawi* with a deservedly laudatory preface by the Series Editors. It was a volume which made one look forward eagerly to further books on Malawi by Andrew Ross. Articles, indeed, on Central Africa were to be written by him and an impressive book on David Livingstone. But his long-projected, detailed and well-documented study of the course of Malawi's history, which culminated in the Cabinet Crisis of 1964 was never to be completed.

Thanks, however, to the skilful editorial work of another distinguished historian of Malawi, Dr T. Jack Thompson, who had been one of Andrew Ross's postgraduate students and, after his return from Malawi became a leading member of the Faculty of Divinity at Edinburgh University, the present book gives the reader not only the feeling of Andrew Ross's highly concerned thought on the creation of the initial and complicated problems of the independent African state of Malawi. It also demonstrates the ambition and range of his research. Furthermore, the present volume is a tribute to one who was a good servant both of Scotland, the land of his birth, and Malawi, the land of his heart, with which he and his devoted wife Joyce, had been associated from the time of their arrival in what was then called Nyasaland, just before the declaration of the State of Emergency in March 1959, as missionaries of the Blantyre Synod of the Church of Central Africa, Presbyterian.

It is given to few to be both makers of history and writers of it. Andrew Ross was one of those few. He made, often behind the scenes, a unique contribution to the achievement of Malawi's independence; and, in its early days, he was chairman of its Lands Tribunal and of its National Tenders Board. Andrew Ross supported the dissident Malawi ministers in the Cabinet Crisis of 1964; and for this, he and his family were forced out of Malawi in May 1965. He could not return to his beloved country until thirty years later.

Even more important, I believe, than Andrew Ross's political role in the making of Malawi was his dedicated pastoral work amongst Malawians at home and abroad. He will always be deeply respected because of his beneficent influence upon their lives. I had a rare glimpse of Andrew's pastoral work when, on a brief visit to Nyasaland in 1960, he took me into the Kanjedza detention centre where he was unofficial chaplain; and when, after his enforced return to Scotland, as an academic colleague and as a friend, I saw how unstintingly he gave of his time, energy and expertise in helping Malawians of many kinds.

The Rev Andrew Christian Ross drew deeply on his political and pastoral experience when he was researching for this present book. One can only regret that he was unable to write directly in it of the Cabinet Crisis of 1964 and thereby reveal his personal experience of its tendencies and tensions.

I cannot help comparing Andrew Ross with that great pro-African Scottish Christian missionary in what was called, in the late nineteenth and early twentieth centuries, British Central Africa: Rev David Clement Scott. I had promised to bequeath to Andrew my rare copy of Scott's *A Cyclopaedic Dictionary of the Mang'anja Language Spoken in British Central Africa* (Edinburgh, 1892) which bears on its flyleaf, in David Scott's firm handwriting, his dedication of this supremely scholarly volume to his sister: 'Margaret Scott from David – November 1892'. It was a book which Andrew Ross, with his admirable command of and interest in the vernacular, admired very much. Alas, that historic volume of mine will now have to find another resting place.

No biography of David Clement Scott exists, largely because so few of his papers have survived. The same cannot be said of Andrew Ross for his future biographer – and he most certainly deserves one. This present volume will surely be an invaluable tool for charting and evaluating the course of his life. For non-biographers I recommend it warmly, not only for its depiction and discussion of colonialism and independence in Malawi; but, above all, for the light which it throws on the life of a good scholar and a good man.

Peterborough,
December 2008

Acknowledgments

While my name appears as the editor of this posthumous publication of Andrew Ross, who died before he had completed the book, I could not have brought the work to completion without the help of many other people. First of all, I must pay tribute to Joyce Ross whose continuing passion and stimulation to get the book out has spurred me on over the last few months. In particular Joyce has been responsible for the time-line and the index, at the end of the book. Patrick Ross (Andrew's grandson) has helped reconcile different versions of chapters which Andrew left behind, and undertaken various electronic corrections. Our thanks are due too to Rachel Edwards, who read and commented on some of Andrew's early drafts. Scott Spurlock has been invaluable, both for his knowledge of computers, and for his willingness to undertake various pieces of last minute research – chasing down missing footnotes, scanning text into the computer, and preparing the bibliography.

Several of Andrew's friends and colleagues have helped me with particular pieces of information, and with general encouragement. Foremost amongst these has been Colin Cameron, who himself played an important part in the story which Andrew tells in the later chapters of the book. As both a defence lawyer for many of the early nationalist leaders, and the only European member of the first Malawi cabinet, Colin's contribution to the struggle for an independent Malawi was considerable, though not always sufficiently recognised. He has been of great help in recalling particular dates, names and incidents mentioned in the text, of which I was not quite sure. Anne Hepburn, a missionary colleague and friend of Andrew and Joyce Ross, has helped me in a similar way, and shown an on-going interest in the progress of the editing. As always, my wife Phyllis has supported and encouraged me in the task. John Lwanda, who has himself written extensively on Malawi's recent political history, has helped with several factual queries to which I needed answers.

If Professor George Shepperson had done nothing else but write the Foreword, I should have been very grateful to him. It is now fifty years since he and Thomas Price published their major study *Independent African: John Chilembwe and the Nyasaland Rising of 1915*, yet it remains a classic to which anyone interested in the period still inevitably and gratefully turns. He is held in very high regard among the historians of Malawi, and, in a real sense may be described as the father of modern Malawian historiography. But, in fact, he has done much more than merely write the Foreword. Following Andrew's death, he was the first person to read his typescript, and advise us on how to proceed. As the supervisor of Andrew's PhD thesis forty years ago, and subsequently as his colleague and friend at the University of Edinburgh, he was deeply concerned that the book should be completed. Though now in his late eighties, he remains deeply interested in Malawi and its people. Throughout the process of editing this volume, I have kept in close contact with him by phone and letter, and, just after Christmas 2008, I visited him at his home in Peterborough, for a discussion which began with Andrew's book, ranged over a wide area of Malawi history (and well beyond) and, though I have known him for many years, left me marvelling at the range of his knowledge and the depth of his memory. His contribution to this book has been much more than I think he himself realises.

Finally, I am particularly grateful for the help of Klaus Fiedler, and his colleagues at Kachere Series. Andrew was keen that this book, in particular, should be published in Malawi, to make it available at a reasonable price for Malawians to read. Though now in a new post at Mzuzu University, Klaus has undertaken to oversee personally the final stages of the publication of the book. Like many of those who have helped with this project, Klaus has done so out of a deep respect for Andrew as a historian and as a person.

T. Jack Thompson

(Editor)

Introduction

I first met Andrew Ross in January 1970 in Edinburgh, as my wife Phyllis and I were preparing to go to Malawi for the first time. Even then, he was talking of writing a book telling the story of the political development of Malawi, and, in particular of the events which occurred in the months immediately after independence, and which have come to be known as the Cabinet Crisis. A number of factors long delayed this enterprise. As a good historian Andrew realised that more time needed to pass before he could assess the most recent of these events more clearly. Then other interests began to come to the fore in his blossoming academic career at the University of Edinburgh. These led over the years, to a number of outstanding publications, as his fascination with the spread of what we now call World Christianity broadened to include other countries and other Christian traditions. Three books in particular stand out: *John Philip: Missions, Race and Politics in South Africa* – his study of the radical Scottish LMS missionary to the Cape in the early 19th century; *A Vision Betrayed: The Jesuits in Japan and China 1549-1742* – a much praised account of early Catholic missions to the Far East; and *David Livingstone: Mission and Empire* – the last book he published before his death, which managed to present a sympathetic yet fresh view of David Livingstone.

Though each of these books deals with a different period and a different area there is one theme running through them all; this is Andrew's deeply held concern for political and social justice, and his belief that, at its best, Christian mission had been (and ought to be) on the side of the people, working with them to struggle against all that de humanized them. This, however, was not just an intellectual idea for Andrew Ross, but a principle which motivated his own missionary career in Malawi between 1958 and 1965, and indeed his whole life subsequently. Like many other Scottish missionaries of the period, Andrew deeply opposed the Central African Federation, and was a strong supporter of the emerging Malawian nationalist movement. When, following the declaration of a State of Emergency in March 1959, many of the political leaders of the Nyasaland African Congress were detained, Andrew regularly visited those held at Kanjedza near Limbe – visits which helped to deepen both his friendship with them, and his commitment to their cause. Thus, when Orton Chirwa was released from detention later in 1959, and persuaded to become the temporary leader of the newly formed Malawi Congress Party, Andrew Ross was one of the first to join, becoming the proud holder of MCP card number six.

Andrew Ross' friendships with several of the nationalist leaders who were later to oppose Kamuzu Banda in the Cabinet Crisis – and, in particular, his close relationship with Masauko Chipembere – meant that he and his family were forced to leave Malawi in May 1965. Though in many respects this was a personal tragedy for Andrew, in one particular way it had a positive outcome, for it enabled him to embark on an academic career at Edinburgh University as a church historian. In particular, it enabled him to concentrate on completing his PhD thesis looking at the historical development of the Blantyre Mission, and, in particular, the work of David Clement Scott (with whom Andrew Ross felt a close personal affinity, though they lived in completely different eras). As Professor Shepperson has pointed out in his Foreword to this book, the resulting thesis was eventually published in Malawi in 1996, thirty years after it was first written.

Following its publication under the title *Blantyre Mission and the Making of Modern Malawi*, Andrew then became deeply involved in researching and writing his biography of David Livingstone, and it was not until around 2005 that he finally began researching and then writing the present volume. Tragically, while he was in the midst of writing it, he was diagnosed with two inoperable brain tumours in March 2008, and while he continued working on the book at a much reduced rate, his death in July 2008 left the work uncompleted.

In the months before he died he had several times asked me to help him finish the book, and I had promised that I would make sure that it was published. Once he had died it became obvious to me that this was very much Andrew's book, written in *his* style, and out of his own personal experiences in Malawi in the period leading up to, and immediately following, independence. In consultation with his wife Joyce and other close friends, I decided that it would be inappropriate for me to try to write extra material to complete the book. We decided that the task at hand was merely to do the best we could to polish (as Malawians would say) what Andrew had already written. At the same time, all who knew Andrew had been looking forward to seeing in print his own personal account of the Cabinet Crisis – a chapter which he had not started when he died. The solution was to use other accounts of the events of August/September 1964 which he had written at various times. The most appropriate of these was a lecture he had given to students at Chancellor College, when, after what I think we can rightly call exile, Andrew was able to return to Malawi for several months in 1997 to teach and meet old friends. This lecture was published in *Religion in Malawi* and in using an edited version of it to make up chapter seven of the book we are still able to hear Andrew's voice on the matter.

In the same way, I have used part of an interview which Andrew Ross gave to the newsletter of the Edinburgh University History Graduates' Association in 1998. In this interview he spoke of the period after the Cabinet Crisis and Chipembere's unsuccessful attempt to march on Zomba, when he had kept in touch with Chipembere (who was hiding in the hills above Mangochi) and helped supply him with food suitable for his diabetic condition. The interview also spoke of the events in May 1965 when Andrew and his family left Malawi. The material contained in the interview seemed to me an appropriate way in which to end the book; but because the literary style of this interview was much more informal and personal than the style in which the rest of the book was written, I have decided to add it as a 'personal postscript' rather than a final chapter.

When Andrew died most of the book had already been written, though a good deal of editing still needed to be done. Most of the footnotes were already complete; some were not, and, where it has been possible to complete these accurately, this has been done. In some cases, however, this has not been possible, and where this is the case, I hope that readers will understand the circumstances, and forgive the occasional lapse from normal academic standards.

While many who will read this book will be familiar with many of the main events in the political history of Malawi, others may not – particularly readers of a younger, post-independence generation in Malawi. It was for such younger people in particular that Andrew Ross wrote this book, since he felt that they had been deprived of much of their own history during the Banda years. For the benefit of such readers (and others less familiar with the details of the story) Joyce Ross suggested that the inclusion of a Time-Line of main events would be helpful, and I was very happy to agree with this suggestion – not least as Joyce did most of the work on it!

Much still remains to be written on the political history of Malawi, not least on what we may call the Banda years. There are still players in the drama alive today who have yet to tell their story. No one account can give us the full picture of what happened (particularly in the years between 1958 and 1965). Andrew Ross would not have made that claim for his book, and neither do I. But I would argue that his account and his views represent an important voice in the debate – a voice which needs to be heard. It is to be hoped that this book, conceived in the 1960s out of a simple desire that the truth be told, and finally written forty years later out of a deep love and concern for Malawi and its people, will encourage others to come forward and tell their own stories.

T. Jack Thompson
Edinburgh
January 2009

Chapter 1

The Creation of Nyasaland and the Threat from the White South

The Early Missions and the Scramble for Africa

The area of land that is modern Malawi was defined by decisions made during what is called in European imperial history, 'the Scramble for Africa'. According to both Portuguese written records and African oral tradition, there was a large African state in the early eighteenth century which included the land east of the Luangwa in modern Zambia and parts of Mozambique as well as modern Malawi. The central political authority was vested in Chief Undi. Although the Portuguese refer to this state as the Maravi or Malawi Empire, it does not appear to have been a centralised state like that of the Mwene Mutapa in Zimbabwe or of Shaka's amaZulu. It would rather appear to have been a much looser type of political organisation of people who shared a common culture and language, while honouring one chieftaincy as primary. This form of organisation is typical of the majority of the peoples of southern Africa. It is one which the eighteenth century Portuguese and the nineteenth century British, used to highly centralised and authoritarian states similar to those of the Europe, did not comprehend. So while they could relate readily to the regime of a Mwene Mutapa or a Shaka, they could not understand the much looser and freer traditional forms of political organisation of the majority of southern African peoples.[1] They had to interpret them as a 'state in decline' or some such analysis because of this inability to appreciate this alternative political structure.

By the last quarter of the nineteenth century the destructive influence of Swahili and Portuguese slave raiding, together with the devastating impact of the Lozi and various Ngoni invading groups from the south, had created turmoil north of the Zambezi. In addition to those invaders, in what is now southern Malawi, the arrival of Yao groups seeking to settle there had added to the political instability of the region. As had often happened in the past, a new more stable situation should have emerged from the various conflicts.

---

[1] 'A classic example is the constant failure of the British in the Cape Colony to understand the political organisation of the Amaxhosa people. They constantly demanded of the paramount chief of the Amaxhosa the exercise of authority over his people as if he were a dictator like Shaka. This was an authority he did not have.'

This did not happen because a new factor appeared on the scene: the sudden increased interest of Britain, France and Germany in Africa.[2]

At one level the story of modern Malawi and the threat to its existence from the white-settlers of the South began in 1875 with the arrival of the Livingstonia Mission of the Free (later United Free) Church of Scotland, followed the next year by the Blantyre Mission of the Church of Scotland. To understand how this particular bit of the old, much bigger Maravi survived to become the Malawi of today, we have to spend some time discussing the Scots and their actions. The aim of these missions was not only to preach the Christian gospel but also with the cooperation of the African Lakes Company of Glasgow, to help develop the economy of what is now Malawi. This was an attempt to fulfil David Livingstone's dream that the people of southern Africa should be prepared to enter the modern world as an equal partner with what we now call the West.[3]

In this period immediately preceding the Scramble, the arrival of the Scottish missions to the shores of Lake Malawi and the Shire Highlands brought a European presence into the area with an attitude that defined their task as helping Africans to develop Africa for themselves. This was in direct opposition to the attitude of Rhodes as he led the expansion of white settlement northwards out of South Africa.

The first challenge to the Scottish hopes for the people of the region came from Swahili slave-raiders seeking to settle at the north end of the Lake and the threat of Portuguese occupation of the land south of the Lake.[4] The missionaries alerted their supporters in Scotland to the threat and they, in turn, mounted an extraordinary political campaign in Scotland: extraordinary because it united Scots across both the then bitter divide between Church of Scotland and the Free Church, and that between Tories and Liberals.[5] This campaign was an exclusively Scottish affair; there was no parallel movement in England. The climax of the campaign was the despatch of a delegation to London to press the Tory government of Lord Salisbury to declare the area of land roughly equivalent to modern Malawi a British sphere of influence. As John McCracken has made clear, in refutation of what has been asserted

---

[2]   In the 'Scramble' the British often supported the claims of the Portuguese to wide swathes of African land where they had no longer an effective presence by the middle of the nineteenth century.

[3]   See Andrew Ross, *David Livingstone: Mission and Empire* (London: Hambledon and London, 2002.

[4]   This was one of a series of fitful Portuguese attempts to assert the authority they claimed over such a vast territory which usually did not come to much.

[5]   At that time the Free Church and elements in the Liberal Party were pressing for the disestablishment of the Church of Scotland.

14

by other historians, this was not a request for British rule over Malawi but rather a request for the British Government to prevent any other colonial power from entering the area.[6]

In response to pressure from leading Scottish politicians, the British Prime Minister, Lord Salisbury, received the delegation courteously but he rebuffed their request equally courteously.

This did not dampen Scottish enthusiasm and the response in Scotland to Salisbury's apparent indifference to this initiative was to intensify the campaign. Large public meetings in each of Scotland's cities - Glasgow, Edinburgh, Aberdeen and Dundee - were addressed by both Scottish Liberal and Scottish Tory leaders. The campaign reached its climax in June 1889 when Lord Balfour of Burleigh, a member of Salisbury's cabinet but acting in his capacity as an elder of the Church of Scotland, presented to the Prime Minister a petition signed by 11,000 prominent Scots. The petition renewed the request for the British Government to declare the land to the east and south of Lake Malawi a British sphere of influence and prevent the Portuguese and Swahili dividing the area between them.

It is an interesting but unresolved question as to how far Salisbury actively encouraged the continuing agitation in Scotland. He certainly had plans for the extension of British influence in southern Africa, an area to which the English public, unlike public opinion in Scotland, appeared indifferent. Salisbury had already in November 1888, appointed H.H. (later Sir Harry) Johnston to be consul at Mozambique and had sent him to Lisbon to negotiate a settlement of Portuguese claims in the area. In April 1889, the Prime Minister received Johnston's report which contained a draft agreement with the Portuguese. This draft agreement stated that Manicaland, Mashonaland, most of what is now Zambia and the lands on the western shore of Lake Malawi were to be deemed a British sphere of influence. However, that part of what is now Malawi from Ntcheu and Mangochi southwards to Nsanje was to be Portuguese. Salisbury then sent Johnston to sell this agreement to the Scots! This was the Scramble at full flood as European powers divided up Africa at will.

Johnston arrived in Scotland in the midst of the widespread campaign to keep the Portuguese out of Malawi. As a result his attempts to influence Scottish political and church leaders to accept the agreement he had negotiated simply infuriated them. Did Salisbury intend this so that he could tell the Portuguese that he would have to placate the Scots in order to achieve any agreement at all? W.P. Livingstone in his biography of Robert Laws,

[6]   J. McCracken, *Politics and Christianity in Malawi*, Cambridge, Cambridge University Press, 1977, p. 158.

head of the Livingstonia Mission, reported a conversation between Burleigh and Salisbury where Salisbury is quoted as admitting this was his motive. However, despite this story being repeated subsequently by a number of historians, as proof of Salisbury's deliberate stoking the fire of Scottish concern, W.P. Livingstone cited no source to authenticate the reported conversation. In any case Salisbury's plans for southern Africa continued to be stalled by the unwillingness of the British Parliament to spend money to implement them.

The situation was all to change in July 1889, when Cecil Rhodes approached Salisbury with an offer to help the Prime Minister achieve his aims in southern Africa. Rhodes suggested that his British South Africa Company would administer Mashonaland, Manicaland and what is now Zambia if the company were granted a Royal Charter to do so, together with all mineral rights in these territories. Rhodes also offered to pay the costs for three years of a British administration of a Protectorate over the area of land that is now modern Malawi.[8] This was part of Rhodes dream of making eastern Africa British from the Cape to Cairo.

Salisbury accepted this offer, which freed him from the restraint imposed on him by the reluctance of Parliament to spend money on southern Africa. He was, as a result, able to bring such pressure to bear on Lisbon that the Portuguese agreed to his plans for the division of southern Africa north of the Limpopo between Britain and Portugal.

The Portuguese, consequently, withdrew their forces from the Shire Valley where hard fighting with the Makololo chiefs had tested them, and in May 1891, the British Central African Protectorate came into being with Harry Johnston as 'Commissioner and Consul-General' for the Protectorate.[9]

The Missions' Relations with the Colonial Administration

Dr David Clement Scott[10] of Blantyre Mission and his associates, however, continued to be deeply suspicious of Johnston and feared that the Protectorate might still become part of Cecil Rhodes's empire. Scott had written to a friend in Scotland some months before the declaration of the Protectorate

---

[7]   See Andrew Ross, 'Scotland and Malawi, 1859-1964' in S.J. Brown and G. Newlands (eds.), *Scottish Christianity in the Modern World*, Edinburgh, T&T Clark, 2000, pp. 292-94.

[8]   The territory was called initially the British Central African Protectorate and then, in 1907, the Nyasaland Protectorate.

[9]   Somewhat bizarrely he was also appointed Agent for the British South Africa Company in what is now Zambia.

[10]   D.C. Scott, head of Blantyre Mission, was the architect and builder of St Michael and All Angels' Church, now a National Monument.

We have heard nothing of any sort of government for this place beyond the Chartered Company. If we have no independent commissioner to whom to appeal for the natives' sake and for the mission, then I fear we look forward to years of darkness from which the only escape will be agitation and political revolution.[11]

The Scots were deeply suspicious of Johnston because of what they perceived as his untenable dual role as Imperial officer and agent of the British South Africa Company. They feared that at the end of the three years of financial support promised by Rhodes, the agitation in Scotland having meanwhile been pacified, the territory would be given over to Rhodes's Chartered Company. Rhodes would then have his greater Rhodesia, consisting of what are now Zimbabwe, Zambia and Malawi.

Both Roland Oliver in his *Missionary Factor in East Africa* and A.J. Wills in his *An Introduction to the History of Central Africa* insist that as an imperial officer Johnston could never have been involved in any such plan with Rhodes, a judgement shaped, at least in part, by Johnston's later vehement and genuine antagonism to Rhodes. Scott and his colleagues, however, were right to be suspicious. This is made clear in Johnston's letter of June 1893 to Rhodes. This letter was not copied to the Foreign Office despite the rule that all Johnston's correspondence with Rhodes should be so copied. In the letter, Johnston wrote of how he still hoped that British Central African Protectorate would become Chartered Company territory in 1894. He went on

I don't think you have ever realised the bitter hatred borne you by these Scotch missionaries of Blantyre ... *Remember that it was mainly Scott and Hetherwick who balked the scheme of 1890 of all BCA coming under the Company's Charter.* They are now up and at it again and are the most serious enemies you possess.[12]

Scott also opposed much of Johnston's policy within the Protectorate. He criticised, for example, Johnston's treatment of many of the chiefs in what is now the Southern Region. Scott insisted that the chiefs had signed treaties with the British believing that the British would interfere only minimally with traditional life while protecting them from the Portuguese and any other external power. Scott was very incensed because he had persuaded a number of these chiefs to sign the agreements with the British on that understanding.

Johnston, however, once installed as Commissioner, almost immediately embarked on a series of military campaigns against some of those very chiefs whom Scott had persuaded to sign, deeming them 'inveterate slavers'. What Scott judged to be most reprehensible was Johnston's attitude to chiefs Mitochi, Chikhumbu, Malemia, Kapeni and other Yao leaders with whom he

---

[11] D.C. Scott to James Robertson. 18 August 1890. Edinburgh University Library. Ms 717/10

[12] Johnston to Rhodes. 7 June 1893. Harare. Zimbabwe National Archives. CT/1/16/4/1 a letter brought to my attention by John McCracken. The emphasis is mine.

had built up good relationships over the previous eleven years. The Scottish Mission had been able to live peaceably with those chiefs for a decade, a feat achieved by Scott's willingness to go through the protracted discussions in public that the *mlandu* tradition of resolving disputes entailed.

Roland Oliver has rejected Scott's complaints of Johnstone's 'unnecessary wars' as essentially unfounded but Cairns in his *Prelude to Imperialism* was able to show that even some senior officials of Johnston's staff agreed with David Scott in his judgement of what Johnston was up to.[13] The most devastating confirmation of Scott's view of Johnston's policy is in an essay by Professor Eric Stokes. This essay shows how after each campaign, the chief's land was declared Crown Land and made available for lease to white planters. By pursuing this policy Johnston was single handedly transforming the Protectorate into something like a Crown Colony, at least in what is now the Southern Region. Stokes makes it clear that Johnston had decided on this policy before the declaration of the Protectorate. As a result of his actions Malawi was not going to be like the other British Protectorates over Lesotho or Swaziland, which were free from the curse of land being made available for white settlement.[14] David Scott wrote at the time

> Our contention is if the Europeans take the land they practically enslave the native population. There is no law to compel them to help the native in his distress, but there is power put into European hands to compel, to force the native to work ... and we uphold this that no civilised power can come into a country, more especially under Christian promises, and turn the natives into slaves on their own holdings ... we cannot treat the land as a conquered country, and we must in every case of confiscation or annexation have the very best proof to show that no other way than fighting the natives was possible.[15]

His words were prophetic: land policy was a source of the people's anger and social tension from the time of the Johnstone settlement on through the whole colonial period of Malawi history and, indeed, even later.[16]

After Scott's departure from the Protectorate in 1898, the Scottish missionaries, both in Blantyre and Livingstonia, settled into a much more cooperative mode with the colonial administration. Their attitude was to help it work efficiently and justly, as much as possible for the benefit of the African peo-

[13] H.A.C. Cairns, *Prelude to Imperialism: British Reaction to Central African Society*, London: Routledge & Keegan Paul, 1965, p. 237.

[14] Eric Stokes, 'Malawi Political Systems and the Introduction of Colonial Rule' in E. Stokes & R. Brown, *The Zambezian Past*, Manchester, the University Press, 1965.

[15] This paragraph also shows Scott's great unease about the role he had played in persuading chiefs to sign up to a 'protectorate'. *Life and Work in British Central Africa*, December issue, 1894.

[16] See Colin Baker, *Seeds of Trouble: Government Policy and Land Rights in Nyasaland*, London, 1993.

ple, as least as perceived by the missions. They certainly criticised the Administration of the Protectorate when they felt that it was necessary but they no longer challenged its very basis as Scott had done.[17]

Although this first attempt by the white south to take control of what is now Malawi occurred in the 1890s when there was hardly yet a modern African consciousness among the local people, Rhodes' effort did have a genuine - if limited - effect on the folk memory of some of the people. The Scots missionaries, who had campaigned so vigorously against the threat presented by Rhodes, published these complaints and criticisms in their journal, *Life and Work in British Central Africa*. This journal, under the editorship of David Scott and his associate editor Dr MacVicar,[18] was a vehicle for their criticism of British policy both in the Protectorate and elsewhere in southern Africa. In particular they published articles critical of the British South Africa Company's war against the amaNdebele in 1893 and the Company's conduct in the subsequent rebellion of 1896, the Chimurenga.

The journal was read by the small but important core of mission educated Africans, who spread the information they gained to a very much wider circle. These men, people like Joseph Bismarck, Harry Matecheta, Mungo Chisuse and John Gray Kufa, were the pioneers of a new Africa. This was the beginning of a development where African people responded to that which they felt was useful and creative in the European presence, and developed it for their own ends. Education and new understanding of the world offered by the missionaries, both Scottish and later by the Catholics as they began to arrive, were used by the people to formulate the vision of a new future both for themselves and their country.

The Concept of Indirect Rule

At the same time there was developing in the Colonial Office in London yet another alternative future for the Protectorate. By the first years of the twentieth century it was clear that the Government in London had little interest in the new Protectorate and was unwilling to spend resources of money, staff or, indeed, thought, on its administration.[19] By 1910 Lord Lugard's theories

---

[17] See, Andrew Ross. *Blantyre Mission and Making of Modern Malawi*, Blantyre. CLAIM-Kachere. 1996, pp. 132-42.

[18] Later head of the hospital at the Lovedale Institution in the Cape, where he trained the first African women nurses to gain the SRN qualification in what was otherwise a whites-only profession.

[19] See the report by the first British High Commissioner to the newly independent Malawi He says in a report how astonished he is on discovering that Britain had done almost nothing during all these years for Malawi. What little external input there had been had come from the missionaries.

of indirect rule had become popular in the Colonial Office, where they were deemed to be very appropriate for the Nyasaland Protectorate.[20] Since the Colonial Office had assigned the Protectorate so very few staff, it was, perhaps, the only way it could be administered. When, however, the Governor-in-Council issued the District Ordinance of 1912, things did not go according to plan.

The theory behind the District Ordinance was that the Protectorate should be divided into districts, each of which was to have a District Resident (later the District Commissioner). Responsible to the Resident, there was to be a Principal Headman, to whom the headmen of the villages in the district would, in turn, be responsible. These headmen would be chosen by the colonial authorities from among the traditional ruling families, although the historic connection was not deemed an absolutely necessary qualification. This pattern of development took no account whatsoever of the growing numbers of educated Africans in the Protectorate who were developing a different picture of the entry of their country into the modern world.

In any case, standing in the way of applying this system to the Protectorate were the problems presented not only by the growing numbers of western educated Africans, but also by the nature of traditional African society in the Protectorate and by the presence of white settlers in the Southern Region.

The concept of Indirect Rule as a means of governing was based upon the existence of a coherent and viable traditional system of authority that could be recruited into the service of the imperial power. In Nigeria the powerful Muslim emirs of northern Nigeria fitted admirably into this system. They willingly cooperated with the imperial authorities and gained greatly from this alliance with the British. Indirect Rule brought them external reinforcement of their authority; it even helped to extend that authority over African peoples in the so-called Middle Belt of Nigeria, who had been resisting both them and Islamisation for generations.

This application of Indirect Rule to Nyasaland was an example of the astonishing lack of understanding of Africa among colonial theorists of the time. They attempted to take a policy from one part of the continent of Africa and apply it without modification to another area a thousand miles away, confident it would work simply because the new context was also African. The Ukraine is much nearer Ireland than Nigeria is to Malawi yet would anyone in London have seriously suggest applying an effective policy shaped in the Ukraine to solve the problems they faced in Ireland, simply because both areas were European?

---

[20] In 1907 the British Central African Protectorate was renamed the Nyasaland Protectorate.

Were there figures in the Protectorate equivalent to the Nigerian emirs? The two Ngoni paramount chiefs, Nkhosi M'mbelwa in the North and Nkhosi Gomani at Ntcheu, were perhaps in a position to play this role, although they had only recently conquered the indigenous Tumbuka, Chewa and Nyanja peoples in their respective areas. Everywhere else in the Protectorate there were serious problems in the way of any attempt to implement such a scheme. The Tonga people on the lake shore did not have, and never had, any kind of paramount chief and their village headmen were more like committee chairmen than the chief envisaged by European ideas of indirect rule. Further south on the lake shore, could the Jumbe of Nkhotakota be used in a system of indirect rule? He was a Muslim interloper, who had conquered the local Chewa population comparatively recently and had been deeply involved in the slave trade?

In the Southern Region, which chiefs were to be chosen? Many of the Yao chiefs had only entered Malawi in the mid-nineteenth century; in the Shire valley many of the chiefs were the sons and grandsons of Livingstone's Kololo followers who had settled there and used their firearms to gain power from the traditional Amang'anja and Nyanja chiefly families who continued to live in both areas. To add to this confusion, across the whole of the Shire Highlands, Lomwe immigrants from Mozambique had for a decade been moving in to seek work, mainly on European estates. They had no tradition of loyalty to any of the local chiefs and headmen whether new, like the Yao or Kololo, or old like the displaced Nyanja and Amang'anja headmen.

In addition to these problems, the European planters in the Blantyre, Chiradzulu, Zomba, Thyolo and Mulanje districts were opposed to any significant authority being granted by the colonial power to chiefs and headmen in 'their' area, they were particularly incensed at the idea of chiefs having any authority over people living on their estates.

The result was that the ordinance was applied in a piecemeal way. It was done at first, with reasonable effectiveness, in the Northern Region where the Ngoni authority structure and the authority of some Nkhonde chiefs in the very north of the territory were still operative. The area was also helped by having almost no resident Europeans other than the missionaries. The pattern of using chiefly authority continued to be expanded slowly into the Central Region, reaching Ntcheu in 1914.

The Beginnings of the Native Associations

Fundamental to the history of Malawi was that at the very same time, another movement began which aimed to provide an alternative channel for African involvement in the political development and governance of their country. This was the Native Association movement, initiated by men (no women at this point) who had been through the educational system inaugurated by the Livingstonia Mission. These men were northern equivalents of the Bismarcks and Gray Kufas of the south. There were, however, many more of them since the Livingstonia Mission had at that time more schools than all the other missions in Malawi put together. The impact of these men would soon stretch into other lands as far as South Africa.

The first Native Association was the North Nyasa Native Association, founded in 1912 by A. Simon Muhango at Karonga with Levi Mumba as its secretary. This was followed by the West Nyasa Native Association, formed at Bandawe in 1914. These Associations were specifically non-tribal and sought to be a vehicle to bring pressure to bear on the colonial authorities to develop policies for the good of the African people of the Protectorate in terms of developing a modern world rather than the traditional world.

The members of the Associations were rightly suspicious of the tentative beginnings of indirect rule. It has often been asserted that this was because the members of the associations would have had no place in any such traditional structure, but this is not a satisfactory explanation. Many of them were from chiefly families and, it should be noted, the third Native Association to be formed was the Mombera Native Association, founded among the northern Ngoni with approval of Nkhosi M'mbelwa.[21]

In fact the primary reason for their suspicion would appear to be that many educated and Christian Africans saw indirect rule as seriously flawed since, under the arrangements developed by the administration, the chiefs and headmen appeared to have become agents of the colonial government rather than leaders of their people. In some ways the structure set up by the 1912 Ordinance was not a system of indirect rule but a form of direct rule on the cheap. As Bridglal Pachai has said, these men were no longer chiefs and headmen in the traditional sense but were primarily government agents who stayed in place so long as they organised the people in a way that evoked the required response to the demands of the colonial administration.[22]

The Associations were, from the beginning, encouraged by Dr Laws, head of Livingstonia Mission, who believed it was important that the voice of the emerging class of literate Africans be heard by the colonial government for the good of the development of the country, if, as Laws hoped, the country was to develop in the direction of modernity. What is notable is that Laws, despite all the sound and fury over the Chilembwe Rising, wrote to the Chief Secretary in Zomba in 1920 attempting to persuade him that it was important to continue listening to the Associations despite the feeling in the admini-

---

[21] Mombera was at that time the way Europeans rendered Nkhosi M'mbelwa's name.
[22] Bridglal Pachai. *Malawi: The History of the Nation.* p. 183.

stration that they were simply a marginal pressure group. Laws even dared to say that these associations, if treated properly could be guided so as to prepare the way for Africans to *elect* first Europeans, but later Africans to represent them in the Legislature.[23] This was an extraordinary statement for 1920, and one which places Laws closer to David Scott of Blantyre than is often recognised.

What is not clear is whether the assertion Professor George Shepperson made in the classic text of modern African historiography *Independent African*, written with Tom Price, about the intention behind the passing of the 1912 Ordinance was accurate or not. Shepperson wrote that the aim

> of building up an organisation to control the rising generation of natives who, finding themselves without the restraining influences to which their parents were accustomed, have of recent years evinced an inclination to emancipate themselves from the disciplinary responsibilities of village life and obedience to authority.[24]

He was quoting *A Handbook of Nyasaland*, published in 1932 by S.S. Murray, a man whose judgement certainly reflected post war official attitudes. The reaction of Robert Laws to the passing of the Ordinance does back up Shepperson's judgement. Laws unambiguously encouraged the new Native Associations because he feared that the colonial authorities were intending to ignore, though perhaps not 'control', the new and expanding number of educated African men and women.

Before the pattern of 'indirect rule' under the 1912 Ordinance could be further implemented and before the Native Association movement could spread out of the north, two major events occurred which put both developments on hold. These were the outbreak of the First World War and the Chilembwe Rising.

The outbreak of the war brought Nyasaland almost immediately into the conflict since its northern frontier was with what was then German East Africa. After the initial brisk fighting near Karonga, however, things became comparatively quiet. This changed when the victory of the South Africans over the Germans in Namibia released South African forces to move north. From then till the end of the war, Nyasaland and Northern Rhodesia were the base for British and South African troops in the southern front of the long drawn out fighting in East Africa. Since the transportation of goods other than on Lakes Tanganyika and Malawi was still primarily by head-load, the people

---

[23] Robert Laws to Chief Secretary, 12 January 1920, SI/2065/19, Malawi Archives.

[24] G. Shepperson and T. Price, *Independent African: John Chilembwe and the Origins, Setting and Significance of the Nyasaland Native Rising*. Edinburgh, Edinburgh University Press, 1958, p. 195.

who suffered in this campaign were the porters, the *tengatenga*. Their losses through disease and malnourishment were severe. In addition their absence from their villages damaged local food production, spreading the misery further. The situation was such that the colonial government had to resort to compelling chiefs and headmen in some areas to produce quotas of recruits for *tengatenga* service. This was a contrast with the brisk recruitment for service as *asikari* with the King's African Rifles.

The war came at a very difficult time for people of the Protectorate. The harvest had been poor over the whole country in 1911, 1912 and 1913 and what had been a comparatively good harvest in 1914 suffered from massive rainstorms in March when the rains should have been light and tapering off. These unseasonable storms not only washed away crops, but also bridges and even part of the railway line from Beira to Limbe.[25]

The storms of 1914 were particularly bad in the Southern Province where European ownership of land was so widespread and where, as David Scott had forewarned, this had been causing increasing unhappiness among local people and increasing tension in relations between European and African. The local people in many instances had refused to work on the estates under the conditions offered by the planters but this had not forced changes in the system. This was because of the massive immigration into the Protectorate of Lomwe people from Mozambique.[26] Shepperson again:

> Some have estimated that in the first twenty years of the twentieth century at least 100,000 Nguru, entered Nyasaland. It is very probable, too, that this emigration increased in intensity as the War approached, owing to the abuses of the semi-feudal system still in existence in the Portuguese territories, the demands of the chartered companies, the increased maladministration which attended the overthrow of the Portuguese monarchy and the disruption of their colonial policy, and the comparative attractions of the more progressive economic and political life in Nyasaland.[27]

The Chilembwe Rising

So in 1914, the African population of the Southern Region was in a disturbed state. Three years of bad harvests, combined with long term unhappiness over the European planters control of so much land and the presence of a large landless immigrant population of rural labourers, all combined to create a situation of serious social dislocation.

---

[25] Alexander Hetherwick, *The Romance of Blantyre*, pp. 205-07.

[26] Known at the time as 'Nguru' and strangely so called by the Protectorate administration, though, like the name 'Ajawa' used previously of the Yao people, it was a derogatory name applied to them by others.

[27] Shepperson and Price, *Inependent* African, p. 121.

In what some have considered the most troubled district in the Region, Chiradzulu, there were two very uncomfortable neighbours: Pastor John Chilembwe, head of the Providence Industrial Mission which was backed by the National Baptist Convention Inc.,[28] and the estates of A.L. Bruce at Magomero. Despite Alexander Livingstone Bruce being the son of David Livingstone's daughter Agnes, and the estate manager being a distant relative of the explorer and missionary, the record of labour relations on the estate was a bad one and, even more remarkably, neither schools nor churches were allowed on the thousands of acres of the estate.

The Reverend John Chilembwe was a Yao who had been profoundly influenced by the radical missionary Joseph Booth and had with the latter's help, gone to the United States where he had been trained for the Baptist ministry at Lynchburg Theological Seminary, Virginia. The story of these two men has been well told in *Independent African* and in Harry Langworthy's *Africa for the African: the Life of Joseph Booth*,[29] but the so-called 'Native Rising' led by Chilembwe has to be reviewed again as an important part of our story.

John Chilembwe did not begin his mission with any of the apocalyptic rhetoric that characterised so many of the so-called 'Wachitawala' preachers who were alarming Colonial officials in both Nyasaland and Northern Rhodesia at the beginning of the twentieth century. These men and women preached that all European governments in Africa were about to be condemned and overthrown by divine intervention. This wide-spread message was the result of a specifically African 'take' on the message found in so much Watchtower Society literature that all earthly governments were corrupt and would be overthrown at a divinely ordained moment in the near future.

Chilembwe, in contrast, was much more the product of one of the major trends in the African American Christianity of his day, a style of Christianity dominated by the message of Booker T. Washington. Like Washington, Chilembwe appeared to believe his task, in addition to preaching the Christian gospel, was to gain for his people social equality with whites by showing the former that Africans could be good industrious sober Christian men and women, worthy of respect. This did not stop him being critical of the use of the King's African Rifles in colonial wars in Ghana and the Sudan, and of what he saw as the cruel behaviour of white estate owners.

---

[28] A major Black Baptist denomination in the United States.

[29] See also G. S. Mwase, *Strike a Blow and Die*, Cambridge, Mass: Harvard University Press, 1967 and B. M. Kavaloh, 'Joseph Booth: an evaluation of his life and thought and their influence on religion and politics in British Central Africa (Malawi) and in South Africa'. PhD dissertation, University of Edinburgh, 1991.

Apart from gaining the respect of his growing congregation, Chilembwe also gained the friendship of many families who belonged to Blantyre Mission congregations: people who belonged to the same social group as those who were forming the Native Associations in the North: schoolteachers, Presbyterian ministers, small businessmen, and the growing group of African cash-crop farmers. Perhaps his closest friend outside his own mission circle was John Gray Kufa, the first African in Central Africa to be trained as a hospital dresser. Kufa was so trusted and respected by the Scottish missionaries that he had been left in sole charge of the Mihekani mission in Mozambique on a number of occasions. Of him David Scott had written

> John Gray Kufa, the physician, Dr Macvicar's ideal of a man. Brave, he stood unarmed in the mission gateway in Lomweland against a yelling crowd of natives with their spears and guns.[30]

Alexander Hetherwick, who had succeeded David Scott as head of the Blantyre Mission, kept up a correspondence with Chilembwe and always treated him as a fellow missionary. It was because of these connections that Hetherwick, in 1914, insisted to the colonial authorities that the rumours that Chilembwe was planning some kind of violent uprising were nonsense.

Hetherwick's dismissal of the assertion that Chilembwe was a secret plotter appeared to be confirmed by the latter's letter of 25th November 1914, sent for publication to *The Nyasaland Times*. In this letter Chilembwe attacked the use of African soldiers and porters in a European war that had nothing to do with them. Chilembwe wrote

> We understand that we have been invited to shed our innocent blood in this world's war which is now in progress throughout the wide world...A number of our people have already shed their blood, while some are crippled for life...We ask the Honourable government of our country which is known as Nyasaland, will there be any good prospects for the natives after the end of the war? ...In time of peace everything for Europeans only. And instead of honour we suffer humiliation with names contemptible. But in time of war it has been found that we are needed to share the hardships and shed our blood in equality...Let the rich men, bankers, titled men, storekeepers, farmers and landlords go to war and get shot. Instead the poor Africans who have nothing to own in this present world, who in death, leave only a long line of widows and orphans in utter want and dire distress are invited to die for a cause which is not theirs.[31]

If he was already plotting an insurrection why on earth would he draw attention to himself with such a letter to the press? Yet for some time there had been rumours that he was plotting an insurrection of some kind. Catholic Christians reported to their priests at the Nguludi Mission that John Chilembwe was planning an uprising, and the rumours were passed to the

---

30   Ross, *Blantyre Mission*, p. 127.
31   The full text of the letter can be found in *Independent African*, pp. 234-35.

authorities. These and other reports were treated as a matter of no consequence until January of 1915 when it was decided to arrest Chilembwe as a precautionary measure, since in wartime the government could not afford to take risks.

Chilembwe was informed, through the grape-vine of African clerks and capitaos, of the plans to arrest him. Whether this provoked him into bringing forward, in a hasty and inefficient manner plans that were in process of being developed for a rising or whether it was the threat of arrest that provoked a rising and that it was never intended to be anything else than a gesture of despair (as Mwase suggests in *Strike a Blow and Die*) will continue to be a subject for debate among historians. In any case, the short-lived armed insurrection, begun on 23rd of January 1915, achieved nothing except the killing of William Jervis Livingstone, the very unpopular manager of the A.L. Bruce estate, and two other European planters. Notably all European women and children were unharmed.

The attacks on European establishments in Ntcheu, Mulanje and Blantyre were suppressed with little or no fighting. The main body of Chilembwe's followers held out briefly at his Providence mission in Chiradzulu then fled eastward towards Mozambique on whose borders three days later, Chilembwe was encountered by a patrol of African policemen who shot him dead.[32]

There then ensued a vigorous campaign to capture every African who could in any way be connected with the Rising. Many were hanged, including John Gray Kufa, 'Dr MacVicar's ideal of a man'; many more flogged and imprisoned. The enthusiasm of the general European population for the punishment of all suspected of collaboration with Chilembwe's plans brought this rebuke from the head of the Blantyre Mission:

> I hear there were six further executions at Zomba on Monday and Zomba camera fiends were on the spot. I wonder what our countrymen and countrywomen are coming to these days. This whole affair is to them a 'Roman Holiday' at Zomba.[33]

Initially the reaction of officials and the European community in general was to blame the influence of the smaller missions and the independent missionaries.[34] Attention soon shifted, however, to focus on educated Africans and so onto the Scottish missions and the churches the Scottish missions had

---

[32] For a detailed exposition of the events of the Rising see *Independent African*. Chapter 6.

[33] Hetherwick to Metcalfe, 17 February 1915. Hetherwick Correspondence. Malawi Archives.

[34] See *Independent African*. Chapter 7 for a detailed description of the treatment of these men and women by the Administration.

produced; after all Blantyre and Livingstonia had produced the vast majority of schools in the Protectorate. Even more significant in European eyes, the nature of the education the Scottish Missions provided was at that time radically different from that given by the other missions.

In their evidence before the Commission of Enquiry into the Rising, the spokesmen of the Roman Catholic, Anglican and Dutch Reformed Missions all insisted on the limited aims of the education they provided, which existed primarily to produce church members literate in the indigenous language. They also emphasized the careful supervision by Europeans of all African catechists and teachers.[35]

This was in sharp contrast with the education system of the Scottish missions whose emphasis was on English and the gaining of skills useful in the modern world. The distinction was equally strong in the area of trust and independence granted the missions' African ministers, teachers and evangelists. Both Blantyre and Livingstonia had allowed a measure of autonomy to their African evangelists and teachers, and more importantly, had already ordained Africans as full 'ministers of word and sacrament'. Classic examples of this were Robert Laws sending of the evangelist David Kaunda as a mission pioneer to Lubwa in Northern Rhodesia and the independent role the Reverend Harry Kwambiri Matecheta played among Gomani's Ngoni.[36]

As a result of this change in focus it appeared that the Nyasaland government might insist that no African minister, evangelist or teacher should work except under close and direct supervision by a European, something that would have closed down the major part of the work of the Scottish missions. It would also have made nonsense of the setting up by these missions of the Church of Central Africa Presbyterian, a legally autonomous African church. Good sense prevailed eventually in Government circles and things were left as they were.

What was much more significant was that the crisis showed that the kind of men who formed the Native Associations in the North did exist in the Southern Province. They came forward to give evidence, in writing or in person, to the Commission of Enquiry into the Rising, an act that required some courage given the ferocious reaction of the European population towards anyone who appeared to support Chilembwe or his views. The most notable contributions were made by the Reverend Stephen Kundecha, Robertson

---

[35] See the evidence given by the representatives of these missions to the Commission of Enquiry in C.O. 525/66 *Nyasaland 1916.* Vol. 1; Nyasaland Native Rising. Commission of Enquiry, 217-664, Public Record Office, London.

[36] David Kaunda was the father of Kenneth Kaunda, the first President of Zambia.

Namate, Joseph Bismarck, the Reverend Harry Kwambiri Matecheta, Mungo Chisuse and Elliot Kamwana Chirwa.

The first five were ministers or elders of the Blantyre Presbytery of the Church of Central Africa Presbyterian, the ecclesiastically autonomous Church formed by the congregations resulting from the work of the Blantyre Mission of the Church of Scotland. The Mission organisation continued to exist in parallel with the CCAP until it's absorption by the CCAP in 1958.[37] The one non-CCAP witness was Elliot Kamwana Chirwa. Kamwana had been a disciple of Joseph Booth's who had sparked off a apocalyptic Christian movement among the Tonga in 1908 and had been exiled for his pains in 1909. Allowed to return to Malawi he had been internally exiled to Mulanje where he was in touch with John Chilembwe. It is important to note, however, that the other five also knew Chilembwe with varying degrees of intimacy, though unlike Kamwana they were not accused of being part of the conspiracy. As we have already noted relations between Chilembwe and the Blantyre Mission had been reasonably cordial throughout, despite the antagonism towards the Blantyre missionaries of Chilembewe's mentor, Joseph Booth. What is to be noted is that the Blantyre ministers and elders were unanimous that though they believed Chilembwe's taking up arms was wrong, his complaints were justified.

What is striking is that while each of these witnesses has something complimentary to say about the results of the arrival of Europeans in their country, they all then turn to complain - in some cases quite bitterly - about the same issues of unjust treatment of the indigenous population that had angered Chilembwe.

The Reverend Stephen Kundecha is particularly direct when he lists as a primary grievance the stealing of the land from the people. Other issues these CCAP leaders raised ranged from the humiliation of the *chotsa chipewa*[38] to the unfairness of the hut tax, from the indignities heaped on Africans by 'certain section of the European population' to the need for the

---

[37] Blantyre and Livingstonia had agreed to the formation of the CCAP by 1914, but the outbreak of the First World War meant that the formal launch of the church did not take place until September 1924.

[38] Many Europeans insisted on Africans removing their hats in their presence, *chotsa chipewa*, (using the second person singular of the verb ku-chotsa which is insulting in itself) and refusing to accord to Africans the European custom of two gentlemen raising their hats in greeting each other on meeting.

Government to consult African opinion about legislation.[39] This last had, of course, been the basis for organising the Native Associations in the North.

Much of their unhappiness with the situation in the Protectorate, as with Chilembwe, focussed on the European ownership of land, the *tangata*, the exaction of labour services instead of rent, and the system of land tenure in general.

Despite the shock of the Rising and the agreement of so many Africans and many colonial officials that land was a key issue nothing of any consequence was done in this area until after the Second World War.[40] What is particularly surprising about the whole situation is that the Colonial Government had instituted a review by Justice Nunan of the land situation in 1910, and that if Nunan's recommendations had been implemented they would have brought about in the second decade of the twentieth century the kind of reforms which were only achieved after the Second World War!

Although historians have argued about the impact of the Rising and its ferocious suppression, Dr Hetherwick's summing up is probably close to the truth. He wrote "nothing came of the commission [which was appointed to enquire into the Rising] and the whole matter was speedily forgotten."[41] Hetherwick was correct in that the Rising soon ceased to be something that the administration factored into their thinking about policy and the Native Association movement, as it developed and grew, did not refer to it. Among Africans in the Shire Highlands, however, Chilembwe was not forgotten nor was John Gray Kufa forgotten among the African leaders of the Presbytery of Blantyre of the CCAP, many of whom had known him well and admired him.[42]

The Growth of a Nyasa National Identity

It has to be noted that it was during the First World War that the threat of white settler domination from south of the Zambezi was raised again for the first time since the 1890s. In a number of influential journals there appeared articles referring to the need to create 'a Confederation of southern African

---

[39]   The evidence of some of these men has been carefully analysed by Shepperson 'The Place of John Chilembwe in Malawi Historiography' in B. Pachai (ed.) *The Early History of Malawi*.

[40]   T. David Williams. *Malawi: The Politics of Despair*. Ithaca NY. Cornell University Press. p. 115.

[41]   Quoted in Shepperson and Price. *Independent African*. p. 388.

[42]   See Lewis Bandawe. *Memoirs of a Malawian*. Bandawe, senior elder of Blantyre Church, whose first steps in the Christian faith were guided by Kufa who was at that time in charge of Mihekani mission of the Church of Scotland in Mozambique.

states owing allegiance to the crown.' The most important of these were two written under the nom de plume 'Africanus' in the *Journal of the Royal Africa Society* in 1917 and in 1919. In reply to the first of these articles, Alexander Hetherwick, David Scott's successor as head of the Blantyre Mission and one of the founders of the CCAP, wrote a passionate article in defence of Nyasaland as a 'Black Man's country'. In particular, Hetherwick insisted that there were no grounds for any association of Nyasaland with territories south of the Zambezi. He wrote

> The conditions of the country are all against any such proposal. Nyasaland is a black man's country ... The place of the European in the Protectorate is that of administrator of its Government or director of its commercial or agricultural enterprises. The work of development will be done by the native himself under the white man's rule and leadership.[43]

Despite its assumption that a handful of expatriates would continue to hold the key positions at the highest level of authority in the land for a long time to come, this was a bold assertion of 'the paramountcy of native interests' the fundamental basis of British policy that was to be asserted in the Devonshire Declaration of 1923[44] and the Passfield Memorandum of 1930.[45] The policy enshrined in these two British documents convinced many Africans - Dr Banda was one as we shall see - that the intentions of the British Government could be trusted. This threat from the South, however, did not appear on the agenda of politics in the Protectorate immediately after the end of the war. As an idea it appeared more and more attractive to the leaders of the white settlers who ruled Southern Rhodesia as the 1920s wore on.

In the north of the Protectorate immediately after the war ended, the North Nyasa and the West Nyasa Associations resumed their meetings and the new Mombera Native Association was formed. In the South, despite the confident and critical contributions of educated Africans to the Commission of Enquiry into the Chilembwe Rising, the development of the Association movement was slower, perhaps the result of a certain nervousness produced by the ferocity shown in the aftermath of the Chilembwe Rising. In 1924, however, an Association was formed in Zomba. Levi Mumba, working in the capital as a civil servant, played a key role in this development actively encouraged by the Reverend James Reid[46] of Domasi Mission of the Church of Scotland. The creation of another Association soon followed in Blantyre, where again it was encouraged by these two men.

---

[43] A. Hetherwick. 'Nyasaland Today and Tomorrow' in *Journal of the Royal Africa Society*. Vol. XVII 1917.

[44] Cmd. 1922, 1923.

[45] *Memorandum on Native Policy in East Africa*, Cmd. 3573, 1930.

[46] Reid was the member of the Legislative Council representing African interests.

In the Central Region (other than in Ntcheu where the CCAP from Blantyre operated and in Lilongwe) the situation was not one conducive to the growth of the Native Association movement. As Roger Tangri has so clearly explained,[47] in the Central Region education was provided by the Dutch Reformed Church, Anglican and Roman Catholic Missions none of whom, at that time, concentrated on education in English. As we have seen the modernizers were almost all products of the Livingstonia or Blantyre Mission school systems. The first Association in the Central Region was formed in Lilongwe but this confirmed the nature of the problem in the Central Region outside Ntcheu, since a majority of the members were northerners or southerners working in the town.

These Associations were the beginnings of an unambiguous nationalist movement in Nyasaland. They shared, as Jap van Velsen has pointed out, common values and appealed to the loyalties of common membership of an embryonic national entity.[48] It is very important to note at this point that because of its ramifications still affecting politics in the 1960s, the various different educational policies of the missions in the Protectorate played an important role in the shaping of nationalism in Nyasaland. The Catholic Missions of the White Fathers and the Montfortians, the mission of the Cape Synod of the Dutch Reformed Church of South Africa, the Anglican mission, Universities Mission to Central Africa - however much they differed in details of policy - all emphasized indigenous language education and played down, (when they had any at all) English medium education. As Roger Tangri has pointed out

The ramifications of such divergent educational and evangelical policies were to be important in the creation of an African elite. Whereas Africans emerging from Livingstonia and Blantyre were to secure the best paid jobs and represent all the main sources of political awareness in Malawi, their counterparts in the Central Region [save Ntcheu District which was in Blantyre mission area] and the Lower and Upper Shire districts were to be less thoroughly involved in the new way of life and less equipped with the skills to proceed to positions of responsibility both in civilian and political life. In consequence modern political groups were to appear late in the Central Region. When they did appear, they were led and controlled by returning migrants who had been trained at one of the Scottish missions and who were sometimes alien to the region. With the departure of these leaders, either to another region or to resume work outside Malawi, the political groups declined quickly and few educated elements remained to ensure their continued operation.[49]

---

[47] Roger Tangri. 'The Development of Modern African Politics and the Emergence of a Nationalist Movement in Colonial Malawi, 1891-1958'. PhD. University of Edinburgh, 1970, pp. 126-27.

[48] J. van Velsen. 'Some Early Pressure Groups in Malawi' in Stokes and Brown (eds.), *The Zambezian Past*, Manchester University Press, 1966, p. 381.

[49] Roger Tangri. 'Modern African Politics', p. 131.

Perhaps the most important factor in the growth of this Nyasa national identity, however, was the massive exodus of men to work on the farms, in commerce in Southern Rhodesia, and in the gold-mines of South Africa. Over 80% of the men working on the European commercial farms in Southern Rhodesia were 'Nyasas', as they were then called. This was a phenomenon about which Mumba and other leaders complained as they felt it weakened the possibility of economic development in the Protectorate, although it strengthened the movement they represented enormously. This was because, as Richard Gray has pointed out

> Wherever they went ... they found higher wages but also restrictive and discriminatory measures: pass laws, a sterner police force, stringent labour regulations, and colour-bar practices which prevented some of them from rising as high as they could at home.[50]

Increasingly through the 1920s Nyasas became sharply aware of the difference between the territories north and south of the Zambezi in the quality of life for Africans. This was a point made very strongly in the *Joint Submission* of Native Authorities and Native Associations of the Northern Region to the Bledisloe Commission of 1938. The commission was set up by the Imperial government in London to investigate the possibility of the Amalgamation of the two Rhodesias and Nyasaland into one white-ruled British Dominion in response to pressure from the Southern Rhodesian Government. This commission is something to which we will return later.

These men who went to the South were not simply an anonymous labour force; they were active in helping create a new sense of African rights in the developing modern world of southern and central Africa. In 1919 in South Africa, Clements Kadalie, a lake-shore Tonga educated at Livingstonia, organised the Industrial and Commercial Workers Union. In the 1920s this union reached the black masses in South Africa on a scale that the older African National Congress did not. Kadalie was the best known of the thousands of Nyasas involved in this massive movement of men between Nyasaland and the lands south of the Zambezi. A very important result of this was, as we have noted, that the people of the Protectorate came to know about the south and what life was like for Africans there. It also meant that close links were forged with the south; Levi Mumba and Kadalie were close friends for most of their lives.

There are many examples of this closely connected Nyasa network which was well established by the late 1920s. Typical is the story of Robert Sambo and Mansell Mphamba. They were two Livingstonia educated Nyasas who formed the ICWU in Bulawayo, having gone first to Cape Town to see

---

[50] Richard Gray, *The Two Nations*. p. 170.

Kadalie and gain formal status as agents of the union. They were subsequently arrested and returned to Nyasaland. Another example is the story of Isaac Lawrence, later Treasurer-General of Nyasaland African Congress, who was sentenced to three years hard labour in September 1926 for importing ICWU literature into Malawi.

Before looking in more detail at how the influence of the men who went south, together with the activities of the Native Association movement, helped bring about the creation of Nyasaland African Congress, we have to digress. We need to look at the politics of Southern Rhodesia, the aims of its leading politicians about which Nyasas were becoming increasingly apprehensive. This apprehension was born out of first hand knowledge of the lands south of the Zambezi, as we have seen, and not as a result of ignorance (as was to be asserted by white politicians and colonial officials from the 1920s and, astonishingly, as late as the 1960s).

The Threat of White Domination

Southern Rhodesia as a political unit had been created by the British South Africa Company in the 1890s and was ruled by the Company until 1923. In 1922 the Europeans in Southern Rhodesia were given the privilege of voting in a referendum where they opted for 'Responsible Government' rather than the one alternative offered: incorporation into the Union of South Africa. This decision led to the country being formally annexed to the British Crown in September 1923. The new 'colony' was immediately granted self-government in domestic matters, modified by a few limitations in the area of African affairs reserved to the government in London. These were meant to protect the rights of the African population but were never effectively invoked. Southern Rhodesia was, as a result, a strange colony whose minority white population had been granted the right of effectively ruling the country in all things other than foreign affairs. Thus Southern Rhodesia was a unique territory in the British Empire; it went from being a territory ruled, somewhat anachronistically, by a commercial company to semi-independent territory ruled by its white minority population without ever having been administered directly by the British government and the officers of its colonial service.

The 1920s were a time when racial segregation was widely held to be the only effective solution to the problems of different ethnic groups living together in the same territory. This widespread intellectual agreement among what are sometimes referred to as the Anglo-Saxon nations, was a result of the domination of the intellectual world of Britain and the United States from the 1870s of the cluster of ideas associated with Scientific Racism and Social Darwinism. It was not surprising then that among the white electorate of Southern Rhodesia some form of racial segregation was the dominant approach to race relations and the future of the territory. However what was to be done in terms of actual legislation saw a variety of approaches adopted by various groups among the settlers.

The white politicians leading Southern Rhodesia, having rejected union with South Africa, did show interest in possible wider relationships, however, when the white settlers in Kenya raised the whole issue of the future of the British East and Central African Territories. These Kenya settlers were challenging the Colonial Office principle of Trusteeship and the idea that the Imperial power should control affairs of a territory as a trust on behalf of the African population. Although allowing that immigrant populations - Asian as well as European - had a part to play in the development of these territories, the interests of the indigenous people had always to be the primary concern of the London government and its Colonial Office. This principle did not mean that the Colonial Office anticipated the coming of Black majority rule in these territories in the next few decades, but only at some vague and distant time in the future. What it did say very firmly was that power was not going to be handed over by London to local white communities as had been done in Southern Rhodesia.[51]

This Colonial Office policy of trusteeship, or 'paramountcy of native interests' so disliked by the Kenya settlers, also alarmed the whites of Northern Rhodesia. With the end of British South Africa Company rule there in 1924, Northern Rhodesia had come under the aegis of the Colonial Office. A Legislative Council had been set up in which the settlers had five seats; the other members were 'officials' who had the majority. The settler leaders, however, were quite clear that the territory should be set on the same track as Southern Rhodesia so that in the not too distant future they also would be granted responsible self-government. The Colonial Office theory of trusteeship stood in their way. As a result, along with their friends in Salisbury (now Harare), they were interested in the protests of the Kenyan settlers.

The Hilton Young and Bledisloe Commissions

There was enough difference of opinion over the future of the British possessions in East and Central Africa that a Commission was appointed by the British Government to review the situation. It was chaired by Sir Edward

---

[51] The idea was enshrined in the Devonshire Declaration of 1924, when, as Colonial Secretary, the Duke of Devonshire laid down this principle as applying to Kenya, and by default to all other territories north of the Zambezi. The Passfield Memorandum of 1930 affirmed this specifically.

Hilton Young and was to consider, among other things, the possibility of closer union between all or some of these British territories.

What the Commission proposed for the East African territories need not detain us. With regard to Northern Rhodesia and Nyasaland, the Commission was so divided that the Chairman's report became the minority report, challenged by the majority report prepared by the other three members, Sir George Schuster, R.A. Mant and J.H. Oldham, a Scotsman who was Secretary of the International Missionary Council.

In his report the chairman, Hilton Young, recommended that the part of Northern Rhodesia between the Luangwa River and the Nyasaland border should become part of the Nyasaland Protectorate and, on the west, Barotseland should also become a Protectorate under the Colonial Office. The rest of Northern Rhodesia, the area of the line of rail, of white settler farms, the mines of Broken Hill and the area where vast copper deposits had just been found on the frontier with the Belgian Congo, should be joined to Southern Rhodesia. In addition the Governor of Southern Rhodesia should become the High Commissioner for the two Protectorates. He added that Southern Rhodesian leaders and representatives of the Northern Rhodesian white settlers were already discussing the possible development of a 'Greater Rhodesia' which might later incorporate Nyasaland.[52]

The majority report submitted by the other three members of the Commission recommended that the 'status quo' be maintained for the government of Northern Rhodesia and Nyasaland. They did say that Nyasaland was not a 'white man's country' in the way that the territories south of the Zambezi were. However, they made a general statement in their 'Summary' with regard to the Central African territories where they stated ominously:

> The independent status of the Governments of Nyasaland and Northern Rhodesia should be maintained pending further development of communications and of mineral exploitation in Northern Rhodesia, both of which may have an important bearing on the settlement of administrative boundaries.[53]

In other words they were suggesting that if the railway system grew and if major mining developments took place with a big increase in the white population north of the Zambezi then something like the arrangements suggested in the chairman's report might be appropriate.

Before returning to this it must be noted that in the list of people interviewed in their travels through Northern Rhodesia and Nyasaland not one African was consulted. No mention was made of the Native Associations in

---

[52] *Report of the Commission on Closer Union of the Dependencies in Eastern and Central Africa* 1929 Cmd 3234 (The Hilton Young Commission) pp. 264-65.
[53] Ibid. p. 296.

Nyasaland, this despite the fact the Levi Mumba had written to the Commission on behalf of the 'Zomba Province Native Association'. His letter was noted, the only African source of opinion to appear anywhere in the 354 pages of the Report. It should be noted that the Scottish Mission Councils backed by other missionary groups, and even one settler group warned the Commission that they believed the African population of Nyasaland was opposed to any development that would link the Protectorate to Southern Rhodesia. The ominous threat in the words in the majority report about the possibility of a reconsideration of the relation of the two northern territories to Southern Rhodesia should there be major mining developments became a lively issue even as the commissioners were preparing their Report, which was published in 1929.

The members of the Commission first arrived in Africa in January 1928 and left in May of that year. At that time rapid developments where taking place in the development of copper mining in Northern Rhodesia. In 1927 10,000 Africans were employed in mining; by 1930 the number had risen to 30,000 and while in 1925 only 260 whites had immigrated to the colony, in 1930 3,600 arrived, most to work in mining and related industries.

This massive change soon had an impact on Southern Rhodesian politicians. Earlier they had had a somewhat tepid interest in the possibility of amalgamation with Northern Rhodesia, but from around 1930 they began to see it differently as the territory gained a larger white population and became one of the principal centres of copper production in the world. These developments in Northern Rhodesia were noticed also in South Africa where Jan Smuts wrote of them as 'another Transvaal on a smaller scale'.[54]

Even as this was happening the Secretary of State for the Colonies, Lord Passfield, issued in June 1930 his 'Memorandum on Native Policy in East Africa' (Cmd 3731). Lord Passfield did no more than re-affirm the 'trusteeship' policy which the imperial government, regardless of which party was in office, had been pursuing since 1920. It did, however, apply these principles which the settlers had previously thought applied to the East African territories and perhaps Nyasaland, explicitly to Northern Rhodesia. The settlers' reactions were instant and furious and they demanded a conference with the London government. This was rejected by London; the Secretary of State saw no point in any discussion since the views the settlers had expressed were, in his view, utterly irreconcilable with the policies of the imperial government. The cable from the Northern Rhodesian white leadership had ended with the threat

---

[54] J.C. Smuts, *Africa and Some World Problems*, Oxford, 1930, p. 43.

> Faced with the declared determination of the Imperial Government to prefer the
> interests of barbarous races to those of their own, they may seek and find sympathy
> and aid (interested though it be) from neighbouring colonies enjoying freer institu-
> tions and more equitable opportunities.[55]

In December 1930 the settler representatives on the Northern Rhodesia Legislative Council began a campaign seeking the amalgamation of their territory with Southern Rhodesia, an approach welcomed with enthusiasm by the
leaders of Southern Rhodesia.

There was an important development taking place in these same years of the
late 1920s and early 1930s among the people of the Nyasaland Protectorate -
the 'Nyasas' as they increasingly called themselves, whether they were
Nyanja, Ngoni, Yao, Chewa, Tumbuka or whatever. As we have seen every
year thousands of 'Nyasas' left home to work in Southern Rhodesia and
South Africa and this level of activity had profound effects in the Protectorate. These men who worked south of the Zambezi discovered a shared
incipient sense of being of one nation and this had its impact back in the
homeland reaching the remotest village. T. Cullen Young, a Scottish missionary who would later jointly produce a book with Kamuzu Banda,
recorded an incident which highlighted this. He wrote of visiting a comparatively isolated area in the Northern Region and of a conversation with a local
elder. The elder was telling Cullen Young that he had heard Africans could
have a union that enabled them to speak to the whites as clans did to each
other through their leaders, that is as equals. At this point a young goatherd
of about twelve broke in and said, 'Yes, it is Kerementi you know'. After a
little puzzlement Young realised the boy was talking about Clements
Kadalie and the Industrial and Commercial Workers' Union.

The men who went to and fro across the Zambezi transmitted this sense of
belonging to one people to their fellows at home on their return and this
sense of oneness was, in turn, encouraged by the Native Association movement. In the 1920s and 30s the Nyasas became increasingly aware of the difference between their situation and that of their brothers and sisters south of
the Zambezi. Wherever they went south of the Zambezi they absorbed the
sense of being in a White Man's country, different from the Nyasaland Protectorate. More than anything the experience of the migrant workers formed
and fed a sense of national consciousness and a pride that Nyasaland, the
homeland about which they sang '*Dziko lathu la Nyasalande liri patari*',[56]
was different.

---

[55] Quoted in Richard Gray, *The Two Nations*, Oxford, 1960 p. 42.
[56] 'Our land of Nyasaland is far away'.

The campaign for amalgamation of the two Rhodesias gathered strength and white Rhodesian leaders wanted to include Nyasaland - the Protectorate was a vital source of labour which might otherwise prefer to go to South Africa. The result was that alarm spread among Nyasas at home and abroad. In the new Copperbelt in Northern Rhodesia, where they provided the majority of foremen, clerks and hospital assistants, Nyasas became well aware of the virulent anger of Northern Rhodesian whites over the Colonial Office stand on its principle of trusteeship which, for all its inadequacies, Nyasas decidedly preferred to the idea of a 'Greater Rhodesia' ruled by a white electorate. As Richard Gray asserted in his study *The Two Nations*, white supremacy was the ideal in Southern Rhodesia, Trusteeship was relatively unchallenged in Nyasaland but the two different philosophies clashed head-on in Northern Rhodesia in the 1930s.[57]

The strength of the call for amalgamation among whites in the two Rhodesias was such that the government in London had to take it seriously. Even before London did anything, the leaders of the Native Association movement in Nyasaland, Levi Mumba and James Frederick Sangala,[58] had raised the alarm there. As early as 1935 the Blantyre Native Association had called a meeting to which all chiefs and headmen in the area were invited to discuss the threat of amalgamation and draft a petition to the Secretary of State for the Colonies opposing any closer association with Southern Rhodesia. This is an example of how the Associations were in close touch with many of the chiefs whose participation in the developing forms of Indirect Rule has often led European observers to mistakenly see them as opposed to the Associations.

As a result of this activity by the Association movement, when the British Government set up the Royal Commission on Rhodesia and Nyasaland, Nyasaland African public opinion was already organised to present to it a united front of opposition to amalgamation. Sangala was the key figure in Blantyre while the influence of Levi Mumba in the rest of the country, particularly in the Northern Region, was fundamental. This united African opposition to any closer association with Southern Rhodesia was presented to the Royal Commission when the members took evidence in Nyasaland in June and July, 1938. Again it is notable that the special memorandum presented to the Commission by Nkhosi Gomani, paramount chief of the southern Ngoni, on behalf of the meeting of chiefs of the Central and Northern Provinces was actually composed by Levi Mumba. The new Governor of the

---

[57] Richard Gray, *The Two Nations*, OUP 1960 p. 181.

[58] Later to be the author's friend and guide through the intricacies of Malawi history and politics.

Protectorate, Kittermaster, saw the Native Associations as a valid channel of African opinion, a majority of his administration, however, looked to the chiefs to reflect the true voice of the people but there was no conflict, African opinion was solidly against amalgamation. It is important to note that even at this date it was pointed out at the Blantyre meeting of chiefs and Association leaders with the Commission and again at the meeting at Lilongwe that the opposition was to *any form of closer association with Southern Rhodesia including a federation!*

Though less well organised than in Nyasaland, African opinion in Northern Rhodesia was also opposed to amalgamation. This was in sharp contrast with the passionate advocacy of amalgamation on the part of the majority of the European population there. European opinion in Nyasaland, despite the efforts of some enthusiasts for amalgamation, was very cautious and suggested nothing should be done against the wishes of the African people. The 'Convention of Associations', the most representative settler body, was quite clear that though they recognised benefits that might accrue from amalgamation, they felt that a move in that direction would so anger and upset the African population as to lead to what they called 'serious trouble'.

Meanwhile the Blantyre and Livingstonia Mission Councils of the Church of Scotland, after consulting the Presbyteries of Blantyre and Livingstonia of the CCAP, each warned the Commission against the imposition of amalgamation against the will of the African people, a warning which the General Assembly of the Church of Scotland had already sent to the Secretary of State for the Colonies in May 1938 in a letter formally approved by a large majority in the Assembly.

The British Government accepted the recommendations of the Commission that amalgamation of the territories, as requested by the white political leaders in Southern and Northern Rhodesia, was not appropriate at that time. Although the immediate reaction in the Protectorate was one of rejoicing - a Blantyre Native Association official even called for 'Three Cheers for the Colonial Office'[59]- the leadership of the movement saw that the road to closer relationship with the South had not been closed once and for all. Even when the Commission was quite clear that amalgamation should not be pursued at that time, their words left it on the agenda for the future.

> The average native is ill-equipped to form a proper appreciation of the effects of amalgamation, either on his own position or on the prospects of the Territories... Nevertheless the striking unanimity, in the northern Territories, of the native opposition to amalgamation, based mainly on dislike of some features of the native policy of Southern Rhodesia, and the anxiety of the natives in Northern Rhodesia and Nyasaland lest there should be any change in the system under which they regard

---

[59] Recounted to me by J.F. Sangala.

themselves as enjoying the direct protection of Your Majesty, are factors which cannot in our judgement be ignored.[60]

However, the Report of the Commission, signed by all its members although some with stated reservations, also stated that the political unity of the three territories would come about sooner or later and that the United Kingdom Government should state its acceptance of the principle of the amalgamation of the three territories.[61] The United Kingdom Government did no such thing, but it was quite clear to perceptive observers that the issue was not closed.

Despite the coming of the Second World War, white Rhodesian political leaders took every available opportunity to press the London government on the issue. The response among Nyasas to the Bledisloe Commission and to this continued Rhodesian lobbying was an increase in radical thinking on the future of their country and the creation of the Nyasaland African Congress.

---

[60] *Bledisloe Report*, p. 218.

[61] *ibid.* p. 214-269. Those with noted reservations were Fitzgerald and Boyd-Orr who did not accept amalgamation as inevitable and Mainwaring who insisted that the interests of the Africans of the Northern Territories would not be served by putting them under the authority of the white Southern Rhodesians.

Chapter 2

The Formation of the Nyasaland African Congress and the Imposition of Federation

There are three threads which are inter-twined inseparably in the story of the struggle of the people of Nyasaland to remain free of political control by the white settlers of Southern Rhodesia. This story runs from 1938, when the people made clear their opposition to amalgamation with the Rhodesias, to 1953 when the British Government imposed the Central African Federation against the will of the Nyasa people. The first thread is the story of the creation and development of the Nyasaland African Congress; the second is the campaign of the Southern Rhodesian leader Godfrey Huggins, (later aided by Roy Welensky, leader of the settler lobby in Northern Rhodesia,) to achieve the amalgamation of the three territories under settler rule. The third is the entry of Dr H. Kamuzu Banda into the affairs of his homeland for the first time.

The Formation of the Nyasaland National Congress

In the classic study of the region in the 1930s and 40s, Richard Gray's *The Two Nations*, the author describes the puzzlement of the senior members of the Nyasaland Protectorate administration over what they saw as the extraordinarily rapid transformation of Nyasa attitudes between 1938 and the end of the Second World War. In 1943 the Nyasaland Educated African Council emerged from discussions among the leaders of the Native Associations; a few months later it renamed itself the Nyasaland African Congress while continuing the former Council's call for rapid constitutional movement towards self-government.[62] In his short biography of James Frederick Sangala, D.D. Phiri asserts that it was Sangala who pressed for the removal of the word 'Educated' from the title of the movement. He had been convinced by the Reverend K.T. Motsetse, a Mosotho teaching at Blantyre Secondary School, of the futility of a movement of the educated elite alone.

It appeared to the colonial administrators that a new radicalism had exploded on the scene with the publication on 1 October 1943 of a circular letter by J.F. Sangala in connection with the creation of the Nyasaland Educated African Council.[63] The letter urged Nyasas to unite to press for self-

---

[62] Gray, *Two Nations*, pp. 337-340.
[63] The Council set up in August 1943 became the Nyasaland African Council and then the Nyasaland African Congress early in 1944.

government for Nyasaland. Indeed Sangala encouraged them to 'Fight for Freedom', though he carefully explained to the District Commissioner, Blantyre, that this did not mean armed conflict. This same radicalism, the administration felt, was also reflected in a speech by Charles Matinga, later to be the second President-General of Congress. His speech bitterly criticized the lack of promotion of African interests on the part of the missions as well as the slowness of the Administration to respond to African demands for advancement. Indeed, Matinga praised the pre-1914 missionaries for their concern for the people and their promotion of African advancement. He specifically accused those who had arrived for the first time after 1918 of bringing with them racist ideas and race prejudice.[64] To the officers of the Administration, all this appeared to be a far cry from the 1938 call of 'three cheers for the Colonial Office'.

In discussing the genesis and development of the Nyasaland African Congress, Gray criticizes the attempt by the officials to explain this apparently sudden radicalisation of African opinion by insisting that a European must be behind it. Their attitude, Gray says, simply exposed how far the officials were, not only from any understanding of the fears and hopes of the people of the Protectorate but also the level of sophistication and understanding they had achieved.

I might add that the officials did not seem to have noticed how, as early as 1938, the Reverend Thomas Maseya of the Blantyre Presbytery of the CCAP, supported by other members of the Blantyre Native Association, dissatisfied with the weak document produced by the Association's chairman Ellerton Mposa, had presented an alternative submission to the Bledisloe Commission. Maseya requested two key things; first a dramatic improvements in the provision of English-medium higher education in the Protectorate and second the immediate empowerment of educated Africans to elect one half of the members of the Nyasaland Legislative Council. This would have given Africans a clear majority over those members representing the white settlers, the so-called 'unofficials' in the Council. Between Maseya's demands of 1938 and Sangala's so-called radical letter in 1943, one can hardly see a dramatic new radicalisation of attitudes among educated Nyasas, but rather a consistent development.

It is significant that in these demands by Sangala and Matinga, radical though they may have been deemed, we see that Nyasas still believed in the British promise that the paramountcy of African interests was the key to British colonial policy in Africa north of the Zambezi. It was, however, also

[64] See Tangri, 'Development of Modern African Politics', (PhD, University of Edinburgh, 1970) p. 277 and Ross, *Blantyre Mission and the Making of Modern Malawi.*

an indication of impatience and that Nyasas felt the British needed to be reminded vigorously that this paramountcy had to be manifested institutionally.

The commitment of Nyasas to totally oppose the threat of amalgamation or, indeed, of any kind of closer relationship with Southern Rhodesia, explains the increased urgency in demanding progress towards self-government, so vigorously begun by Maseya in 1938. The very next year the publication of the Bledisloe Report meant that Nyasas realised with grave disappointment, that the threat of amalgamation had not been removed. Although the Report insisted that amalgamation was not to be imposed so long as the people of Nyasaland opposed it, a majority of the Commission still approved it in principle. Furthermore, Nyasas scattered across southern Africa read the local newspapers, *The Johannesburg Star, the Bulawayo Chronicle* and *The Rhodesia Herald,* and knew what was being said by the white Rhodesian politicians. They knew that these men, led by Huggins, were continuing to press Britain for the amalgamation of the three territories under settler rule and the Nyasas saw them continue to do so despite the outbreak of the Second World War. Indeed during the war the new leader of the Northern Rhodesian settler community, Roy Welensky, became Huggins' most effective ally in this campaign.

What always astonishes anyone reviewing this period of the history of the region is the way the leaders of the settler communities in Southern and Northern Rhodesia would, in local constituency meetings and in interviews with the local press, articulate their commitment to white supremacy and segregation and then appear to be puzzled when Nyasas were able to quote these speeches and interviews when protesting to the London government about the aims of Huggins and his allies. Nyasas knew through the simple exercise of reading the local newspapers that whatever they might say to London, the aim of Huggins, Welensky and company was the extension of white domination north of the Zambezi. They knew this was so whether it was voiced in terms of amalgamation or federation.

The greater astonishment for the historian, however, is how through the nineteen forties and early fifties British officials in the Colonial Office and Commonwealth Relations Office, continued to accept at face value the white Rhodesian politicians' plans about the place of African people in society. The senior British officials charged with responsibility of advising the British government on policy for the area seemed unaware of the glaring discrepancy between what was said to them and what these same politicians said to their home audience. Yet this was a discrepancy of which many ordinary Nyasas, so often declared to be not yet sophisticated enough to understand the issues, were well aware.

War Service, Work Experience and Growing Self-Consciousness

With the outbreak of the Second World War in 1939 an important new influence on the self-understanding of Nyasas came into play. This was the extraordinarily large part played by Nyasa soldiers in the world-wide conflict. One out of three male Nyasas of the required age-group served in the army, all volunteers. The result was that not only did nine battalions of the Nyasaland King's African Rifles fight in Ethiopia, North Africa and Burma but also many other Nyasas served in the Northern Rhodesia Regiment in these same campaigns.

During the Second World War, the Army Education Corps gave lessons on Allied war aims to all British and Commonwealth troops in training. Thus these KAR and NRR *asikari* were taught that they were fighting for liberty and for 'the self-determination of subject peoples'! The impact of this was immediately reflected in the first Annual Conference of the NAC, when the president referred to 'the support of our soldiers who are *fighting for the cause of liberty.*'[65]

All of this appears to have been missed by the Administration when casting around to find an external left-wing European influence on the Congress leaders to explain what they saw as the radicalisation of the movement. Colonial officials appeared to be incapable of understanding that Africans could think things through for themselves using the world of knowledge available to them through an English medium education system.[66] They discussed the possibility that it was W.H. Timcke, a local white planter sympathetic to African advancement and who certainly sought to radicalise people like Sangala; some officials even suggested that the root of the radicalisation came from the contacts between James Sangala and Arthur Creech-Jones of the British Labour Party, or his contacts with Senator Margaret Ballinger, the South African white radical politician. Since these latter connections were a matter of a few letters, the officials do appear to have been clutching at straws.

There was, however, one European intellectual influence on some of the leaders of Congress, which the British officials in the Protectorate missed completely, as have historians of the period like Richard Gray, Robert Rot-

---

[65] I remember well the Reverend Jonathan Sangaya, General Secretary of the Blantyre Synod of the CCAP, telling me how important to him and his comrades in the KAR was their victory over the Italian colonialists in Ethiopia, as he said, 'an African army freeing an African country'.

[66] It was only in the late 1940s that the Dutch Reformed Missions and the Roman Catholic Missions began to develop education in English. Until then they had concentrated on 'native tongue' education.

berg and Roger Tangri: and that was Jim Rodgers of the Blantyre Mission, an elder of the CCAP. In the run up to the visit of the Bledisloe Commission in 1938 and continuing intermittently until 1948, this agriculturalist missionary made available to Sangala and his circle books from the *Left Wing Book Club*, publications which, at that time, were banned from the Protectorate. Sangala and his friends met intermittently at Rodger's house on Blantyre Mission, usually on Sunday evenings, to discuss issues raised in these books.

Rodgers was a quiet man; not a political activist but rather an educator. He believed in exposing important ideas to his African friends who would make of them what *they* wished.[67] His involvement began in 1935 when, in response to the white settler agitation that led to the setting up of the Bledisloe Commission, he published an essay which was read by many Nyasas. In the essay he compared the current situation in Central Africa to the situation in South Africa in the years leading up to the Union of 1910. He pointed out that after the Union was achieved, all the rights of the Africans of the old Cape Colony, supposedly guaranteed in the new constitution by the Imperial government, had been swept away without any interference from London. Such guarantees, he insisted, were exposed as being not worth the paper they were written on.

There is no doubt that Sangala and others picked up a certain vocabulary from these meetings, and that they felt affirmed in their political stance by what they read, but the radicalisation of Nyasa politics was an indigenous phenomenon. It was shaped by the fear of amalgamation which so many Nyasas well understood was intended to achieve the permanent imposition of white supremacy in the region and the end of 'the paramountcy of native interests', the policy of the Colonial Office enshrined in the Passfield Memorandum. Modern writers can rightly say that the 'paramountcy of native interests' was not all that it should have been in practice, but it continued to articulate a principle which appeared threatening to the settler community.

The concept of the paramountcy of African interests had already been articulated in the Devonshire Declaration of 1922 where it related only to Kenya. In 1930 Lord Passfield, the Secretary of State for the Colonies, ruled that the principle should apply to Nyasaland and Northern Rhodesia also. If there was a conflict between the needs of an immigrant community and that

---

67 Interviews with Jim Rodgers in May 1966.

46

of the people native to the territory then the needs of the people native to the territory must have priority.[68]

For all the slowness of African advancement under the Colonial Office, the Northern Rhodesian settlers and a minority of Nyasaland settlers saw the doctrine of the 'paramountcy of native interests' as real enough to make its removal one of their primary political aims. As W. Tait Bowie of the Cholo Settlers Association, at that time one of the few pro-amalgamation activists in the Protectorate, said in May 1938

> Do we consider the ideal is one strong British self-governing community in Central Africa, or do we wish to remain forever the vassals of the Colonial Office?[69]

It is clear which of the two opinions he preferred!

The removal of the authority of the Colonial Office from Central Africa was the key reason for the white settlers in Northern Rhodesia to seek the amalgamation of the three territories. Support for the idea of amalgamation or federation among the small number of settlers in Nyasaland varied and was never a majority until the eve of the imposition of federation in 1953.

When we turn to what Congress was actually doing and thinking and leave the speculation of the officials to one side, we find that in addition to the opposition to amalgamation or federation, three themes run through the thinking and the activities of Congress between 1944 and 1951. These were first, a demand for direct representation in the Nyasaland Legislative Council as the first step towards self-government; second, a significant increase in the quantity and quality of the English language education available to the people, and third, the encouragement and growth of a sense of supra-tribal unity.

It should be noted that Nyasas vigorously propagated their ideas wherever they went. For example, it was a groups of Nyasas who, in 1946, played a significant part in the creation of the Reformed Industrial and Commercial Workers' Union in Southern Rhodesia, which instantly became the focus there of non-tribal African radicalism in the territory. Indeed, until the mid-fifties, it surpassed in numbers and in effective action the far more moderate Southern Rhodesian African Congress. This is not so surprising when it is realised that something over twenty per cent of all Africans in paid employment in Southern Rhodesia were Nyasas.

---

[68] The profound impact this had on settler opinion, particularly in Northern Rhodesia, is well described and documented in Rotberg's *The Rise of Nationalism in Central Africa*, pp. 102-104.

[69] Quoted in Tangri, 'Modern African Politics', p. 265.

A national loyalty beyond traditional local or 'tribal' loyalties was not simply an idea propounded by a few leaders of Congress. By 1948 tens of thousands of Nyasas who had either worked in the south or served in the army undoubtedly felt they were 'Nyasas' rather than simply Nyanja, Chewa, Ngoni, Yao, Tumbuka, Tonga or Lomwe.[70] Even the Annual Report on Nyasaland, issued by the Colonial Office in London in 1946, recognises this new sense of a supra-tribal sense of national unity among the people of the Protectorate.

It is somewhat ironic that this recognition of Nyasa national self-consciousness was made officially in a British Government publication on the eve of the initiation of a major shift in British policy. This shift fatefully linked Nyasaland to the two Rhodesias in a way that, had it succeeded in the long term, would have prevented the coming into existence of their nation, the Malawi of today.

We should note, and this is something we will return to on a number of occasions later, that the growth of this strong Nyasa self-consciousness was an experience that was not shared by the most famous *mchona* of all, Dr H.K. Banda.[71] Although from 1938, while living in Britain, he had begun to take an interest in Nyasa affairs and supported diligently Nyasaland African Congress with funds and advice, Banda's absence from the country from 1915 until 1958 meant that he had not been part of the community of people who experienced the growing sense of Nyasa identity. He was not one of the tens of thousands who came to feel that they were Nyasa rather than Chewa or Tumbuka, Nyanja, Ngoni or Yao. Kamuzu Banda never escaped a deep sense of being Chewa. It is perhaps understandable that Mark H. Watkins' *A Grammar of Chichewa*, published in Chicago in 1937 might include the words 'All the information was gained from Kamuzu Banda, a native Chewa'. What is much more significant, however, is that when publishing with Cullen Young the volume of essays *Our African Way of Life*, Banda was so emphatic that he was Chewa and that the essays were about the Chewa way of life. This volume was published in 1946 when, as we have seen, even the Colonial Government was remarking on the wide spread sense of being Nyasa in the Protectorate.

---

[70] In 1962 while talking with some ANC activists in London, one said to me 'You are lucky in Nyasaland, you have only one tribe, we see them all over South Africa, the Nyasas.'

[71] *Mchona* (for non-ciNyanja speakers) means one of those Nyasas who left the Protectorate to seek work and didn't return.

White Settler Pressure for Amalgamation

Before we can pursue further the story of the development of the Nyasaland African Congress and the problems it faced during the first years of its existence, we need to turn to the second thread of our story. We need to examine the continuing campaign for the amalgamation of the three territories and how its aims remained the same even as it was reshaped as a campaign for the federation of the three territories. More importantly we must consider how and why the British Government became willing to reverse its previous policies and impose federation against the express wishes of the Nyasa people.

As early as 1944, two events took place that appeared to indicate some sympathy in Whitehall for the pleas of the settler politicians. The first was a major change in the Northern Rhodesian constitution whereby the Colonial Office increased the number of settler members, giving them a majority in the Northern Rhodesia Legislative Council. In the same document, it was announced that three additional seats in Legco were to be filled by Europeans nominated by the Governor to represent African interests, and that these were to be replaced by Africans when a suitable form of election could be developed. This was little more than a gesture to show that trusteeship was still British policy. Most people in the region assumed that this was a step in the direction of settler control and the beginning of the removal of Northern Rhodesia from what Southern Rhodesians thought of as the 'Black North' controlled by the Colonial Office.[72]

The second development, also in 1944, was the setting up of the Central African Council, a move that had been recommended by the Bledisloe Commission. The Council was to facilitate cooperation between the three territories in areas of mutual interest. The impact of the Council on the politics of the region was twofold and contradictory. Although the British Government had said specifically that this Council was not meant to develop into the amalgamation or federation of the three territories, most white politicians and most Nyasas saw it as a first step in that direction. Its existence also meant that a number of key officials from all three territories became used to working together and seeing the area as one rather than three units.

There was also, however, a contrary impact that the Council made on the politics of the region of which little notice was taken by so many officials in London who were more and more supportive of some sort of union of the three territories. This was that the very success of the Council in promoting

---

[72] Colin Leys, 'The Making of the Federation', Conference paper delivered at Rhodes House, Oxford, 17 April 1959.

joint ventures, both economic and administrative, showed that all the gains that amalgamation or federation was needed to achieve could be and indeed were being achieved without closer constitutional links. In 1958 the Jack Report would point out the positive economic development that had taken place in Nyasaland in the five years since the creation of the Federation in 1953. What it failed to point out was that an equal volume of economic development had already taken place in the previous five years. Geoffrey Colby the Governor from 1948 to 1956 devoted himself to the economic development of Nyasaland using all the opportunities that the Council gave him for the economic development of the territory. This same distinguished British civil servant was opposed to the creation of the Federation. He pointed out the serious error of imposing it in the face of the opposition of the African people, and although doing his duty in trying to make it work after Federation was imposed, he forecast its failure. Roy Welensky later wrote of him:

> he felt from the word go – and I go back to the conference – that it wouldn't work. He thought – when I talked privately – he didn't see the day would ever dawn when the Africans would accept the kind of constitution that men like Huggins and I wanted for the Federation.[73]

Yet, it was the assertion that federation was necessary to gain these economic and administrative advantages that was to be the key argument which led many moderate figures in the UK to support federation in the debate that went on in Britain from 1950 to 1953. Indeed the idea that a federal union was essential for economic development and to gain an increase in the standard of living of Africans was what persuaded some in the United Kingdom, who had opposed federation previously, to contemplate the possibility of supporting the scheme. These economic advantages which could only be achieved by the federation of the territories were seen to be so obvious as to need no detailed explanation and, indeed, at no point was any formal paper written to explain them in the debates that went on through these three fraught years.[74]

Although Colin Leys traces the drive for amalgamation back to 1915,[75] we only need take up the story with a conference held in January 1936 at Victoria Falls, the first of three famous (or infamous) conferences there. All the settler representatives on the Northern Rhodesian Legislative Council sup-

[73] Letter from Welensky to Colin Baker, quoted in the latter's biography of Colby *Development Governor*, p. 339.

[74] A. Hazlewood, 'The Economics of Federation and Dissolution,' in A. Hazlewood, (ed.) *African Integration and Disintegration*, Oxford, 1967.

[75] Chapter One of Colin Leys and Cranfors Pratt (eds.) *A New Deal in Central Africa*, London, 1960.

ported amalgamation and met with representatives of all the white political parties of Southern Rhodesia. No firm agreement on proposals to be put to the British Government was produced by these discussions, however, as the Southern Rhodesian Labour Party, which represented white artisans and small shopkeepers there, would only agree to support such a plan if the proposed new central government was given 'a complete free hand over "native policy"'. This Southern Rhodesian group were upset by the presence of Africans in skilled trades in Nyasaland and, to a lesser extent, in Northern Rhodesia. Delegates had been warned that such a public and total abdication of previous traditions of the Colonial Office was something that the British Government was unwilling to countenance. Although it was to be wiped out as a party within the decade, the Southern Rhodesian Labour Party's objections at that point, when added to other areas of contention, led to the conference breaking up without the formulation of any firm resolutions.

Godfrey Huggins, however, continued his lobbying of London and the result was the creation of the Bledisloe Commission which visited all three Central African territories in 1938 and reported to the UK parliament in 1939. After wide consultations in the three territories, the Commission, as we have seen, recommended that amalgamation must not be imposed against the wishes of the African population of the two Protectorates. From the Nyasa point of view, what was ominous was the agreement of a majority of the Commission that amalgamation was a worthwhile objective in principle. This encouraged Huggins and other settler leaders to continue lobbying London throughout the Second World War.

The war created a substantial and continuing demand for Northern Rhodesian copper which led to a massive growth in white immigration; significantly most of the immigrants came from the south. Perhaps even more important was that these developments led to Northern Rhodesia having, year by year, a massive budgetary surplus.

This new prosperous white community wanted security for their way of life and they saw the old Colonial Office mantra of the paramountcy of native interests as a threat. Their apprehension increased markedly when, after granting independence to what are now Pakistan, India, Sri Lanka and Burma, the Labour administration in Britain began to talk of democratic self-government in Africa. The white population of Southern Rhodesia increasingly saw the policy of the 'Paramountcy of Native Interests' north of the Zambezi as a threat to them also. Colin Leys has summed up the attitude of the majority of whites in the two Rhodesias in 1948 to the Colonial Office and its policies.

This had its greatest effect on the most recently settled Europeans, over 60% of whom in the war years had come from the Union of South Africa. They had no par-

51

ticular interest in Northern Rhodesian independence, but they had strong views on white supremacy. .... If a system of racial equality were introduced in Northern Rhodesia and Nyasaland, white supremacy would become insecure in any neighbouring state – especially if, as in Southern Rhodesia about 20% of the labour force came from Nyasaland. It was logical for Southern Rhodesian settlers to try to prevent this by extending the system of white supremacy to these territories by uniting with them. The way Huggins put it was: 'We do not want our grandchildren to have as neighbours a state such as Liberia...'[76]

This sense of urgency was intensified by two other factors. The first was the massive victory of Dr Malan's National Party in South Africa in 1948. For the anti-Afrikaner majority of Southern Rhodesian whites, this closed off any resort to closer association with South Africa as a means of maintaining white supremacy. The second factor was one which the Huggins' cabinet kept confidential but which was an important influence on them. This was threat to the stability of Southern Rhodesia, created by its running short of the development funds necessary to sustain the prosperity of the sizeably increased white population of the colony. Union with Northern Rhodesia and its massive budgetary surpluses now seemed doubly attractive.

By 1948 the majority of whites in both Rhodesias were agreed on the need for amalgamation and set about campaigning effectively for it. It should be noted that the minority of whites in Southern Rhodesia who opposed amalgamation and subsequently also opposed the amalgamation or federation of the territories, did so on the grounds that such developments did not go far enough to maintain white supremacy.

From Amalgamation towards Federation

The leaders of the settlers of both Rhodesias met in Lusaka in October 1948. It was at this meeting that the decision was taken to change the tactics, though not the ultimate aim, of the campaign. Huggins and others had learned that the Tory Opposition in Britain agreed with the Labour Government that British pubic opinion would not tolerate amalgamation because of the history of opposition to it by the people of Nyasaland and Northern Rhodesia. However, Col. Stanley, a former Tory Cabinet Minster, suggested to the white Rhodesian leaders that the federation of the three territories was something that both the Conservative and Labour parties in Britain might accept.[77]

At the Lusaka meeting it was agreed to begin a campaign to persuade the British government to accept a scheme for the federation of the three territories. Initially Huggins was opposed to this change but was finally persuaded

---

[76] Leys. Ibid.
[77] Don Taylor. The Rhodesian. London. 1955. p. 105.

to back the scheme when it was pointed out that the constitutional arrangements could be so manipulated as to give preponderance of power to the Federal Government, which would be controlled by settler votes. In any case, as Huggins himself was to remind the Matebeleland Executive of his own party in 1951, the arrangements to be made by Britain to ensure African rights in the proposed federation should be seen in the light of what happened to the safeguards of African interests in the Cape in the setting up of the Union of South Africa and the fate of similar safeguards in the original 1924 constitution of Southern Rhodesia. These, as his audience well knew, had proved worthless. Huggins insisted that even the British Government knew this. If full Dominion status - which would bring with it full political autonomy - could be gained by the white government of the new federation reasonably soon after its establishment, then everything they had hoped for from amalgamation would be achieved.

The next step for Huggins was to call a second Victoria Falls Conference which met in February 1949. The leaders of the settlers of the two Rhodesias attended, this time along with three Nyasaland settler representatives, to draw up a federal scheme to be presented to the British Government. They failed to reach an agreement because Huggins would not budge from his draft for a 'federal scheme' which was so obviously just amalgamation under another name. The other problem was Huggins' insistence that any African representation in the proposed Federal Parliament would, in his words, 'be a farce'. As the *Bulawayo Chronicle* reported on 17 February, 1949, he went on, 'For the time being the native must be ruled by a benevolent aristocracy in the real sense of the word'.

As I have pointed out already this was one of the newspapers which were widely read by Nyasas in order to gauge what the settlers were up to. Almost as soon as the federal scheme was broached they knew from the mouths of the settler leaders themselves that this was simply another, if slower, way to achieve amalgamation and the expansion of settler supremacy. Yet the senior officials of the Colonial and Commonwealth Relations Offices did not seem to notice the discrepancy between what was officially said to the British Government and what was said by the same white politicians at home in the Rhodesias.

These senior officials were intelligent and able men, so of course they noticed the discrepancy but they appear to have changed their understanding of the traditional Colonial Office policy enshrined in the Passfield Declaration. The change was signalled by the statement of the Chief Secretary in the Northern Rhodesia Legislative Council on 24th June 1949 in which he said that 'if by paramountcy is meant a policy of subordinating the interests of one section of the community to those of another, then I can say that paramountcy is dead.' The interpretation of paramountcy which he was declaring dead was exactly what the Passfield Declaration had meant, and the Devonshire declaration before that.

Thus, already in mid-summer 1949, we have a very senior British colonial officer extolling the 'partnership of the races' rather than 'the paramountcy of native interests'; indeed he was using the 'partnership' phrase for the first time in the political discussion on the future of Central Africa. This concept of 'partnership' was to become the key concept used by Huggins and Welensky to 'sell' the idea of the federation of the three territories to the British public.

How do we account for this change which left the Congress leaders in Nyasaland in a very difficult situation? People like James Sangala had, until then, taken as given that the future freedom of their country depended on staying under British Colonial Office authority while pressing for more rapid advance towards self-government. He and other Congress leaders took for granted that the Colonial Office was their ally against the expansion of white settler rule from the south into the lands north of the Zambezi. The leaders of these same settlers were insistent in their dislike of the Colonial Office and their desire to remove the authority of the Colonial Office from the region, hence the shouts by Africans in Blantyre in 1938 of 'Long Live the Colonial Office'.

Back in London, in the letter he wrote to the Colonial Office which he later published as a pamphlet in 1951 entitled *Federation in Central Africa*, Dr Banda expressed the same trust in Britain and articulated the same understanding of the situation as Sangala and the other congressmen in Nyasaland.[78] He wrote

> We Africans of Nyasaland and Northern Rhodesia value highly our direct political and cultural connexion with the United Kingdom. We value the steps that have been taken to give us lessons in government. We value the steps that have been taken to widen our educational and cultural horizons by allowing us to study in Britain.
>
> If we accept the proposed federation we shall cut ourselves away from the United Kingdom...[79]

---

[78] Both the letter and the pamphlet list Harry Nkumbula as joint author but he contributed nothing to the text.

[79] H.K. Banda and H. Nkumbula. *Federation in Central Africa*. A meeting of Nyasa and Northern Rhodesian students in London in 1949 commissioned Nkumbula and Banda to write on their behalf to the Colonial Office protesting against federation. Nkumbula left the writing to Banda, who published it privately in February 1951 for distribution in the two Protectorates.

If 'the paramountcy of native interests' was dead this was not just a problem for Northern Rhodesia but a massive one for Nyasaland.

It has been suggested that the change in the attitude of a number of senior key officials in the Colonial Office and the Commonwealth Relations Office came from their interpretation of the conclusions drawn by Lord Hailey in his highly regarded report made to the British Government during the War, *Native Administration and Political Development in British Tropical Africa*, (London, HMSO, 1944). From the late nineteen thirties onwards, Hailey's judgement was trusted by many people with influence on colonial policy, politicians and officials as well as academics. In his policy-shaping report, Hailey drew two conclusions which had profound effect on the history of Central Africa. The first was his assertion that the export of replicas of British parliamentary democracy was not necessarily the way ahead for Africa, and the second that economic development and a decent standard of living were far more important to ordinary Africans than was political advance: bread was more important than the vote!

These two conclusions were seized on by the supporters of the federal idea and used again and again in their discussions with British politicians and officials. Federation would raise dramatically the standard of living of the Africans in the Protectorates and that was what really mattered to them. If one really had the good of the Africans in the Protectorates at heart, one supported federation, which alone could improve their standard of living.

Federation would, it was pointed out tellingly, also help Britain economically at a time when Britain was in profound economic difficulties as a result of the enormous debts accumulated during the Second World War. Getting rid of the burden of Northern Rhodesia and Nyasaland while retaining close economic links with a new white Dominion was an objective that senior British officials and some politicians pursued, but rarely, if ever, admitted during the years leading up to the creation of the Federation of Nyasaland and the Rhodesias.

Equally important to an understanding of the impact of Haley's ideas on traditional Colonial Office policy is the fact that these ideas appear to have been appropriated by two very important British civil servants, Andrew Cohen in the Colonial Office and G.H. Baxter in the Commonwealth Relations Office. After meeting these two men in London, Roy Welensky made a most revealing remark which illuminated the thinking of these officials and what 'federation' and 'partnership' meant to all three. Welensky asserted that he was now convinced 'that the stage had arrived when the dream of a British Central African Dominion could become a reality'. In other words, the way ahead was opened up for a white settler ruled self-governing state;

what Tait Bowie had, back in 1938, called 'one strong self-governing British Community'.[80]

After the 1949 Victoria Falls Conference ended without effective results there was a period of calm and apparent inactivity. The Secretary of State for the Colonies, Mr Creech-Jones, stated in the House of Commons soon after that the British Government did not consider it advisable to call a conference on the possible federation of the Rhodesias and Nyasaland and that seemed to be that.

As Griff Jones, then a District Commissioner serving in Nyasaland, has suggested Huggins and Welensky were simply biding their time.[81] They believed that very soon the Labour Government would have to go to the polls and that if the Conservatives won the General Election, they had a better chance of achieving their aims. Certainly, as long as Creech-Jones was Colonial Secretary they felt their way was blocked. The series of conversations he had had with African leaders in Nyasaland and Northern Rhodesia had re-affirmed his belief that Federation was not 'on'.[82]

In December 1949 Huggins, with a British General Election certain to be called soon, made his move and said he would withdraw Southern Rhodesia from the Central African Council within the next twelve months, effectively destroying the Council. Creech-Jones understood this to be an ultimatum to the British Government; they had to listen to the demands for Federation or Southern Rhodesia might look to closer union with the Union of South Africa. This was a bluff as most Rhodesians were hostile to the now Afrikaner dominated South Africa. However it seems that the senior officials in the Colonial and Commonwealth Relations Office, whose job it was to advise the British Government, took Huggins' threat very seriously.

The British General election took place in February 1950. Not only did Creech-Jones lose his seat but the Labour Government was returned with only a very narrow majority in the House of Commons. A Labour government, in danger of defeat at every division in the House of Commons, had much more to worry about than the fate of a small Protectorate in Central Africa. Of course the traditional colonial affairs pressure groups in Britain were concerned but they too had other problems to deal with, the fate of the South African Protectorates and armed insurgency both in Malaya and Kenya. It was only in Scotland that there was a continuing significant and

---

[80] Colin Leys reported Welensky saying this, without citing a reference, in his paper to the Conference on the Federation at Rhodes House in April, 1959.

[81] Griff Jones, *Britain and Nyasaland*, London, George Allen and Unwin, 1964, p. 134.

[82] D.D. Phiri, *James Frederick Sangala*, p. 38.

widespread popular cross-party concern over the threat of Nyasaland being incorporated into a new state against the wishes of the African people.[83]

The new Secretary of State for the Colonies, Jim Griffiths, had little or no experience of African affairs. Unlike Creech-Jones, who had the knowledge and experience to assess the advice he got from his senior civil servants, Griffiths was at their mercy. Thus it was that, as a result of these events, Huggins, Welensky and the British senior civil servants sympathetic to the federal concept had a massive opportunity to push for the rapid creation of the federation of the three territories. Griffiths, distracted by the problems presented to him by serious difficulties across the colonial Empire, fell into the trap set by Huggins.

The Prime Minister of Southern Rhodesia had written to the British Government calling for a conference of officials whose task was, as he put it, simply to review the technical problems faced in any attempt to create a federation of the territories. Creech-Jones had responded with a firm 'no' to any such conference but things were now different. On the 8th of November 1950, Griffiths announced to the House of Commons that in response to the request from the Southern Rhodesian Prime Minister, he was setting up a conference of officials from the three Central African territories together with others from the Colonial Office and the Commonwealth Relations Office. Their remit was to

> Examine the problem in all its aspects and consider whether it is possible, in the light of this examination, for them to formulate proposals for a further advance in the closer association of the three Central African territories.[84]

Although Griffiths went on to say in that speech that the work to be done was purely exploratory and did not commit the British Government to anything, from the Nyasa point of view, it appeared as if the game was lost.

Nyasas already knew that in March of that year Huggins had visited London for talks with Griffiths. At that meeting the two men appeared to have come to some sort of agreement. As Colin Leys has pointed out, only the existence of such an agreement can explain Griffiths setting up working parties of officials from the three territories with instructions to produce a survey of the 'native policies' of the three territories, particularly since the decision was taken almost immediately after Huggins visit to London.

The contrast between the 'Native Policies' north and south of the Zambezi was the nub of the matter on which the Hilton Young and Bledisloe Commissions had rejected amalgamation of the territories, something of which

---

[83] See my 'The Kirk and colonial policy 1864-1964' in *The Scottish Churches and the Union Parliament, 1707-1999.*

[84] Hansard for 8.11.50 quoted in Griff Jones, p. 135.

Creech-Jones had been very well aware. Consistently in all discussions about the political future of the region, this issue had been held to be one of fundamental difference. It was a clash between white supremacy and the paramountcy of native interests; a clash between no skilled jobs for 'natives' in the south and African engine-drivers and telegraphists in Nyasaland, between Sangala hopefully pressing for an African majority in Legco in Nyasaland and Huggins asserting that the natives must be ruled by 'a benevolent aristocracy'. It was that very 'native policy' of Southern Rhodesia, so dramatically different in their view from what they knew at home, that from the mid 1920s onwards made Nyasas certain that they wanted no closer association with that territory.

Griffith's official working parties of civil servants produced a document entitled *Comparative Survey of Native Policy*. This document became the principle working paper of the 'Conference of Officials' when it convened in London in January 1951. It was published later that year along with the Report of the conference. The talks among the officials that produced the *Comparative Survey* were hardly confidential, since the *Johannesburg Star* of the 14th July 1950 could assert that the report was going to show that the differences in 'native policy' between the three territories were fewer than was generally believed. That was, of course, the conclusion that did emerge from the document, one of the most astonishing documents produced by British civil servants in the twentieth century.

What is so astonishing is that the *Comparative Survey* shows, in meticulous detail, that there were profound differences in 'native policy' between Southern Rhodesia on the one hand and the two northern Protectorates on the other, with Nyasaland in particular. Yet the key conclusion of the document was that it was the similarities which were significant while the differences were merely a matter of method and timing! **The evidence the civil servants carefully explored and clearly and conscientiously laid out in their report itself gives the lie to the conclusions they then drew.** The report was printed and then, as we have seen, became the working paper for the Conference of Officials of January 1951.

As many commentators have noted, the officials who gathered round the conference table in January knew that the conclusions in the conference working paper were 'rubbish', the word chosen by one of their own, Griff Jones, who was serving in the Nyasaland administration at that time.[85] It was this document, however, which justified the setting up of the Conference of Officials in the first place and enabled the members of that conference to

---

[85] Jones, *Britain and Nyasaland*, p. 137.

create a model federal constitution and present it to the Government of the UK.

Griffiths had said that the Conference of Officials was to assess the feasibility of creating a federal constitution and they assessed that possibility in the only rational way open to them, which was to attempt to draw one up. That is what they did. They did more than that, however. When C.R. Baxter, their chairman, who had already so raised Welensky's hopes, presented their report, not only did he outline a draft federal constitution but he warmly commended this draft constitution to the Secretary of State and to the British Government. He went so far as to suggest it ought to be implemented and implemented urgently.

Opposition in Britain and Nyasaland

Things now moved forward at a remarkably fast pace. There was very vocal opposition in Britain to the Government even considering the idea but this was largely ineffective since both the major parties, Labour and Conservative, were willing to consider at least the possibilities of the scheme. It should be noted that at that time in Scotland, leading members of both the Labour and Conservative parties defied their London leaders and opposed any consideration of the plan. There was also a rapid increase in African opposition in Nyasaland which we will consider later.

Meanwhile planning went on in London which led to James Griffiths, the Colonial Secretary, and Patrick Gordon-Walker, the Commonwealth Relations Secretary, deciding to tour Central Africa. They travelled extensively in Nyasaland and Northern Rhodesia when James Griffiths, as he recorded in his memoirs later, came to see the reality of the African opposition to the scheme and to accept the quality and dignity of the people who opposed the scheme.[86] It was at this point that it became clear that if Labour stayed in power there would not be a federation. Griffiths and Gordon-Walker, both of whom, but particularly Gordon-Walker, had been initially sympathetic to the scheme, were persuaded by their talks in Nyasaland and Northern Rhodesia to change their minds. Their meetings with African people in both Northern Rhodesia and Nyasaland left them firmly persuaded that it would be wrong to impose federation against the wishes of the African people of the two Protectorates.

The two ministers and their staff then went to the Victoria Falls to meet in conference with Huggins and his Southern Rhodesian ministers together with leaders of the white opposition parties there. The Governors and senior

---

[86] James Griffiths, *Pages from Memory*, pp. 115-118.

59

officials as well as settler representatives from Northern Rhodesia and Nyasaland attended and, for the first time at such a meeting, African representatives from the two northern territories were also present.[87]

The Southern Rhodesians brought with them an all-party agreed set of minimum changes to the officials' draft constitution which they insisted would have to be met if it was to go ahead.

The Northern Rhodesian African delegation insisted they could not begin any discussions until 'partnership' was spelt out clearly.

The Nyasas, Edward K.Gondwe, Clement Kumbikano and Chief Mwase, went further and said that their people were united in opposition to any closer political or constitutional relationship with Southern Rhodesia. Their stand re-affirmed what Griffiths had come to believe already; that the gulf between what the Southern Rhodesian and Northern Rhodesian whites wanted and what the African people north of the Zambezi wanted was an unbridgeable one.

Huggins then suggested that the meeting should continue with neither the African delegates nor the Nyasaland and Northern Rhodesian colonial officials present. The British Ministers refused and so the conference was deadlocked and then technically adjourned. In reporting on the conference to the Southern Rhodesian Assembly on 19 November 1951, Huggins said that the conference had 'degenerated into a Native Benefit Society Meeting led by the Secretary of State for the Colonies'.

Huggins was by then hoping for a change in Government in Britain as it had been announced while the conference was meeting that another General Election had been called. The two Labour ministers had decided it would be wrong to push through Federation against the wishes of the people of the two northern Protectorates; however, Huggins was hoping for better things from the Conservatives.

He was not disappointed. The Conservative Party won the British General Election and the new Government announced in November that the federation of the three Central African territories was a matter of urgency. They then called for the Victoria Falls Conference to be re-convened in July 1952. Huggins, however, visited London and pressed hard for the process to be speeded up and so it was decided that the Conference should be re-convened in April, but at Lancaster House in London, not the Victoria Falls.

---

[87] The Africans were hardly 'representatives' in the normal sense. NAC had refused to be represented at the Victoria Falls but the African Protectorate Council had accepted Griffith's invitation and chose the three Nyasa delegates, who, it must be pointed out, *opposed federation as firmly as any Congress delegation would have done.*

What is so extraordinary about this decision is that the Colonial Office in London knew very well that African opposition to federation in Nyasaland was massively supported and was not a matter of a few agitators. Geoffrey Colby the Governor knew this and sent a secret cable to Andrew Cohen saying that the Colonial Office should take the initiative and pull Nyasaland out of the negotiations for the proposed federation. This was at a time when even the settler newspaper the *Nyasaland Times* insisted that the Nyasa people were 100% against the proposed federation. Cohen was, as we have seen, a dedicated supporter of the proposed Federation, and turned down the suggestion.[88]

The conference met in April 1952 and African delegations from Northern Rhodesia and Nyasaland arrived to attend but with real reluctance and hesitation since they feared that federation was going to be imposed whether they liked it or not. After a meeting with the Secretary of State for the Colonies, Oliver Lyttleton, someone who in his cultured way was as scornful of African people as the most reactionary settler, they were convinced that this was so and they decided to boycott the conference. They were criticised widely for this, even in the liberal press in Britain. Their defence was why should they give even indirect endorsement of this federation, against which they were opposed in principle, by attending the conference? Trying to get the best deal possible in a federal scheme, as they were urged to do, was to accept something they had been opposing consistently since the 1920s.

At the conference many of the so-called safeguards of African rights in the original proposals were dramatically watered down - some would say washed away. There was no longer to be a Minister of African Affairs and critically, the Federal Parliament was now given authority to make constitutional and electoral law changes so long as these were supported by a two thirds majority in the Federal Assembly. Since over three quarters of the seats in the Federal Assembly were settler controlled, this was a granting of real power to the Assembly which the original draft of the Officials Conference had not granted.

In January 1953 the final conference was held in London at Carlton House Terrace. The meetings were held in secret and two more important changes were agreed to the constitution of the new state that would come into being in August 1953. One was that the African Affairs Board was no longer to be a board of independent people of standing but was to become a committee of the Federal Assembly. Very ominously, it was agreed also that the constitution would be reviewed at a conference in not later than ten years and no sooner that seven years' time. The implication was that full Commonwealth

---

[88]   Colin Baker. *Development Governor: A Biography of Sir Geoffrey Colby.*

status - that is, full political autonomy - would be granted at that time if all had gone well meantime.

The new powerful line that was adopted by the supporters of Federation in their pro-federation campaign in the United Kingdom was that the concept of racial partnership was the guiding principle of the new federation. This would save Central Africa from the extremism of South African apartheid on the one hand and of African nationalism on the other. This was listened to widely in the United Kingdom despite the fact that in the two Rhodesias the same protagonists of 'partnership' were re-assuring their white electorate that white supremacy was secure under the new proposals.

What embittered the Nyasas was that they were very well aware of this but only a very few in Britain paid any attention when they pointed this discrepancy out. A classic example of what the pro-federation white politicians meant by 'partnership' is the speech by G.F.M. van Eeden, one of Welensky's close allies in the Northern Rhodesian Legco. In a report of his speech at Enkeldoorn in the *Rhodesia Herald* of 24 February 1953 we read, as did Nyasas,

> Turning to relations between Europeans and Natives Mr van Eeden did not agree that federation would weaken the European position in Central Africa. 'I believe the only thing that can strengthen and consolidate the position of the European in Central Africa is federation', he said ... the only thing that could enable the Europeans to maintain their position of leadership was to bring in as many immigrants as possible. At present N. and S. Rhodesia could take about 20,000 immigrants a year, but that was not enough to ensure European survival in Central Africa. 'I would like to see 50,000 immigrants a year coming to Central Africa. In 15 or 16 years time we would have a white population of something like 1 million and then we will be able to ensure that the Europeans maintain that position of leadership. Mr van Eeden said that the Federation would have near Dominion status and no Minister in the United Kingdom would argue with the Federal Prime Minister. Most of the reservations and entrenchments in the constitution would be merely formalities.[89]

Attempts by Congress to Stop the Imposition of Federation

We can now look at what Nyasaland African Congress was doing while this dramatic change in British policy was taking place, a change which Nyasas saw as a betrayal of the trust they had always had in the good intentions of the British Government. Where did all this leave J.F. Sangala, Charles Matinga, Chief Mwase and their UK representative, H.K. Banda? This was a betrayal, throwing into the dustbin the Colonial Office policy of the paramountcy of native interests which the old Native Associations and the new

---

[89] Newspaper cutting in *Nyasaland and Federation File* in D.S. Lyon Papers held in Centre for Study of Christianity in the Non-Western World, University of Edinburgh.

Nyasaland African Congress had always taken for granted in the political situation.

Congress policy had been, from the very beginning, to hurry the Colonial Office along, to make it live up to its own declared policies. It was not seen as an enemy to be fought, as Dr Banda made so clear in his famous pamphlet, but an ally - though a dilatory one that had to be nudged regularly to keep it up to the mark. The Colonial Office had indeed been an ally and, although doing little about development in Malawi, undoubtedly had helped in the long term struggle against the attempts of settler power from south of the Zambezi to get a foothold in Nyasaland.[90] Already in 1952, however, it was clear that the old friend had turned traitor!

As we have already noted it was not just J.F. Sangala, Charles Matinga, Clement Kumbikano and that generation of Nyasa leaders who believed the essentially beneficent nature of British Colonial policy in Africa. Their friend and official representative in London, Dr Banda, also saw the Colonial Office in that light. The leadership of Congress in this period from 1944 to 1953, so often written off as discredited and misguided, were at one with their adviser in London, Dr Banda. They shared the same attitude to Britain and the same attitude to the situation in general. The later much maligned Clement Kumbikano said nothing at the Victoria Falls Conference that was not echoed in Banda's pamphlet, whose genesis we now consider.

When, in 1949, news of the second Victoria Falls conference reached London, a meeting of students and others from Nyasaland and Northern Rhodesia was held. They unanimously opposed amalgamation and asked Banda, then working as a doctor in general practice in London, and Harry Nkumbula from Northern Rhodesia, who was studying at the London School of Economics, to prepare a protest to be sent to the Colonial Office. Banda was the author of this document since Nkumbula left the writing to him; Nkumbula's name was left on the letter as a gesture to the other Protectorate. Dr Banda had the letter of protest published, at his own expense, as a pamphlet in 1951, to aid the re-invigorated anti-federation campaign.

The original production of the pamphlet was also partly Banda's response to a letter from Charles Matinga conveying the NAC's request for help from Banda over the threat of the imposition of federation. The pamphlet expresses sentiments which J.F. Sangala and the other original Congress leaders readily recognised as their own when copies of the printed edition were sent to them by Banda.

---

[90] The first British High Commissioner to the newly independent Malawi in his 4th Despatch to London commented on what he called "the almost inexplicable neglect of the Territory until the 1950s." DO 183/457.

In the document, the first reason Banda gives for rejecting federation is that

It would deprive the Africans of Nyasaland and Northern Rhodesia of direct political and cultural ties with the United Kingdom, and would mean a discontinuation of the policy of deliberate tutelage of Africans now pursued by the Government of the United Kingdom in these two territories.

This was an articulation of the foundation stone upon which the early Congress leaders had built all their plans and policies. Banda went on to insist that there was 'no disloyalty to His Majesty the King'. Banda's pamphlet exhibited the attitude of the original founders and early leaders of Congress; men who were to feel utterly let down and betrayed by Britain with the imposition of Federation in 1953. These were also the men who were to be cast aside by the new breed of young Congress leaders who emerged after the imposition of Federation. In 1953, the older leaders had failed to prevent the imposition of the Federation and had no idea of what to do next. They rightly had to make way for others. However, they failed because one of the secure pillars upon which they had built their whole understanding of political reality had been torn down by the British Government.

The Colonial Office, their trusted ally against the threat from the white south suddenly became a supporter of the white south. Congress then faced a situation it had not been organised for to deal with. We shall look a little later at how that unpreparedness was exposed. Perhaps there were only two survivors of the early leaders of Congress who remained effective. One was Congress's London representative, Kamuzu Banda; the other was J.F. Sangala, who, as Masauko Chipembere records in his *Autobiography*, was his mentor when 'Chip' was stationed at Domasi.[91]

The picture that Congress presented to the observer during these years that led up to the imposition of Federation was one full of contradictions. The most prominent was the contrast between a lack of a coherent organisational structure at the centre of the movement and the rapid growth of the movement across the country with thousands signing up and creating a multitude of local branches of Congress.

To understand what was happening we need to go back to the beginning with the first annual conference of Nyasaland African Congress held in Blantyre in October 1944. The veteran inspirer of nationalism in Nyasaland, Levi Mumba, was elected President-General. James F. Sangala the other key figure behind the creation of Congress had recently been transferred to Dedza and was unable to get to Blantyre for the meeting. He was elected to the central committee but not to an office. The other office-holders were:

---

91   Robert I. Rotberg (ed.). *Hero of the Nation: Chipembere of Malawi. an Autobiography*. pp. 167-69.

Charles Matinga, (Vice President), Charles Mlanga, (Secretary-General), J.D. Phiri, (Asst Secretary), H.Z. Tung'ande, (second Asst Secretary) and Isaac Lawrence, another nationalist veteran, Treasurer General.

It is important to note that Congress was an entirely northern - southern affair. As we have seen already the Central Region, other than Lilongwe and the Ntcheu district, had not had many effective Native Associations. This was also the case in the Upper and Lower Shire valley areas of the Southern Region. This later area has a social and cultural history in the first half of the twentieth century different from the rest of the Southern Province. As a result, the effective drive to create Congress came from the alliance of the southern region Native Associations with Levi Mumba and I.M. Jere's Representative Committee of Northern Province Native Associations.

Tragically, very soon after the creation of Congress, Levi Mumba and Isaac Lawrence died and without the skilled leadership of these two veterans, a lack of clear direction at the centre of the movement became apparent. The Blantyre Native Association had long been riven by factional disputes. We have seen the Rev Thomas Maseya had been forced to send an alternative submission to the Bledisloe Commission because of the anger felt by so many at the pusillanimous submission by the chairman of the Blantyre N.A., Ellerton Mposa. These divisions, tragically, continued to bedevil the central leadership of the new movement when Charles Matinga was elected to succeed Levi Mumba and the distinguished northerner, the Reverend Charles Chinula, became Vice President.

Some academic writers have joined other modern critics in condemning these men for not setting up a modern political party. What model were they supposed to follow of which they had any real knowledge? In any case they were not thinking of setting up a political party but rather an effective pressure group to represent African interests to the essentially authoritarian colonial authorities. The critics of these men have not attempted to understand what it was that the founders actually set up in 1944.[92]

The NAC was seen by the original founders - Mumba, Lawrence and Sangala - as an umbrella organisation designed to pull together and coordinate at Protectorate level the efforts of the many Native Associations and other local organisations concerned with the welfare of the indigenous people of the Protectorate. The Mulanje Foodstuff Growers' Association was a classic example of the kind of group which was still sending delegations to Congress meetings through 1946. These varied organisations, as well as the local Native Associations, affiliated with the NAC when it was set up and

---

[92] Though this was clearly explained with full references to Congress minutes in Robert Rotberg's *The Rise of Nationalism in Central Africa* pp. 192-4.

were then called branches of Congress. They were, clearly, not in any way like the local branches of a modern political party.

What might be raised more tellingly against the founders of the movement was that no effective central organisation was set up; there was not even an office or any permanent staff. Even an umbrella coordinating body ought to have had at least a permanent office with a full-time secretary. This was, in fact, what Dr Banda recommended to Matinga on the eve of the Congress annual convention meeting at Salima in September 1946. The executive committee of Congress had already agreed to Dr Banda's suggestions with regard to their financial arrangements.[93] Until then each branch had kept its own funds and spent them as it wished and the Blantyre branch had financed whatever central activities were undertaken by Congress. From the spring of that year, branches paid certain limited dues to the centre where the Treasurer-General kept them as a central fund for the organisation.

At the Salima convention a special committee, including Sangala and Chinula, recommended that in response to Banda's suggestion, there should be a full-time secretary/organiser employed by Congress to run a central office. Banda had guaranteed an annual salary of £68 and G.W. Mwase had already promised to build the office.

Banda's biographer, Philip Short, sees Matinga's fear of Banda's influence on Congress as the reason why the full meeting of the conference turned down this suggestion by a huge majority. It is clear that Matinga did fear Banda's influence. He had been disconcerted at the previous year's conference by the plethora of motions of thanks to Banda for his interest in and help to the organisation. Matinga's suspicions of Banda's intentions, however, are hardly enough themselves to explain the massive vote by the delegates to turn down the suggestion of a full time secretary, especially when that suggestion had been endorsed by a committee containing popular leaders like Sangala and Chinula. No satisfactory explanation, in my judgement, has been proposed by those who have written about this period, but the size of the vote would indicate that there was both a suspicion of centralisation, and of Banda, that was widespread, despite the latter's prestige among the Congress elite.

This popularity among the Congress elite was undoubtedly merited. Banda had already done much for Congress in linking them with the British Labour Party and effectively lobbying the party so that questions about the Protectorate's affairs were raised in the House of Commons.

---

[93] Though Short in his biography *Banda* asserts they did not. p. 49.

So Congress struggled on, with some centralisation of funds but with no permanent secretariat. Again this is a period when Sangala's untiring enthusiasm and energy helped hold things together. This was despite the Protectorate government often paying no attention whatsoever to submissions made to them by Congress. This was at least in part because the administration had already begun the process of creating its own channel for African opinion. This initiative consisted of three regional councils whose establishment would be followed by that of a Protectorate African Council, a structure which would be, as far as the Government was concerned, the effective channel for the expression of African opinion in the Protectorate.

Despite Government's apparent indifference towards Congress, it was at this time that Congress had its first real success. The decision of the Salima conference to seek the agreement of the Governor for a Congress delegation to go to London to meet with the Colonial Secretary and discuss the educational provision for Africans in the Protectorate came to fruition. By May 1947 sufficient funds for the trip were accumulated by Congress. At the Zomba conference of Congress in September 1947, the Governor accepted an invitation to address the gathering and six weeks later Congress was informed that the Secretary of State was willing to receive a Nyasaland African Congress delegation. This was a high spot for the movement which the administration had, hitherto, tended to ignore or even deride.

The executive of Congress decided that there would be a delegation of three members. Charles Matinga, the President, and the Reverend Charles Chinula, the Vice-President, would go to London where they would be joined by Dr H.K. Banda to complete the delegation. There then followed, unfortunately, a series of events with disastrous consequences for Congress. Matinga left for Cape Town to catch the ship to the UK, not with Charles Chinula but with Andrew Mponda, the new Secretary-General. Chinula, with the aid of travel documents and funds provided through the initiative of Sangala, pursued them to Cape Town but failed to prevent their going. With the meagre funds granted him by Congress expended, he was left penniless in Cape Town. Fortunately the local community of Nyasas looked after him and paid his fare back to the Protectorate.

In London, meanwhile, Banda, a little taken aback at the turn of events, joined Matinga and Mponda to complete the delegation. Despite Banda having some arguments with Matinga, the three men worked well together and negotiated successfully with the Colonial Secretary. They did gain worthwhile results. The British Government agreed to the creation of a new secondary school at Dedza and a new Teacher Training College to be situated at Domasi.

Whether or not these meetings helped the Colonial Office to make its mind up on the delicate issue of African membership of the Legislative Council, a matter that had been on the agenda for a number of years without any decision being given, is not clear. The decision, however, to have two African members in the Nyasaland Legislative Council did emerge soon after this visit.

Back in Nyasaland there was still widespread anger and embarrassment over Matinga's high-handed action. This was compounded by accusations made while Matinga was en route to Cape Town that he had misappropriated Congress funds. Sangala, for the sake of the mission, persuaded the Nyasaland Police not to pursue the matter at that time, but the shadow still hung over Matinga. The whole situation was made worse by Mponda and Matinga refusing, after their return, to attend Congress meetings to report on their mission, a mission that, after all, had been paid for by the membership of the movement.

It was not until the spring of 1949 at a meeting called by the acting President W.J. Manda, who had been appointed to hold the fort while the senior officials were in London that Matinga appeared and gave a verbal report only. This infuriated the delegates who demanded a full written report. To this Matinga responded by walking out. As an effective political organisation, Nyasaland African Congress had ceased to function.

The Rebirth of Congress and Continuing Opposition to Federation

Sangala was appealed to by many to step forward and take over the leadership. Always the stickler for procedure Sangala hesitated but was convinced to act by a letter from Dr Banda pleading with him to act. Otherwise it would appear, Banda wrote, that Congress was dead. Sangala then circulated a request for the branches to send delegates to what he deemed the Sixth Annual Conference of the NAC to be held in Blantyre on New Year's Day 1950.

The situation was urgent because the activities of Huggins and the settlers of the two Rhodesias had raised the threat of amalgamation again. As we have seen, Creech-Jones appeared to have successfully resisted the pressure of Huggins and Welensky but in December Huggins had returned to the fray. What complicated matters further was that, because of the disastrous state of Congress, many educated and uneducated Nyasas had come to pin their hopes instead on the Protectorate African Council as the effective medium for influencing their political future.

To everyone's astonishment at the Blantyre meeting Matinga turned up and chaired the first session. This was his last fling before being dismissed for the misuse of Congress funds. The meeting resolved, in the words of one veteran delegate 'not to waste time on the broken Congress of Matinga, let us start things afresh.'[94] Sangala committed himself completely to the task of virtually re-creating Congress from scratch. His efforts paid off when, in August 1950, a genuinely representative meeting of delegates met at Mzimba. James Chinyama, the son of Filipo Chinyama who was one of Chilembwe's supporters executed after the Rising in 1915, was elected President with Sangala as Vice-President. Chinyama's appointment has been seen by historians as marking the new dominance of prosperous farmers and small businessmen in the movement, taking over the leadership from the civil servants, schoolteachers and Protestant clergy who dominated hitherto.

The rebirth of Congress was just in time to allow it to face the challenge of Huggins and Welensky's campaign to obtain British agreement to the creation of a Central African Federation. We have already seen above Congress's reaction to the various developments of campaign for federation. There was initial success. The unanimity and the political awareness of the leaders of the NAC, the chiefs who were interviewed and the members of the Protectorate Council convinced the Secretary State for the Colonies, James Griffiths, and his colleague, Patrick Gordon Walker, that the attitude of the NAC did reflect the opinion of the Nyasa people and converted them from a position of sympathy towards the federal idea to one of opposition to it being imposed against the wishes of the people of the Protectorate.

All was to no avail, however, when the Conservative Party, fully committed to the scheme and with key figures in its leadership closely allied to Huggins and Welensky, won the British General Election of October 1951. The creation of a federal constitution uniting the three territories and its imposition now became something that the Conservative government in London sought to achieve as quickly as possible.

Initially Congress petitioned and protested against the scheme but their long term trust in the sympathy of the Colonial office blinded them to the new situation which amounted to a revolution in British colonial policy in Africa. Thus Congress sent a delegation to the Lancaster House Conference of April 1952 and then and only then did the full realisation that they faced a *fait accompli* come home to them. The federation was going to come into being whatever they said. Their response was to refuse to attend the conference, which alienated a great deal of hitherto sympathetic British public opinion.

---

[94] D.D. Phiri, *James Frederick Sangala*, p. 34.

Most British observers did not understand the profound sense of betrayal and the bewilderment experienced by the people of the Protectorate (who had always relied on London against Salisbury) when it became blindingly clear to them that Salisbury and London were united. To their profound dismay they came to realise they were no longer a people under British protection from external threats including those from the British settlers in Rhodesia. Through 1952 and 1953 the Nyasa people had consistently been portrayed by British officials, who in the past had been their 'protectors', as a simple people who, out of ignorance and the influence of a small number of extremists, were delaying a programme that was for their own good. This was the Colonial Office now working in concert with the propagandists on behalf of the Rhodesian politicians who went even further. They portrayed the Nyasa people as blindly following a handful of dangerous fanatics who were attempting to prevent a sensible moderate scheme of partnership between the races in Central Africa.

It was at that time that the long relationship between Scotland and the 'land of the lake' stood out clearly. Not only did the Mission Council of the Church of Scotland consistently insist that African opinion in Nyasaland was informed not uninformed and united in opposition to the imposition of Federation, but in Scotland there was also a cross-party movement in opposition to Federation that had a massive influence on that small country. It was a Scottish missionary and a member of the CCAP, the Reverend Andrew Doig, member of the Nyasaland Legco for African Interests, who, in December 1951, joined with Ellerton Mposa and E.A. Muwamba in moving a motion in the Legislative Council in Zomba urging the British Government not to go back on its past commitment to give up its authority only to the people of the Protectorate. Through 1952 Dr Banda had many well attended speaking engagements organised for him across Scotland and a delegation of chiefs, having been refused permission to present a petition to the Queen, had a very successful tour in Scotland. A classic example of the Scottish situation in contrast with the cross-party attitude in England of 'give federation a chance' was a mass meeting in the Hall of the General Assembly of the Church of Scotland on 26 January 1953 entitled 'Crisis in Central Africa'. It was presided over by the Very Reverend Dr John Baillie, an ex-Moderator of the Church of Scotland and a President of the World Council of Churches. The speakers were Nkhosi ya Makhosi M'mbelwa, Lord Hemingford, a Conservative Peer and John Dugdale, a Labour MP.

The campaign in Scotland which was across party lines and had the backing of the Church of Scotland reached its climax with the attempt to present a petition from the 'People of Scotland' to the Queen. This petition had twenty-seven thousand signatures; many of these were of a minister and one of his elders signing on behalf of a church congregation. The Honourable Margaret Herbison, George Thompson and Sir Richard Acland, all of whom had served as Government ministers in the past, attempted to present the petition on May 5th 1953, but were refused access to the Queen on the advice of the Conservative Government, so determined was the Government to establish the Federation.

As Professor George Shepperson has pointed out this cross-party and well supported movement in Scotland was a product of the way in which the crisis in the affairs of the Nyasaland Protectorate had touched a nationalist nerve in the Scottish people. That this feeling was communicated to Nyasa visitors can be seen in the letter Chief Kuntaja wrote after his return to the Protectorate to the Reverend Duncan Finlayson, one of the leaders of the Scottish movement. Mfumu Kuntaja wrote thanking the 'Scotch' people for their hospitality and their support and made great play with the need to pray that the 'English' leaders in Parliament might change their mind about Federation.[95] Certainly a groundswell of opposition to the imposition of federation occurred in Scotland across party divisions, while in the rest of the United Kingdom more and more people, hitherto suspicious of the proposed Federation, were coming to accept the economic and partnership arguments for federation and were urging the peoples of the two northern Protectorates to enter into the new situation and to make it work. Indeed even Clement Attlee, the Labour Party leader and ex-Prime Minister, called on people to stop opposing Federation and instead to try to make it work.

In Nyasaland, in face of the decisions taken in London, Congress had to develop a new style of action in this new world where they felt betrayed in a way that is difficult for people in the twenty-first century to understand and appreciate. Initially they had campaigned in the old way by petition and appeals to London. Funds had been raised to send a delegation of chiefs to London. They had sought permission to present to the Queen a petition requesting her intervention to prevent the imposition of the Federal scheme upon people who had voluntarily come under the protection of the Crown. As we have already seen, the Government in London persuaded the Queen not to receive the petition. The delegation illustrated that the majority of the chiefs, indeed all of the important chiefs, supported Congress throughout this campaign.

This is notable for it had been to the chiefs that the leading thinkers among the Colonial Service officers had looked for the shaping of Africa's future,

---

[95] Chief Kuntaja to Duncan Finlayson, 11/3/53. Box 3 David Lyon Papers, New College Library, University of Edinburgh. Kuntaja had been one of a group of chiefs who had toured Scotland speaking against the proposed federation.

rather than the new African politicians.[96] The gulf seen as existing between these two groups in the various colonial territories in Africa was made much of in policy documents. In the case of Nyasaland, however, this division between Congress and chiefs had never been straightforward as it was in some colonial territories and as it was envisioned by Colonial Office planners. Some of the most important chiefly families in the Protectorate, notably those of the two Ngoni Paramount chiefs M'mbelwa and Gomani, had from the beginning supported the Native Associations and then the new Congress. Thus it was these Ngoni chiefs and Chief Mwase, the most prestigious of the Chewa chiefs, who played a leading part in the formation of the Council of Chiefs. The Council was created specifically to cooperate with Congress in resisting the imposition of Federation.

The Imposition of Federation in 1953

None of the traditional forms of activity made any difference though, because of the new alignment of London and Salisbury. These actions had been based on the presumption of a not unsympathetic reception of their petitions and complaints by the Colonial Office in London. The Colonial Office was no longer the ally of the Nyasa people but rather of the white Rhodesian politicians.

This was brought home to the Nyasa people when Harry Hopkinson, the Minister of State for Colonial Affairs in the new Conservative Government, came to Nyasaland in August 1952 to assess Nyasa opposition to the federal proposals. At the end of his visit to the Protectorate he declared to the reporter of the influential journal, *East Africa and Rhodesia*, that Congress's claim that African opinion was solidly against Federation was untrue. Indeed he insisted that African opinion on the subject hardly existed. His attitude shows how determined the new Conservative Government of the UK was to push through Federation. Hopkinson must have known, as his officials certainly knew, that as recently as January the settler newspaper in the Protectorate, the *Nyasaland Times*, had insisted on the unanimity of all sections of Nyasaland African opinion in opposition to the proposed Federation. The *Times* went on to say that this was known to the government in London and 'to all the people of Southern Africa'. As we have seen, the Governor, Sir Geoffrey Colby, was convinced of the strength of African opposition in Nyasaland and had informed London of this. Despite all this, Hopkinson

---

[96]   Sir Glyn Jones in the notes he kept of a long meeting with a Granada Television Director on May 31, 1983 about his career in Africa confessed that he still believed that through most of his earlier career in Northern Rhodesia. Sir Glyn Jones Papers, Rhodes House Library, University of Oxford.

insisted on a lack of opinion about the Federation among the African people of Nyasaland.

New methods of action needed to be found by Congress. The problem was that the loose structure of the NAC was not of much use in planning nationwide resistance to the Government, violent or non-violent, as its leaders soon found out.

On the fifth and sixth of April, 1953, a special national conference of the Nyasaland African Congress was held in Blantyre. Although the President, James Chinyama, perhaps remembering the fate of his father Filipo, had earlier voiced his opposition to any form of civil disobedience, the conference agreed to a national programme of non-violent resistance.[97] The conference heard speeches from some of the chiefs returned from their fruitless visit to the UK and the Reverend Michael Scott, a Church of England priest and Director of the London-based Africa Bureau, among others. Congress also agreed to appeal to the United Nations and to the International Court of Justice. Senior legal advice which was sought on these two appeals declared that it would be a waste of resources since neither appeal had a legal basis enabling it to be received by the international bodies concerned.

The people wanted something done. They were deeply frustrated and showed it by boycott of public functions like the Queen's Birthday celebrations, which was all very well but achieved nothing.

What forms of civil disobedience would have effect? Delegates at the Blantyre Conference had talked of a national withdrawal of labour, but how was that to be organised? It was also thought that there could be a programme of refusal to pay taxes, but again, how was this to be organised on a national scale?

In reality nothing was organised on a national scale, despite many speeches about resistance. In Thyolo, Mulanje and Chiradzulu there were a number of violent incidents and rioting. These events, though undoubtedly triggered off by the frustration and tensions of the situation, all occurred where there was long-term bitterness about the European ownership of so much good land and were not part of any organised campaign. They were also suppressed firmly and quickly.

The only attempt at organised resistance came from a chief, Nkhosi ya Makhosi Gomani. In many ways Gomani had been a model chief. He had encouraged the implementation of all the soil erosion and other agricultural

---

[97] In January 1953, Mikeka Mkandawire, a northerner but leader of the radical wing of Congress in Blantyre had advocated a campaign of non-violent civil disobedience and this had been publicly repudiated by Chinyama in a letter to the *Nyasaland Times*.

reforms instituted by government. The result was that erosion of the soil had been halted in Ntcheu and agricultural production had increased there. It was Gomani, however, who in May 1953 called on his people to refuse to pay taxes and to disregard the structure of agricultural and forestry procedures which he and they had so effectively implemented in the past. When police came to arrest him there was serious rioting. In the midst of the chaos, the Nkhosi Gomani, his heir Willard, along with Michael Scott who had been staying at the chief's home, fled into Mozambique only to be arrested by the Portuguese and handed back to the British authorities.

A number of other Congress activists, most notably Qabaniso Chibambo, were arrested and imprisoned and some, as in Chibambo's case, sent into internal exile. Chibambo, a northern Ngoni, was forced to live at Nsanje, then known as Port Herald, and report regularly to the police there.

Chinyama was interviewed by the Governor and warned of severe consequences if the disturbances continued. He and the other Congress leaders came to see that their rhetoric had connected with the sense of bitter frustration felt by so many, which had led to some deaths and a lot of violence which had achieved nothing. Thus the coming into being of the Federation of Rhodesia and Nyasaland progressed smoothly despite all the people of Nyasaland could do.

In September 1953, in a joint statement, the Nyasaland African Congress and the Council of Chiefs called on people to end all forms of civil disobedience. Congress and the Council of Chiefs then united in calling for all literate Africans over 21 years old to have the right to vote and that half of the members of Legco should be elected by them. It is astonishing that this is not much more than the Reverend Thomas Maseya was asking for in 1939. It also ignored the new reality that Nyasaland Legco, although theoretically having still a link with the Colonial Office in London (its civil servants were still British colonial officers) was now also a territorial authority within the new Federal state. The only reference to the Federation in the Congress statement was again to the people's opposition to its existence.

Perhaps the Congress leaders had spotted an inherent flaw in the Federal Scheme. This stemmed from the fact that Nyasaland was both a province of the new Federation but was still administered by British civil servants appointed by the Colonial Office. The Governor was also appointed by London. Nyasaland was not simply a province of the new Federation, it still, in its internal affairs, was directly linked to London. Could this be exploited to bring about change?

The call by Congress for reform of the Nyasaland Legislative Council was getting at that connection. If there was real progress in the Africanisation and democratisation of the Nyasaland Legislative Council then what? If London gave in to this kind of pressure to any degree it would raise a serious problem for the federal experiment and the Federal Government did not have the authority to stop it. It was a loophole for Congress to exploit, were it able. J.D. Sangala's great contribution was that he did realise the potential of the situation. We shall see in the next chapter how he exploited it.

This rather bewildering state of affairs, however, provoked a number of other leaders to begin an alternative political party. This was the Nyasaland Progressive Association, which accepted the need to work within the reality of the new situation and was led by the previously disgraced leader, Charles Matinga, with the help of Andrew Mponda and Orton Ching'oli Chirwa (later to be the first Malawian to reach the legal rank of Queen's Counsel and Malawi's first Minister of Justice.)

The leadership of Congress in the next few months underwent massive changes and, at a National Conference of Congress in January 1954, Wellington Manoah Chirwa (a graduate of University College, Fort Hare where he had befriended the young Masauko Chipembere) and Clement Kumbikano became the leading figures in the movement. Their view was that a new policy had to be worked out for Congress to act in the new situation; people simply had to accept the reality of the new federal state, though not necessarily its permanence. But what was that policy to be?

Widely in Britain and Nyasaland the line being taken was that now that the Federation was established there was no way back and what had to be done was to strive to make it work, to make the partnership of the races real and not a cover for the extension of settler power. As Lord Milverton, chairman of the United Central Africa Association, said in press statement

> Is it too much to hope that all sections of opinion in Church and State will accept the decision and devote their energies to making the Federation successful? It is surely fair to suggest that all who claim to be true friends of the African should shew that friendship by advising him to accept the decision and work to secure its benefits for the African people of the three territories.[98]

It is astonishing that this attitude was accepted so widely in Britain. Many people must have been hoping with fingers crossed that somehow it would all turn out for the best. The behaviour and attitude of the ruling United Federal Party under Geoffrey Huggins (later Lord Malvern) showed little or no sign of meaningful 'partnership' between the races. In a famous speech in the Federal Parliament on July 28th 1954 his views on race relations were made only too clear. In calling for the rejection of a motion requesting the

---

[98] Issued on 10 April 1953.

federal enforcement of equal treatment of all races in all public places throughout the Federation Huggins made his party's attitude clear.

> You cannot expect Europeans to form in a queue with dirty people, possibly an old mfazi with an infant on her back, mewling and puking and making a mess of everything ... It is perfectly obvious to anyone that the system we have in Southern Rhodesia at the present time is the most satisfactory to both sides and it is certainly impossible to alter it until the hon. leaders of the African people have cleaned up their brother Africans a bit; and then we can perhaps consider it.[99]

This was not a one-off aberration, it was a statement in Parliament by the Federation's Prime Minister. Yet in the UK people were insisting on the bold initiative that the Federation represented of racial partnership. So successful was this campaign that a large number of those who had opposed Federation reluctantly concluded that it was the way ahead. Others agreed to give the experiment a trial but with the proviso that if it became apparent that 'partnership' was a farce then they would have to think again.

Both in Britain and, more importantly, in Nyasaland there were people still determined that Federation should not be treated as an accepted fact of life but rather as something that could and should be dismantled.

[99] Quoted in Harry Franklin. *Unholy Wedlock*. p. 100.

Chapter 3

Congress Recovers and Goes on the Offensive

In January 1954 J.D. Sangala was yet again trying to pull Congress together after what can only be considered another debacle. We must always keep in mind, however, that Congress had not been developed to deal with a situation where they were expected to organise passive resistance to the Protectorate Government. To be in direct opposition to the Government in London and Zomba was a profound shock to the fundamental understanding of politics held by Nyasa people. People could hardly believe that in a few brief months the British Government could ditch its thirty year old policy of the 'Paramountcy of Native Interests' and hurriedly force through the creation of the Federation over the expressed opposition of the Nyasa people. Congress had been created and developed on the basic assumption that the British Government could be trusted, that the task of Congress was to agitate and pressure the Colonial Office to accelerate the pace of African advancement. This could not be stated more clearly than it was by Dr Banda in his famous pamphlet, *Federation in Central Africa.*

A measure of the disarray that the collapse of the initial resistance campaign into random unorganised bouts of violence brought to Congress can be seen from the story of Sangala's arrest and subsequent trial at the end of 1953.[100] While hurrying across the Southern Region (this was at his own expense) trying to keep passive resistance alive while also trying to prevent violence, he always managed to escape arrest.[101] When eventually he was arrested late in September 1953, he had no money left for a lawyer or indeed for anything else, and neither had Congress. It was then that two Nyasa businessmen and lifelong supporters of Congress came to his aid. These men, Lali Lubani and Lewis Mataka, gave fifty pounds themselves and, with the help of the Mashonaland branch of Nyasaland African Congress, raised the sum of one hundred pounds for Sangala's defence. When Sangala handed over the money, the lawyer thanked him and said he would put it to clearing the debt that Congress had already built up with him for defending other congressmen. Sangala still had no money for his defence or for anything else. It was

---

[100] D.D. Phiri, *James Frederick Sangala* pp. 46-48.

[101] Phiri says that this gained him the nickname Pyagusi which he translates 'slippery feet'. However members of Sangala's wife's family and Sangala's son James insist that the name's meaning is clear and could be translated 'one that perseveres' or 'one that has stamina for the fight' which would certainly fit J.F. Sangala's life and career.

77

just as well that at his trial in November 1953 the charges against him were dismissed by the magistrate.

In the hectic and confused situation of the last months of 1953 and early 1954, Sangala began to steer Congress along what appeared to be two diametrically opposed policies at the same time. The need for this dual strategy stemmed from an event in October 1953. Sangala, while in custody awaiting trial, had been informed by Manoah Chirwa that he and Kumbikano were going to stand for the two seats reserved for Nyasas in the Federal Parliament. As he later told his biographer, D.D. Phiri, Sangala was surprised at the enthusiasm with which Manoah and Kumbikano, who only weeks before had been advocating civil disobedience, were now seeking seats in the Federal Parliament.

Their decision worried Sangala but, when he was elected President of Congress in January 1954, he didn't oppose their decision. Manoah Chirwa and Clement Kumbikano were clearly so popular with the delegates who attended the Conference that it would have been futile to oppose them. More importantly it would have provided yet another excuse for Congress to split into factions, a tendency which Sangala had been fighting to contain since the late1940s.

Pyagusi went along with Manoah's argument to Congress, one that did have some merit, as both Dr Banda and Chipembere agreed as we shall see later. His argument was that it was better that these seats were filled by candidates approved by Congress than that they should filled by members of the Nyasaland African Progressive Association of Matinga and Orton Chirwa. More than that, Manoah insisted that they could publicise more effectively from the inside the fraud that Partnership was than by complaining from the outside. This latter course would look particularly pathetic while other Nyasas sat in the parliament in Salisbury and appeared to represent the Nyasa people. Manoah and Kumbikano also assured Sangala and the delegates at the Conference that, having made the Nyasa case effectively with maximum publicity, they would then resign their seats. It was typical of the political subtlety of Manoah that no firm time limit was set for that withdrawal, leaving Manoah master of the situation.

Meanwhile, Sangala travelled all over the Southern and as much of the Central Region as his finances would allow, trying to re-invigorate the local branches of Congress. Despite his efforts, outside Lilongwe and Ntcheu Congress as a formally structured organisation hardly existed in the Central Region. In the Southern Region, the densely populated Blantyre - Mulanje-Zomba triangle was where Congress had great strength and this area provided a strong national base for Congress with a concentration of many of the best educated Nyasas from all districts working there. Outside that triangle, however, Congress was still seeking to establish an effective presence.[102] In contrast, by the end of 1955 in the Northern Region, Congress had again become an organisation to be reckoned with.

In the south the Blantyre branch was the lively branch of Congress and in 1954 showed a liveliness and initiative in stark contrast with the sense of defeat displayed elsewhere. That year, Blantyre branch elected as its Treasurer Mrs Rose Chibambo, whose husband Edwin was a young civil servant, the son of the Reverend Yesaya Chibambo, one of the first Malawians to be ordained as a minister of the Christian church. Rose had the previous year started an informal group of women activists in Zomba before Edwin was transferred to Blantyre. In the new situation, Rose, aided later by other future women leaders, notably Vera Chirwa, started what was in effect, though not yet in name, the Women's League of Congress So powerful and independent were the Blantyre women that it was they, not the men, who sent a delegation to Zomba to protest outside the High Court at the trial of Sangala for sedition in May 1956.

However, it is wrong to measure Nyasa resistance simply by the numbers of formally organised Congress branches. In the Southern and Northern Regions there was continuous scattered resistance to Government measures of various sorts. This resistance often took the form of refusal to comply with Government agricultural and forestry rules. This phenomenon has usually been seen as sporadic and unorganised and simply an expression of peasant conservatism, and so it was in the Southern Region until late in 1957 when Congress began a programme of encouraging it there. However, as McCracken and others have indicated, by 1955 this resistance was a planned political programme of self-conscious political resistance in the Northern Region.[103] The central role in this development was taken by another young man returning to the homeland, not from university studies but from active participation in the Defiance Campaign in South Africa - Flax Musopole. Building on the widespread unrest in the area and using the members of the revived branches of Congress set up by Chiume and Dunduzu Chisiza in 1955-56, he created a situation where increasingly the Nyasaland Government was close to powerless in many parts of the Northern Region.

---

[102] As late as February 1959 I was told by a village headman at Chikwawa in the Lower River, 'Sitifuna macalici, masukulu, Kongressi, tingofuna mtendere basi.' We do not want churches, schools, Congress, we just want peace'.

[103] John McCracken, 'Ambiguities of Nationalism: Flax Musopole and the Northern Factor in Malawi Politics, c. 1956-1966.' In *Journal of Southern African Studies*, Vol. 28, No. 1, 2002.

Agricultural procedures had been resisted sporadically for years but it was Musopole who organised these protests into a massive refusal by the chiefs and the population at large to obey the Nyasaland Government. A devastatingly frank witness to this can be found in the letter of T.R. Wade, the Federal Intelligence and Security Bureau officer liaising with the Nyasaland Government, to his boss in Salisbury. In this letter of October 1958 he reports that the Nyasaland Government was hesitant about taking any action in the North where all the chiefs were deemed to be pro-Congress.[104] Musopole's efforts were significantly, though unintentionally, aided by the Nyasaland Government concentrating its police and military resources in the south.

In the Southern Region this popular unrest was sporadic and never as effectively organised as in the North. However, in the sprawling and constantly growing Blantyre-Limbe urban area, Mikeka Mkandawire led an effective movement to resist urban planning developments. A classic example of these campaigns was that pursued after Chief Kapeni resigned as Native Authority in 1954 in protest against the forced resettlement of many of his people. Mikeka Mkandawire effectively organised resistance for more than two years to the Government's attempts to set up a government approved council to replace Kapeni. His dismissal from Congress over his opposition to Manoah did not inhibit Mikeka. He continued as a leader of campaigns of opposition to the Nyasaland Government in the Blantyre-Limbe urban area, particularly with regard to the forcible removal of people both from traditional villages in the urban area and from squatter settlements. Much of this urban planning which he opposed and sought to sabotage he deemed to be a covert attempt to create residential racial segregation.[105]

We have to keep in mind, as a background to any discussion of the formal politics of the period, this grass-root resistance to the Government of the Protectorate; it was sporadic in the South but was becoming increasingly well-organised in the North.

Turning to the activities of Congress after 1953 we find Sangala concentrating the activities of the slowly reviving Congress on the second line of the dual approach to the Federal problem, one which completely ignored the other approach exemplified by Manoah's and Kumbikano's role in Salisbury. Sangala's policy was that of encouraging Nyasas to behave as if the Nyasaland Legislative Council and the Protectorate Government were still answerable only to London. Thus the task of Congress was to campaign for rapid progress toward a democratically elected Legislative Council with an

---

[104] Quoted in Colin Baker, *State of Emergency*, p. 6.
[105] Conversations with Mikeka over the years 1958 to 1966.

African majority which would be followed by the granting of Responsible Government.

Sangala was able to adopt this approach because of the peculiarity of the constitution of the Federation. Nyasaland became a province of the new Federation, but its Governor was still responsible to the British Government for those functions of Government in Nyasaland that did not belong to the Federal Government. Thus the imposition of Federation in 1953 did not entirely get rid of the Colonial Office's influence in Nyasaland. Sangala attempted to exploit this somewhat bizarre element in the Federal Constitution to the full. It created a legitimate channel for Nyasas to continually appeal to London and thus exploit potential tensions between Salisbury and London. It gave them a channel through which to constantly complain to the British public against Federation and push their case for secession from the Federation.

Sangala led Congress in pressing the Colonial Office for democratic elections to Legco, as the Legislative Council was referred to normally at that time. He also vigorously lobbied London for the rapid development of African education in Nyasaland. He was so effective in this latter task that in December 1954, Sir Charles Cox, the Special Adviser to the Colonial Office on Education, visited Nyasaland. Pyagusi presented him with a long memorandum on education and reminded him that the same problems he, Sangala, had presented to Cox's predecessor in 1942 were still in existence in 1954!

Thus, at the same time as allowing two congressmen to serve in the Federal Parliament, Sangala had Congress deal with the Protectorate Government and the Colonial Office as if the Federation did not exist, emphasizing Nyasaland's Protectorate status which enabled Congress to continue to appeal for change to the British Government and British public opinion. The bitter complaints made by Roy Welensky, the second Prime Minister of the Federation, about the focus of Nyasas on this London connection is confirmation of the correctness of Sangala's judgement.

Sangala also had clear ideas on what had to be done to make Congress a truly effective political organisation but he had very scant financial resources for any kind of development. (One source of advice and of some limited financial support had now dried up. On going to live in Ghana in August 1953, Kamuzu Banda ceased to have any regular contact with Congress.) Sangala saw correctly that a newspaper was vital to keep people and the Party well informed, particularly at a time when the Federal and Protectorate Governments were spending a great deal on pro-Federation propaganda in Nyasaland. Alas, as with so much he tried, the financial resources were simply not there. He did start a Congress newspaper by turning a mimeographed newsletter, *Kwacha*, which had been put out by Congress headquarters intermittently since 1952, into a weekly newssheet. Without serious advertising revenue, which was not forthcoming in this case, no newspaper could survive and *Kwacha* died after less than a year in existence.

Sangala's continued and vociferous campaign of insistence that Nyasaland was a British Protectorate and ignoring the Federation except in seeking to secede from it was one which troubled the Federal Prime Minister Huggins and his successor, Roy Welensky.[106] In Welensky's eyes the activities of Manoah Chirwa and Kumbikano were a marginal sideshow in comparison.

This focus by Congress on London's obligation to Nyasaland constantly reminded the Colonial Office of its responsibilities towards Nyasaland as a 'Protectorate' and it reminded the Colonial Service officers in Nyasaland of the older Colonial Office traditions of the 'paramountcy of native interests' at a time when some were becoming distinctly uneasy about the way the Federation was developing.[107]

Sangala's approach was in harmony with some of the views of the Governor of Nyasaland, Sir Geoffrey Colby. In 1952 and 1953, Colby had expressed grave doubts about the imposition of federation again the wishes of the African people and was now pressing ahead, as much as his limited resources allowed, with development in Nyasaland, both economic and constitutional.

Sangala's approach also helped to keep alive the attention of the anti-federation groups in the United Kingdom. In Scotland particularly, Nyasaland became the focus of their anti-federation agitation as a result of Sangala's persistence.

To return to the Governor for a moment, he was a complex character but saw very clearly, more so than most Europeans, whether Colonial Service or settler, that the African opposition to Federation had a valid and important point in its criticism of the Southern Rhodesian Government and Southern Rhodesian society.[108] As he said in a letter to his successor, Sir Robert Armitage,

> I advised originally against the inclusion of Nyasaland not because I objected so much to the idea of federation but rather because I was convinced that there was no goodwill toward us or understanding of our problem in Salisbury. I fear I have to say that this has been borne out in practice. I do not believe that federation can succeed unless there is a complete change of heart in Salisbury – at present I see no sign of this.[109]

---

[106] Huggins was later made Lord Malvern and Welensky was later knighted.

[107] Griff Jones, *Britain and Nyasaland*.

[108] There is an excellent biography of Colby by Colin Baker, *Development Governor*, 1994.

[109] Quoted in Colin Baker, *Retreat from Empire: Sir Robert Armitage in Africa and Cyprus*, p. 181.

In different words Colby was expressing agreement with views of the majority of the people of Nyasaland. It was the nature of Southern Rhodesian society and the policies of its government that lay behind their long term opposition to any closer political relationship with Southern Rhodesia, and along with the Governor the Nyasa people saw no sign of change.

To the delight of Sangala and other Congress leaders, Colby, in the months after the creation of the Federation, proceeded to pursue a policy in his administration of the Protectorate that fitted in with Sangala's policy as leader of Congress. Although trying to persuade Africans to accept the Federation, Colby also insisted on developing all that could be done by the Government of Nyasaland within its own sphere, including constitutional advance. Equally important was his adamant insistence that there should be no expansion whatever of the Federal Government sphere of authority or influence in the Protectorate.

All of this fitted well into Sangala's policy of concentrating Congress activity on what lay within the authority of the Nyasaland administration and London, behaving as if there was no Federation. This was a policy which, to Sangala's delight, also served to infuriate the white politicians in the Federation, both those in government and in opposition.[110] The Rhodesian politicians were so upset that they discussed seriously the possibility that the Federal Government should seek to have the status of the Nyasaland Protectorate changed to negate this Congress policy. To attempt that was to stray into dangerous territory since, on the setting up of the Federation, it had been agreed that there would be no constitutional changes whatsoever until the Constitutional Review scheduled for not less than seven and not more than ten years after the creation of the new state.

When, at a meeting in Lilongwe, Julian Greenfield, the Federal Minister for Justice and Internal Affairs, made a statement on the status of Nyasaland as a British Protectorate and the need for change, Sangala wrote a piece in *Kwacha* challenging Greenfield's status and authority. He asserted that Greenfield had no right to make such statements or to think he had any place in the Protectorate and its affairs at all. Sangala wrote

Mr Greenfield would be well advised to confine his activities to his own territory and leave the solution of the Protectorate problems to the Nyasaland residents, their government and the Colonial Office. Accordingly the people of the Protectorate wish to remind Mr Greenfield and his government that Nyasaland is not a conquered country.[111]

[110] Welensky to Joelson, 3 Jan. 1957, The Welensky Papers, Coffin 9.
[111] *Kwacha*, 26 January 1955.

Sangala also made sure that sympathetic Labour members of the UK Parliament and pressure groups like the Scottish Council on African Questions, which continued an effective cross-party lobby in opposition to Federation, were informed regularly about the affairs of the Protectorate. For example, he made great play in communications to his allies in London and Scotland with the fact that previous to the coming of Federation, Africans could move freely within the area of the three constituent territories of the Federation. Since the coming of Federation this right had been curtailed. The arrival of federation meant that Africans were immediately deprived of rights they had enjoyed before the creation of this new state which, it was asserted, had come into being to improve their condition! Sangala and Kenneth Kaunda both sought to exercise their old right of freedom of movement and were arrested for their pains, Kaunda in Southern Rhodesia and Sangala in Northern Rhodesia Sangala made sure that observers in Britain were kept up to date with these events and others that he felt showed the Federation in its true anti-African colours.[112]

Sangala also sought to prevent any violent disorder that could possibly be seen as provoked by Congress activity lest it led to Federal military interference in Nyasaland. That would be an outcome Congress had neither the organisation nor plans to deal with. Violence would also have an unfortunate impact on British public opinion, whose sympathy was important if Congress was to achieve Nyasaland's secession from the Federation. Pyagusi therefore insisted that everything had to be done constitutionally.

At the annual meeting of Congress at Lilongwe in April 1955, in keeping with this policy of Sangala's, Congress called upon the British Government to restore Nyasaland's proper status as an African Protectorate and to grant it the right to secede from the Federation. This has often been seen as a product of the arrival on the scene of Masauko Chipembere and Kanyama Chiume, but it was the policy that Sangala had been pursuing for the previous fourteen months.

What is often seen as more clearly attributable to the influence of Chiume and Chipembere was the call at the next annual conference of Congress in 1956 for Manoah Chirwa and Clement Kumbikano to resign their seats in the Federal Assembly. We shall see, however, that at that time both 'Chip' and Chiume were still persuaded of the usefulness of the role played by the two Federal MPs and that it was other Congressmen who campaigned vociferously for Manoah and Kumbikano to withdraw.

It was in the last months of 1955 that many supporters and members of Congress concluded that Manoah's and Kumbikano's continued presence in the

112 Robert Rotberg. *The Rise of Nationalism in Central Africa*. pp. 267-68.

Salisbury Parliament was a mistake. They had come to believe that it gravely weakened the seriousness with which Congress's call for Nyasaland's secession was received both by friend and foe. The critics who began this increasingly bitter attack on the continued presence of members of Congress as Federal MPs were not the new arrivals like Chipembere and Chiume but the radicals in the Blantyre and Johannesburg branches of Nyasaland African Congress, notably Mikeka Mkandawire, Rose Chibambo, Solomon Hartwell and Mwezi Mhango backed by some delegates from the Northern Region branches.

In retrospect it might appear that taking part in the Federal structure of government was clearly the wrong thing for anyone concerned with the self-determination of the Nyasa people to do. It was, however, a more complicated decision to make at the time than it appears to people in the twenty-first century. As we have seen, Federation had been rapidly and forcibly imposed on a Nyasa people whose opposition had been quickly and effectively crushed. It really did look as if Federation were 'here to stay'. To many, Manoah's argument appeared correct, that to boycott the Federal Parliament and leave stooges to represent the Protectorate might mean that Nyasaland, more than ever, would be at the unchallenged mercy of the settler politicians of the two Rhodesias. The presence of Congress MPs in the Federal Parliament was very important. It showed clearly that the claim by Congress that they represented the Nyasa people was true. It also gave Congress a platform on which to plead their case, a plea that would be heard not only in Salisbury but by the outside world.

In order to cut through the deliberately distorted understanding of the later history of the Congress movement in Nyasaland, it must be understood that as late as the meeting of national delegates of Nyasaland African Congress in April *1956*, Kanyama Chiume, Masauko Chipembere and Dr Banda supported Manoah Chirwa's position.

The dilemma that faced all opponents of Federation with regard to what to do about participation in Federal structures can be illustrated very clearly in the situation of the Reverend Andrew Doig. Doig, with the sympathy of Congress, had represented African interests in the old Nyasaland Legco. In 1953 he had to decide whether to accept the invitation of the Governor of Nyasaland to fill the seat in the Federal Parliament and on its African Affairs Board, which was in the Governor's gift. If he accepted, Doig would sit in support of the two Nyasa African elected members of the Federal Parliament. Doig, who had drafted the Blantyre Mission Council's statement of total opposition to the imposition of Federation against the wishes of the Nyasa people and who had opposed federation of the three territories vigorously whenever the opportunity arose in Legco, nevertheless believed that there was a case for going to Salisbury.

If the whole scheme was as much a betrayal of the Nyasa people as he thought it was, arguably it could best be exposed from inside by someone having shown a willingness to give it a trial. After all, Dr Banda had reluctantly expressed a similar sentiment on his departure from London for Kumasi.

In this difficult situation Doig sought advice from Dr James Dougal, Secretary of the Foreign Mission Committee of the Church of Scotland. Dougal summed up the situation with great perception. Indeed when he wrote in 1953 he anticipated what was only to become the firm Congress position at the end of 1956:

> Whatever answer you give it is going to be liable to misinterpretation. If you decline your answer can be construed as definite non-co-operation. The Mission itself might be accused of trying to sabotage the Federation scheme. [*It already was being so accused*] If you accept you will be charged with betraying African interests and I don't suppose you have the slightest hope of making your position understood by the Congress. What might be even more serious would be that in the event of an African boycott of the Federal Assembly you might find yourself without any representative African colleagues in the Federal Parliament or in the African Affairs Board. The Africans who would consent to act would be 'stooges' of the Government who did not represent African opinion in the slightest.[113]

The position adopted by Manoah Chirwa and Clement Kumbikano with the support of Congress gave Doig the confidence to go ahead and appeared to answer Dr Dougal's doubts which were only to be vindicated later. Doig, in his role in the Federal Parliament continued to have good relations with Congress even after Congress came to decide that the two African members of the Federal Parliament should resign. For a time at least, Congress felt that Doig's presence in Salisbury did not undermine their call for secession and that he could still be of some use to the cause, operating in the Parliament and on the African Affairs Board.[114] Lord Malvern's opinion of him is confirmation of the service Doig provided for the Nyasa cause. With regard to the African Affairs Board, the British Government had said it was to provide the African MPs with guidance and restraint. 'In Malvern's view, Doig, in particular, had never provided either guidance or restraint and indeed had only tried to lead every extremist movement.'[115]

---

[113] J.C. Dougal to Andrew Doig. 26 June 1953. in Federation File. D.S. Lyon Papers. University of Edinburgh.

[114] Conversations with Dunduzu Chisiza and Masauko Chipembere in Kanjedza Detention Centre.

[115] J.R.T. Wood. *The Welensky Papers*, Durban, 1983. p. 574.

It is not clear how far Sangala's active pursuing of Congress's old campaign for a democratically elected Legislative Council for Nyasaland affected the Colonial Office but it did chime in with the ideas of Geoffrey Colby, as we have seen. In early 1955, the Governor with the agreement of the Colonial Office initiated a massive change in the constitution of the Nyasaland Legislative Council with important long-term results.[116]

Hitherto the Nyasaland Legco had consisted of ten 'official' members - Colonial Office officers - and ten 'unofficial' members. These latter had consisted of three Africans nominated by the Protectorate Council, one Asian appointed by the Protectorate Asian Association, five Europeans nominated by the various European organisations in the Protectorate and one European nominated by the Governor.

In July 1955 Colby announced a radical new structure for Legco; it was now to contain elected members for the first time. The Executive Council – the Governor's cabinet as it were – was, however, to remain unchanged.[117] After elections to be held in 1956, Legco was to consist of eleven 'official members' and eleven 'unofficials'. The latter group would consist of six Europeans and five Africans. The six Europeans were to be elected by the existing European Voters' Roll created by the Federal Constitution and which barely reached two thousand in number! The five African members, representing three million people, were to be elected by the membership of the three Provincial Councils, the same councils which had been created by government to provide an alternative African voice to that of Congress.

This decision created a potentially effective platform for the continuation on a new and more effective level of Sangala's policy of concentrating on Nyasaland and its institutions as the means of fighting federation and gaining the right to secede. The new Legislative Council could be used not only as an effective platform upon which to express opposition to Federation but also the elections created an opportunity to show that, even with a conservative electorate, the members of the three Provincial African Councils, Congress represented the voice of the Nyasa people. All this could be achieved so long as Congress candidates won the five African seats.

It was at this point that the young men who had returned to their homeland and had become Congress activists came into their own. It has been usually understood by writers on this period of Malawi history - Baker, Short, Tangri and even the most perceptive of them, Robert Rotberg - that the new dynamism of Nyasa nationalism that occurs at this time was a product of the initiative of these new men. They did play a very important role, without any

---

[116] Colin Baker entitled his biography of Colby, *The Development Governor.*
[117] It consisted of officials with two European unofficials.

doubt. Their opportunity to lead and gain the attention of all Nyasas, however, only came into being with the new situation created by Colby's reform
of the Legislative Council. This reform created an extraordinarily effective
channel to further Sangala's existing policy of concentrating on democratisation and reform in Nyasaland as a prelude to secession and eventual independence. It created an opportunity which the new Congress members of the
Legislative Council exploited to the full.

The importance of Colby's reform of Legco can hardly be exaggerated. It
created a completely new situation for Congress, for Nyasaland and for the
Federation. Gaining seats in Legco enabled the new Legco members to take
Sangala's policy onto an entirely new level. A further radically new element
in Nyasa politics also emerged with the creation of the new Legco. This was
the opportunity to turn the Legco Hansard into a vehicle of Congress propaganda; an opportunity the elected members made full use of, as we shall discuss later.

Without the new platform that the reformed Legco provided them, what
exactly could anyone have done that Sangala was not already doing? Colby's
reforming zeal led to a turning point in the history of Congress and of the
Protectorate.

The Governor had hoped that the new Legco would be a means of appeasing
Nyasas and of allowing an alternative voice to that of Congress to be heard.
He saw it as part of what he held to be his task which was, as he told the old
Legco in April 1955, to convince the Nyasa people that Federation was in
their best interests. He, as we have seen, did not believe the propaganda
claim made both by London and Salisbury that Congress's total opposition
to Federation was not the majority view of the Nyasa people. He did believe
that the people's opinion might be changed, though he feared that Salisbury's policies rather than Congress might prevent that. The new members
of Legco elected by the Provincial Councils he hoped might provide a more
moderate Nyasa voice, though he did not doubt it would still be a voice critical of Federation.

Astonishingly, however, officials in London and white politicians in Central
Africa thought the essentially conservative Provincial Councils would elect
men to Legco who would cooperate with the Federation, thus showing that
Congress did not represent the Nyasa people!

Who were these young men who had arrived and through the new constitutional changes were enabled to make such an impact on the political scene in
Nyasaland? Before we look at them we need to remember that two Nyasas
returning from university had already made their presence felt in the politics
of their homeland. The first had been Orton Edward Ching'oli Chirwa who,

already in 1952, had been a member of the NAC delegation that went to the United Kingdom to publicise the Nyasa opposition to Federation. He was seen as the Party's 'intellectual' until he was replaced in that role, in 1953, by Wellington Manoah Chirwa. Manoah had been the leader of the considerable body of Nyasa students at Fort Hare University College in what was then the Cape Province of South Africa and had been a mentor to Masauko Chipembere when the latter arrived there.[118]

The key figures among the young men who returned to Nyasaland and who rose to positions of leadership with astonishing rapidity were Henry Blasius Masauko Chipembere, Murray William Kanyama Chiume and Dunduzu Kaluli Chisiza.

Chipembere was a southerner and the son of an Episcopal priest. His father and mother were both from the Maravi people who, in the nineteenth century, had fled to the east side of the Lake to escape Ngoni raids. One of his grandparents was a Yao, which perhaps explains why he has been referred to in some of the literature as if he were a Yao. The fact that both his parents, although Maravi, were born on the east side of the Lake, allowed Dr Banda to assert later that Chipembere was not a true Malawian. After spells at Blantyre Secondary School and Goromonzi High School, Chipembere went to Fort Hare where he joined a politically significant group of Nyasa students led by Manoah Chirwa. He returned to Nyasaland in 1954 to enter the Protectorate civil service.

Chiume was a northerner, a Tonga from Usisya. Chiume spent most of his school days in Tanganyika where his uncle had taken him in 1938 after the death of his mother. After village school and a time at High School in Dar-es-Salaam, he was one of the academically outstanding boys who were admitted to Tabora Government High School to complete Standards XI and XII. From there he went to Makerere University College in Uganda. In 1949, while still a student at Makerere he returned to Nyasaland to visit his family for the first time since he had left in 1938. After leaving Makerere, Chiume went to teach at Alliance High School at Dodoma in Tanganyika. In December 1953 he returned to Malawi and immersed himself in the work of Congress. He also committed a vast amount of energy to a campaign to spread the cultivation of coffee as a cash crop. This project, by mid-1955, could claim real success in the Nkhata Bay district and adjacent communities. In the next two years, alongside his political campaigning, Chiume continued to spread his message about coffee cultivation in every area in the Northern Region where the soil was suitable.

---

[118] Robert I. Rotberg (ed.) *Hero of the Nation: Chipembere of Malawi.* Chapter 4, *passim.*

In their attempts to bring new life to Sangala's struggling NAC, Chipembere and Chiume also had the support of a small but growing group of Nyasa university graduates who were returning to their homeland at this time. Their closest ally in this group was Augustine Bwanausi; among the others were Dr Harry Bwanausi, Vincent Gondwe, Moir Chisuse and Edwin Mwase.

Dunduzu Kaluli Chisiza was also a northerner, a Tumbuka from Chitimba, or Florence Bay as it was then called.[119] He arrived on the scene nearly two years after Chiume and Chipembere returned to Nyasaland. We will look at his life in more detail later. Suffice it to note that though academically the least formally qualified of the bright young men who rallied to the cause of secession and independence, yet he was later the Nyasa leader most admired intellectually by outside academic observers.[120] His three essays on the situation in Malawi and Africa generally are still essential reading by anyone concerned about Malawi's future; they present a vision that can still inspire.[121]

On the basis of the little that has been written about the years 1954 to 1957 the story has too often been understood as one where the young men arrive and are almost immediately disillusioned with the leadership of Congress under Sangala and the continuing presence of Manoah Chirwa and Kumbikano in the Federal Parliament. They then got rid of Sangala, pressed for the dismissal of Chirwa and Kumbikano from Congress, got themselves elected to the new Legco and then transformed the whole political situation in preparation for the return of Dr Banda.[122]

What actually happened is a somewhat different story. Chipembere and Chiume were welcomed by Sangala and Manoah - after all Manoah and Chipembere had been good friends at Fort Hare. Manoah Chirwa was still the dominant figure in Congress and at any meeting of delegates he always commanded a majority of the votes even though home-grown radicals like

---

[119] Because his parents moved to Karonga district some authorities have referred to him an Nkhonde. However the Chisizas belong to the Mkandawire clan of the Tumbuka speaking-people. See Austin Mkandawire. 'A Short History of the Chisiza Clan' in *The Society of Malawi Journal* Vol. 58 (2). 2005.

[120] In 1960. when the Governor of Kanjedza Detention Centre allowed me to arrange Dunduzu's essays on economics to go to Professor W.W. Rostow of the Massachusetts Institute of Technology. later Special Adviser to President John Kennedy. and for the Professor's comments to be given to 'Du'. Professor Rostow remarked to me in a covering letter that Dunduzu's was one of the sharpest and most perceptive minds that he had encountered in southern Africa.

[121] See bibliography for the titles of these essays.

[122] This glib misunderstanding even reaches a sort of academic endorsement by the acceptance of Yacub A. Adams' MSc thesis at University of Edinburgh in 1976.

Mikeka Mkandawire and Masopera Gondwe were already constantly challenging him.

Meanwhile Sangala, ever struggling to prevent a repeat of the disastrous splits of the past and because of Manoah's power over the delegates to Congress meetings, often had to give way to Manoah even when he disagreed with him. A clear example of this is when he agreed to Manoah's continuing longer in the Federal Parliament than was initially anticipated. Sangala even dismissed from the Executive Committee of Congress members who too actively challenged Manoah, most notably Masopera Gondwe, the eccentric but talented Assistant General Secretary of Congress, something Sangala later admitted he bitterly regretted.[123]

Ever since the foundation of the movement Sangala had struggled to keep it alive and united. He was most happy when organising things behind the scenes, never wavering from his commitment to the cause despite being, at times, near bankruptcy as a result of personally subsidizing the movement. Twice he served the movement as President but this was only when he deemed that it was essential for the survival of Congress At no time was Sangala ever one of 'the older men holding back the radicals', which even as perceptive an observer as Rotberg sometimes implies in his earlier writing. Far from being one of the old conservatives holding back the movement and a stumbling block that Chipembere and Chiume had to remove, this is what Chipembere wrote of him.

> He was a man I deeply respected and loved. In my great nationalist feeling of those days, he personified all that I held dear. The fact that he was living on the verge of bankruptcy and sometimes having hardly enough to eat endeared him even more to me. He was utterly selfless, and his financial problems did not shake his great faith in his own mission or in the cause he led.[124] One of my greatest disappointments was that I was never able to demonstrate my gratitude to this man for his great service to the nation.[125]

As we have seen, although Congress protested that the new constitution of Legco did not even begin to approach their demands for its democratization, it was decided they should contest the election. When the Executive Committee of Congress discussed whom they should put forward as Congress candidates, it was Manoah Chirwa who suggested Chipembere as a candidate for one of the Southern Province seats. This was immediately and enthusiastically endorsed by Sangala. 'Let him stand as a candidate. He will

---

[123] I gained this information through conversations with Atate Sangala in 1960 and 61.

[124] These troubles were partly because of Sangala's spending so much of his resources on behalf of Congress but also because his transport business, run by his oldest son Gibrea, had suffered badly after the young man's tragic death in an accident.

[125] Chipembere. *Hero*. p. 168.

do great things – he is highly educated, and yet he used to eat *nsima* at my house with me, sitting on a dusty mat. He has the right type of humility.'[126]

The Executive formally endorsed three candidates, Kanyama Chiume for the North, ex-NAC president Ralph Chinyama for the Central Region and Chipembere for the Southern. They could not agree about whom Congress should endorse for the other two seats; a number of Congress members and Congress supporters put themselves forward and it was difficult in these circumstances for the committee to make a decision about endorsement.

This lack of decision stemmed partly from Manoah's consistent policy which was to avoid, unless in extreme circumstances, making a decision that might annoy an important figure whom he might need to call upon for help later. Despite his oratorical powers which enabled him to sway crowds, it was not by speeches that Manoah exercised his leadership in Congress. He always preferred to operate in a 'Godfather' mode, a purveyor of influence, patronage and favours, a style Chipembere graphically describes

> He called upon personal friends, acquaintances, relatives, business associates, favour-seekers, and past recipients of favours – and the wives, husbands, lovers and the illicit associates of such men or women. The machine, which he himself used to prefer to call 'machinery', had men and women of all races, skills and walks of life.[127]

The other reason for not making a decision about the other two seats was that whoever won them, the Congress members could never win a vote in Legco against six European members and eleven officials, dedicated, as Colby put it, to convincing Nyasas that Federation was good for them. The point about getting into Legco was not to pass legislation but to use the meetings of Legco as a platform from which to preach Congress's case against Federation and for claiming the right to secede. That did not prevent the new members from pressing for local reform once they did become members of Legco, as we shall see.

When the elections were held in the three Provincial Councils, the three Nyasaland African Congress approved candidates were elected - Chiume, Chinyama and Chipembere - and the other two seats were won by committed Congress supporters, N.W. Kwenje and Dunstan Chijosi. As 'Chip' makes clear in his autobiography, it was 'the old men', Sangala, Manoah and Reverend Charles Chinula, who achieved both his electoral victory and that of Chiume, through their prestige and influence with the chiefs who were the majority in the councils which constituted the electorate.[128]

---

[126] *Ibid.* p. 169.
[127] Ibid. p. 203.
[128] Ibid. p. 203-212 passim.

The victory of the five Congressmen in these elections came as a shock to the Federal Government and to the Colonial and Commonwealth Relations Offices in London. After all the British administration of the Protectorate had created the three Provincial Councils as vehicles for a more conservative and traditionalist public opinion to be heard, a public opinion that would show that Congress did not represent the majority of the Nyasa people. Again this wishful thinking was exposed as nonsense, as it had been again and again in the past. Steadily from 1938 the Nyasa people had expressed their opposition to any political involvement with the settler dominated south, yet some British officials, who, as we have seen, ought to have known better, clung to the myth that anti-federal feeling was restricted to a radical minority and those misled by them. The new Legislative Council which came into being in 1956 exposed their wishful thinking for what it was and in a form that could not be explained away.

It was that same year that Dunduzu Chisiza returned to his homeland to work for the Congress cause. After a short period in Tanganyika as a police clerk, the young man who had whiled away his time at Livingstonia, playing football and writing and acting in plays, gained a place at Aggrey Memorial College, near Kampala, Uganda. At Kampala not only did he excel in his schoolwork but he became a voracious reader in the fields of history and economics. Aggrey's was an extraordinary school where each 'boy' (they were usually young men like 'Du') had to build for himself a small daub and wattle house in which to live and also each 'boy' had to grow some of the vegetables for his own sustenance.

In 1955 he came back to Malawi, having gained his Cambridge School Certificate and, despite still being a 'schoolboy', having played a very active role in the Makerere Nyasa Students' Association with Chiume and Augustine Bwanausi. On his return, he almost immediately went to Salisbury as a clerk in the Indian High Commission there. In Salisbury he joined the Mashonaland branch of Nyasaland African Congress, which was the NAC's main source of funds. More significantly he joined a group of Shona and Ndebele young men to form the Youth Wing of the Southern Rhodesian African Congress. These young men, including James Chikarema, Edson Sithole and George Nyandoro, brought new life to Congress and seriously alarmed the Southern Rhodesian Government, a government which was headed at that time by the most liberal prime minister that country had had, Garfield Todd. It was also, however, a government which acted firmly against Congress and deported Dunduzu back to Malawi.

On his return home 'Du' decided to stay in Blantyre and got part time work with a butcher in Blantyre market so as to have more time to serve the cause. Subsisting on this meagre income, he pursued an even more Spartan life-style than he had at Aggrey College which confirmed Dunduzu's commitment to the simple way of life which he followed for the rest of his tragically short life.

His energy and abilities as a speaker and an organiser soon made a strong impact upon supporters of Congress. The loose organisation of Congress at that time enabled him to act in an almost freelance capacity. Soon after the elections to the new Legco, the Congress members of Legco urged him to stand for the post of Secretary General in the coming NAC elections. This was part of Chiume and Chipembere's plans for the further development of Congress activity. The Congress members of Legco promised they would provide a salary for Dunduzu from their own salaries if he was elected, so the new Legco would help fund the usually cash-strapped Congress.

Clearly a group of well-educated young men from all over the Protectorate were coming together to demand more determined action from Congress. The role of these young men was not as straightforward as the literature on the period suggests, as we have already seen. It was not a matter of them instantly uniting in pressing for the withdrawal of Manoah Chirwa and Kumbikano from the Federal Parliament and the ousting of the previous leadership, those 'old men' who were holding everything back.

Of Manoah Chirwa and his role in the Federal Parliament, Chipembere has written

> Not only were his speeches intellectually well-organised and well thought-out; they were also deeply radical ...Chirwa became the symbol of Malawi nationalism and its undying opposition to Federation. For us, the radical Malawi youth of the time, he was a hero.[129]

It was Manoah and Pyagusi, after all, who managed the electoral victory of the Congress candidates at the 1956 elections for the new Legco. Chipembere and Chiume recognised Manoah as the real power in Congress as well as admiring him and his political skills. Just as we have seen how Sangala was unable to challenge Manoah because of this power, Chipembere goes further and continues to call Manoah, 'my much respected leader' through most of 1956.

The first moves demanding the withdrawal of the two Federal MPs from the Federal Parliament came from other sources, **not** from the new young graduate group. As we have seen it was Masopera Gondwe who first forced the issue in August 1955. His dismissal, forced on Sangala by Manoah, then triggered the resignations from their various official posts in Congress of Mikeka Mkandawire, K.W. Kulujili (until then Sangala's right-hand man, and J.A. Pambala, the Treasurer-General.

---

[129] Ibid. p, 201.

It was the impact of these resignations and the continued activities of Gondwe's new party, the Congress People's Party (popularly referred to as Chipipi), which created a crisis over membership of the Federal Parliament but which, initially at least, Manoah rode out successfully. The critical moment came in March 1956 at the Annual Conference of Congress. The revision of the party's constitution was first on the agenda, but delegates rapidly put this matter aside to get onto the burning issue of the day, the continued presence of Nyasaland Congressmen in the Federal Parliament. It was the delegates from the Johannesburg Branch of the NAC, led by Mwesi Mhango, a friend of Mikeka Mkandawire and Rose Chibambo, who began the attack, vigorously supported by northern delegates led by Patrick Kaunda from Ekwendeni.

Manoah sat passively through these speeches and relied, as he so often did, on others to defend his position. These spokesmen he had carefully primed with the arguments they were to use. He had also worked hard in his usual 'Godfather' way to make sure that delegates were committed to support him before the Conference had convened. What is important to note is that the young graduate group was solid in its support of Manoah at this conference.

His case, ably put over by his well-briefed allies, had three elements. The first was that the resignation of the two Nyasa Congress MPs was pointless if it were not followed up by a well planned and effectively executed campaign to force Nyasaland's secession from the Federation. The second point was that the danger of stooges taking Manoah's and Kumbikano's seats in Parliament was still a possibility. What a blow that would be to their claim that Congress spoke for the Nyasa people.

The third element in his argument was that even if Congress did decide to mount a massive campaign for secession following the resignation of the two MPs, nothing was planned or prepared. They might be able to mount a campaign to prevent anyone playing the stooge role in the Federal Parliament. The danger was that if any violence occurred in that campaign, then the Federal authorities would have all the excuse they needed to drastically intervene in the affairs of the Protectorate. This was, of course, precisely the pattern of events that Sangala had all along feared might happen and which he had been struggling to prevent for the previous three years.

Chipembere and Chiume both thought these arguments were worthy of serious consideration and came down on Manoah's side. Indeed Chiume spoke passionately and at length in defence of Manoah and Kumbikano staying on in the Salisbury Parliament. He did, however, also go on to suggest that a committee be set up to plan, in secret, an effective secessionist campaign to be ready to be put into action when the time did come for the Nyasa Federal

MPs to resign. The result of the debate was that the call for the two MPs to resign was decisively defeated.

It was at this conference that those elected to Legco put up Dunduzu as a candidate for Secretary of the Party. His youth, and, most tellingly, the fact that almost none of the old guard knew him combined with his overt and very articulate radicalism meant he was defeated. This did not deter him from continuing his freelance speaking and organising in the pro-Congress and anti-Federation cause.

So, as a result of this conference it was an older group of radicals, the most outstanding being Masopera Gondwe and Mikeka Mkandawire, who were left out in the cold and the so-called 'young men on-fire with the white-heat of radical nationalism' who helped ensure their defeat and the continuance of Manoah's dominance over Congress.

At the same time the 'grand old man' of Congress, James Sangala, was becoming increasingly perturbed by the situation. He also continued to be deeply distressed by his son's death and troubled by the near collapse of his business. He made it clear that he would not seek re-election to office and that he was going to retire from public affairs.[130]

The issue of Manoah and Kumbikano's position as federal MPs, however, did not go away. Indeed anger continued to spread and, in August 1956, Chiume made it clear that he had changed his mind and was now on the side of those who wished the immediate resignation from Parliament of the two MPs. In contrast, Chipembere only slowly came to agree. He tried initially to use his long friendship with Manoah to persuade him to resign voluntarily. Indeed in November and December of 1956 he pled with Manoah on numerous occasions to resign before he was forced to resign or was expelled from Congress.

The critical moment was reached at a special conference of Congress which took place on 31st December 1956 and 1st January 1957. In the closed session of the conference on the first day, Chiume and Chipembere were attacked for their stand on the need for the Federal MPs to resign and the delegates overwhelmingly defeated the motion calling for Kumbikano and Manoah's resignation from the Federal Parliament. What should be noted particularly about that first day of debates was how again and again Chiume and Chipembere were referred to as 'boys' and 'children'. This may be seen as the beginning of what became Chipembere's deep conviction that to have the

---

[130] Of course he never did. He was always willing to listen to people and give advice while keeping a shrewd eye on affairs. He also contributed, as an elder, his energy and skills to the work of the Blantyre Synod of the CCAP. It was in that capacity that I first met him and gained his friendship.

widest appeal to the people an older man was always necessary. In addition, it is very significant that the leading Central Region delegate, James Chinyama, their fellow member of Legco. referred to Chipembere and Chiume several times as *atumbidwa*. In his memoir Chipembere says the literal translation is 'uninitiated' but what was meant was a 'young person'.[131] So it was understood, probably, by most southerners and northerners who were there, but did not Chinyama mean much more? After all Chinyama could have used *anyamata* – boys, or *ana*-children; *atumbidwa*, unlike those two general words, is very specific. Was Chinyama's use of that word a foreshadowing of what was to come under Kamuzu Banda? Was it an outburst of the Chewa chauvinism that Banda was later to play upon? In the famous book he edited with Cullen Young which was published in 1947, had Kamuzu not said that no Nyasa could be counted a man unless he was initiated into the Nyau Society, that is to say, had become *mtumbidwa*? To become so would be an unlikely happening for the son of an Episcopal priest, and impossible for a lakeshore Tonga!

On the second day of the conference, 1 January 1957, the meetings were open to the public. A large contingent of radical young people from the Blantyre-Limbe urban area attended. These were young men who had been influenced by Mikeka Mkandawire and other leaders who had been forced to carry on their political campaign outside the formal ranks of Congress. As we have seen, they had been meeting regularly at the house of J.B. Msiska, always known as Stenning; they were well prepared and vociferously called for Manoah's resignation from the Federal Parliament. Indeed when the time came for Manoah to speak he was unable to make any kind of impact because of the constant interruptions and jeering by these young men.

Earlier in the day, T.D.T. Banda had been elected President of Congress, and was given a new power by the conference, the ability to nominate additional members of his own choice to the executive committee of Congress. This gave Banda more power over the executive than previous presidents who had had to put up with their failed rivals for the President's chair getting elected to other positions on the Executive.

It seems clear that Manoah felt that he would be able to manipulate the new President, but the scenes at that last session of the conference on January 1st gave 'T.D.T.' the confidence to be independent of the old 'Godfather' of Congress, to the latter's surprise.

As we have seen, another important result of those fateful meetings was the impact that the constant harping on about their youth had on both Chipembere and Chiume. This litany of complaint about their youth during confer-

---

[131] Chipembere, *Hero*, p. 229.

ence further compounded the impact on them of the similar reaction they had experienced from time to time in the villages they visited in their work. Neither in the North nor in the South where each operated did they meet opposition because they were not Nyau initiates, but they were made to feel that they were somehow inadequate simply because of their age. This was a reflection of the fact that in traditional village society in which the vast majority of Nyasas lived, age did continue to matter in terms of suitability for leadership.[132] We will return to this issue later.

It is, however, important to note that, breaking a long silence which had begun on leaving London for Kumasi, it was at this time that Dr Banda re-entered the affairs of Nyasaland. Hitherto, as we have seen, he had simply ignored letters sent to him from Nyasaland. On this issue of Manoah's continued membership of the Federal Parliament, Kamuzu had at last entered into correspondence with Chipembere. Their correspondence on this matter was reviewed by the Devlin Commission and from it we see that Banda had initially supported the line taken by Manoah and Kumbikano and continued to do so even after Chipembere had, at last, changed his mind and sought the resignation of the two Federal MPs.

As we have seen, despite the success of the 'behind the scenes' manipulation of the delegates to the conference by Manoah on the first day, all was not lost as far as the young men were concerned. The election of T.D.T. Banda to succeed Sangala with the new powers of cooption granted the president was a victory for their cause since 'T.D.T.' no longer felt he need bow down to Manoah. His position was strengthened by the fact that the new Secretary-General and Treasurer were men sympathetic to the cause of the Blantyre radicals who had jeered Manoah on the second day of the Conference. Confirmation of the new President's independence from Manoah came when he exercised his right to co-opt new members to the Executive Committee. In the exercise of this power, the new President chose radicals sympathetic to Chipembere and Chiume to expand the new Executive of Congress.

Thus, although Manoah appeared to have won in that he was not forced to resign his seat and was not expelled from Congress, he had lost the main battle. The new Executive Committee was one which believed that the time had come for the disassociation of Nyasaland African Congress from the Federal Parliament. This had been a long and difficult struggle and not the instant transformation that has been assumed in the writing of many commentators.

---

[132] In the fifties and early sixties, both in Balaka and Ntcheu, although I was married with children, my session-clerks would refer to me thus – 'ngakhale mbusa wathu ndi mnyamata basi'...– although our pastor is just a boy...

When the results of the January conference are viewed together with the victory of the Congress candidates in the election for the new Nyasaland Legislative Council, it is clear that a new style leadership had emerged in Nyasaland politics. We should note, however, that although Sangala was about to bow out of holding office in Congress, the campaign that Chipembere and Chiume waged once the new Legislative Council came into being was a direct continuation of the policy initiated by Sangala. It was the opportunity afforded by the decision of the Governor and the Colonial Office to reform the Legislative Council that gave the two 'atumbidwa ' the opportunity to raise that policy to a new level of visibility and effectiveness.

As Chipembere has recorded in his memoirs, they were ably assisted by the other three Congress members, including James Chinyama although he differed with them over Manoah.[133] The Colonial Office and its officials in Nyasaland were not going to be allowed to forget for a minute their responsibility for the Protectorate which they had so dramatically forsaken in agreeing to the creation of the Federation.

The Congress members were well aware that as well as reaching their own constituency - the Nyasa people - their role in the Legco was also going to be carefully studied in London where not everyone in the Colonial Office was entirely a convinced supporter of the Federation. Indeed, although Chipembere did not appear to be aware of it, as we shall see, there were Colonial Service Officers in the Protectorate who were not by any means committed supporters of the Federation which they viewed as an experiment. Its existence, after all, was to be reviewed in seven to ten years to see how it was progressing and decide about its future.

To Huggins, Welensky, and their settler supporters the review was something quite different. It was the vehicle by which the white-ruled Federation would be granted Dominion status and become, effectively, a sovereign nation. For the white settlers, the Federation was not, and must not appear to be an experiment. They were also adamant there must not appear to be any doubts about its viability among British officials of the Nyasaland Government.

It was in exploiting this incipient conflict that Chipembere scored a spectacular victory in Legco, one which had a widespread impact in the Protectorate and in the UK when publicised there. He was given a letter, marked 'SECRET', which had been sent out in September 1957 by the Director of Education, (African education that is, since the education of white children came under the Federal Government). The letter was addressed to the Director's white staff and read

---

[133] Chipembere. *Hero,* p. 263.

Government is concerned to learn that on occasion Nyasaland Government officers have failed to do their utmost to stimulate confidence in Federation.... I must ask you to ensure that you and all European officers serving under you are fully aware that it is the duty of every officer to promote great confidence in Federation, and in particular to take the greatest care that any personal fears or doubts are never publicly expressed.[134]

Chipembere managed to get round the problem that the reading of a 'SECRET' document was forbidden in Legco, since it would be published in the daily Hansard, the verbatim record of the proceedings of the Council, and so cease to be secret. Chip prepared for his coup by asking permission of the presiding officer before the debate opened to read a letter as part of his speech. This permission was granted. After he began to read the letter, the Director of Education attempted to stop him by raising the point of order that he believed the letter being read was one officially marked 'SECRET'. Chipembere brushed him aside by saying he had permission to read the letter and finished reading it. The full text of the letter then appeared in the daily Hansard.

Chip rightly pointed out that this letter exposed the commitment of Protectorate Civil Service to the promotion of the cause of Federation, something that was, in his view, contrary to British Civil Service tradition. In 1953, Sir Geoffrey Colby had said his role and that of his civil servants was to persuade Nyasas of the value of the Federation; that was Government policy, which civil servants were duty bound to serve. What Chip does not mention and this represents a blind spot in his thinking, is that the letter was written in the first place because there were Colonial Service Officers with fears and doubts about Federation.

It was the duty of Colonial Office officials to uphold the policy of the government of the day. After all the legal situation was, as they assured themselves and African audiences they addressed in the early 1950s, that London had the power to strike down Federal legislation if it were appealed against by the African Affairs Board. They went on to assure African audiences that the future of the Federation was still under review. However, events in 1957, made them appear duped and provoked these bitter words from Griff Jones, one of the most perceptive District Commissioners of the period, in his *Britain and Nyasaland*. He writes

The British Government had not deserted them, but had kept power to kill any bad law the Federal Government made. Such promises were usually met with unhappy silence: they had learned to trust us, but knew the most trusted can err and forget. In 1957 Mr Lennox-Boyd made an agreement with Sir Roy Welensky that Federal legislation would not be repealed by the British Government. Those who remem-

---

[134] Quoted in Clyde Sanger, *Central African Emergency*, p. 72.

bered making promises to village people five years before felt nausea for which the best remedy was cynicism, until the memory faded in longer time.[135]

Chip's reading of the letter and so publicising it was a triumph for the Congress cause but in the comments on the event in his autobiography Chip exposes a blind spot in his understanding. He does not understand the position of a significant number of expatriate civil servants like Jones, and he treats all Europeans as actively pro-federation. Throughout the otherwise attractive book, those Europeans in the Protectorate who opposed Federation are ignored by Chip. He does not, for example, mention the missionaries of the Church of Scotland working in the CCAP, whom the Special Branch of the Nyasaland Police saw as a group dedicated to the undermining of the Federation and the secession of Nyasaland from it.[136] Indeed, in 1958 every monthly security report on the situation in the Protectorate complained about the attitude and activities of the Scottish missionaries in this regard.[137]

The propaganda victory Chipembere scored through his exposure of the secret letter was the highest spot in the very successful campaign which the Congress members of Legco waged in the Council chamber. Under the Federal Constitution of 1953, the Nyasaland Legislative Council had a restricted remit. As Chipembere records

> The government had expected us ... to focus our attention on questions relating to the educational, economic, and social problems of our people; it also expected us to keep out of the Legislative Council and leave to the Federal Assembly in Harare all matters falling under the jurisdiction of the Federal departments.[138]

On the contrary, the Congress members consistently brought up the issue of secession from the Federation and the rapid advance of Nyasaland towards self-government and they simply refused to accept the rules of debate of the Council which forbade the raising of Federal topics. This was, of course, carrying on J.F Sangala's policy of treating the Nyasaland Legco as still the supreme authority under London for the governance of Nyasaland.

The new members of Legco had a new stage, however, upon which to act out this policy in sharp and aggressive terms while reaching an audience far beyond that which Sangala or any previous African spokesman could have reached. The Congress members made such a fuss that Legco became a really lively political debating chamber, perhaps for the first time in its exis-

---

[135] Griff Jones, *Britain and Nyasaland*, p. 152.

[136] 'Secret Report on the Church of Scotland Mission and the CCAP.' Government Printers, Zomba, March 1959. The Report accuses the Church of Scotland of sending missionaries of radical left-wing views deliberately to strengthen CCAP opposition to Federation.

[137] John McCracken in his article, 'The Ambiguities of Nationalism,' in the *Journal of Southern African Studies*, Volume 28, No 1, 2002.

[138] Chipembere, *Hero*, p. 255.

tence. Very soon after their new aggressive campaign started, the stir they had created hit the local white press and radio. As a result interested people began to buy the daily issue of Hansard which gave the verbatim reports of the previous day's proceedings in the Legco. Chiume and Chipembere soon realised that this gave them a new well-printed propaganda sheet, at no cost to Congress.

In the past the speeches of previous Congress leaders had never been effectively reported in the white dominated press and had a very limited ability to reach any kind of mass audience. Suddenly, at 3 pence a copy, every word that Chipembere, Chiume, Chinyama and the others uttered in the Legco was available to the general public. The Government Press could not keep up with the demand for these daily reports during the sessions of Legco. Even when the government put up the price to one shilling, its popularity continued.

It was not, of course, only those who bought Hansard who got to know what Congress wanted them to hear. People would get together in the house of someone who had bought or borrowed a copy and there it was read aloud, and its contents eagerly analysed and discussed.

It was an extraordinary situation upon which Lord Devlin commented in his classic *Report of the Nyasaland Commission of Enquiry* (1959). Congress, which had chronically failed to produce an effective newspaper or newssheet of any kind, was suddenly provided with one at no cost to itself, and this done by an administration that was committed to supporting the very Federation from which Congress was determined to gain Nyasaland's secession.

The Congress members of Legco did more than create propaganda for the cause, important though that was. They forced both the official and unofficial members to really work at making Legco effective. This was a new phenomenon since in the past Legco had been very much a laid back institution, where business was done expeditiously, with only a few problems caused occasionally by the African members or by their colleague Andrew Doig. In those days Officials were readily able to return to their offices and what they saw as their real work and Unofficials, eager to look after their own businesses were not troubled by long and demanding sittings of the Council which Chipembere and the others now made the order of the day. Chipembere described the new situation they created thus

> We refused to accept the rule of debate under which we were forbidden to introduce Federal subjects. The white officials and unofficials always combined their votes to defeat our motions, but we brought them up again and again ... Chiume and I were often ordered to stop talking, because we would not obey the governor's or, later,

the Speaker's order to refrain from such disallowed topics, and, at times, we were expelled from the House; but we did not give up.[139]

Ralph Chinyama alone of the five African members did not take much part in the sort of verbal guerrilla warfare in which Chipembere led the others. He spoke very soberly and seriously on issues of injustice or on issues where the welfare of the Nyasa people needed protection from harm or could be improved. On one very notable occasion, Chipembere joined him in what turned out to be a very successful campaign. Their joint efforts led to the creation of a system of Government-provided small loans to encourage African small businesses. It worked well for a time but then it was abused. Government defence of what happened was that known troublemakers were not given loans; Chipembere rightly saw the situation had become one where only politically 'safe' persons received a loan. It should be noted that this, as well as a number of other traditional practices of the Colonial authorities, was one of the practices continued under the later regime of Kamuzu Banda in its descent into tyranny and dictatorship.

There were other victories achieved by the Congress members in Legco in terms of the normal business of the legislature, quite apart from their very effective guerrilla campaign to achieve maximum Congress coverage in the daily Hansard. One was the defeat of the attempts by the white 'unofficials' to have so-called 'European agriculture' transferred from the remit of the Legislative Council of the Protectorate into the remit of the Ministry of Agriculture of the Federal Government. This was not, they insisted, a constitutional change; in 1953 any constitutional change had been declared out of order until after the Constitutional Review. This suggested change was one allowed for in the founding documents as long as what was called the Territorial Legislature, i.e. Legco, agreed.

Indignation that such a thing should be brought before the house sparked a walk-out by the NAC members, led by the tall, always dignified Ralph Chinyama, he who only weeks before had been berating Chiume and Chipembere as *atumbidwa* in the bitter arguments over the role of Manoah and Kumbikano in the Federal Parliament. Eventually the Congress members returned to the chamber and a debate on the matter ensued. The motion to change control of 'European' agriculture made by the white unofficials was defeated. This was achieved because the majority of the 'officials' voted with Congress because they agreed that this was an unacceptable and illegitimate attempt to increase the powers of the Federal government.

Another example of white officials taking a stand in agreement with the policy of Congress is reported by Chipembere in his discussion of his work

---

[139] Chipembere, *Hero*, p. 256.

on the committee of Legco on the reform of traditional land tenure. He was well prepared for his role on that committee because he had attended a conference at Kings College, Cambridge on land tenure during August and September 1956. He notes that the West African delegations, including members of Kwame Nkrumah's Convention People's Party, were enthusiastically in favour of radical reform of traditional African land tenure. In contrast with these fellow Africans, 'Chip' took a stand supported only by the other delegate from Nyasaland, who was a white official. Chipembere writes

> I had been very surprised to find that a British administrative official from Malawi, who made an eloquent and moving speech, and I, were the only ones who raised a dissenting voice in the final plenary session against the otherwise unanimously accepted resolution recommending the adoption of a reorganisation of African traditional land tenure.[140]

On the issue of traditional land tenure Chipembere expressed clearly the need for reform if there was to be an increase in agricultural productivity. He could not support the reforms suggested at the time, particularly in the context of the Southern Region where so much land had been alienated into settler hands and in the context of the struggle against the imposition of the Federation and the widespread fear that Federation was intended to produce more alienation of land. Altogether he had no option other than to lead NAC opposition to the proposed reforms in the Protectorate.

The only land reforms of which he approved and which he supported vigorously were to do with the acquisition and placing into African hands of tracts of land which were deemed unused or underused by their European or Asian owners.

Fears among village people about land were inextricably bound up with other fears about a changing world which constantly challenged the social values they felt essential to their identity. The young Congress leaders, in particular Chiume and Chipembere, who had now co-opted Dunduzu Chisiza informally into the leadership group, ran into this social conservatism again and again as they moved around the country. When they put these experiences together with the constant refrain about their youth, they came to the decision that an older man had to be leader of the movement and the focus of popular loyalty. Their immediate problem was, could T.D.T. Banda fulfil this role?

There is no doubt that the young men hoped that he could. Initially he had shown great promise. He backed the young radicals and broke clear from the influence of Manoah Chirwa, to the latter's astonishment. What followed however, was gravely disappointing to Chipembere and company. Although

---

[140] Chipembere, *Hero*, p268.

an older figure who had more appeal than the young men to many in village society, 'T.D.T.' gradually came to be exposed as an ineffective leader when attempting to deal with the problems Congress faced both in their campaign to achieve responsible government within the Protectorate and in the fight to gain the right to secede from the Federation. 'T.D.T.' was a superb crowd-pleasing orator, which was important, but a leader had also to be able to negotiate effectively with European politicians and officials from Salisbury and London as well as Zomba. More and more, in the judgement of the young men, 'T.D.T.' showed himself gravely inadequate in this field.

What was equally damaging to his position as an effective leader was that he showed no capacity to heal the growing rift within Nyasa nationalism. After the meeting of Congress on January 1, many people had continued to press for Manoah Chirwa and Clement Kumbikano to resign from their seats in the Federal Parliament or be expelled from Congress. Pressure was particularly strong in Chirwa's own Northern Region. This pressure was effective within Congress at least, and in April 1957 the two Nyasa Federal MPs were for-mally requested to resign with the promise of their expulsion if they did not comply promptly. On July 9 1957, having scorned the previous directive, the two men were expelled from the NAC.

This, however, caused a serious rift in the support of the NAC, rather to the surprise of the young men and the one young woman who was beginning to make her presence felt in the movement, Mrs Rose Chibambo.

The three older members of Legco, Chinyama, Chijosi and Kwenje, all stayed loyal to Manoah, as did several wealthy businessmen upon whose generosity Congress relied. A further blow, one of great importance, came when the Mashonaland Branch of Congress, by far its richest branch, also supported the old 'Godfather' of Congress. This rift was very important financially but even more importantly, it weakened the Congress case for secession and independence. Just when a united African front needed to be shown to the world, the Congress members of Legco were divided, just as the membership of Congress was divided. This was a massive crisis in the face of which T.D.T. Banda appeared totally helpless.

It was then that Chipembere, Chiume and Chisiza became certain that only a person who was of great prestige from both a modern and a traditional per-spective, one who was also detached from the conflicts that had led to the split, or at least appeared so to be, was needed to lead a united Congress. Dr Hastings Kamuzu Banda was the only man to fit this bill, they believed. They therefore pressed the August 1957 conference of Congress to formally invite Dr Banda to return to Nyasaland.

The motion, which Chipembere drafted and which was passed unanimously by the executive and then by the full conference, stated that Dr Banda was to be invited to return to Malawi 'to help in the work of leadership'. That was also the wording of the cable to Kamuzu and the long letter which was sent to supplement the cable, both of which were also scrutinised and passed by the conference. Chipembere has stated that although he intended Kamuzu to become the President of Congress as soon as possible after his arrival, he had chosen these words carefully to meet the feelings of those who had doubts. These doubts ranged from some who feared that a *mchona* would simply not be acceptable to the majority of people, to others who felt that Dr Banda should be tried out for a time in the hurly-burly of the politics of his homeland before being endorsed as leader. There were also a number of people, including some older men in his home area, Kasungu, who firmly disagreed about Kamuzu's suitability to be leader.[141]

The August 1957 conference agreed to call on Dr H.K. Banda to return to assume some form of leadership in the movement for secession and independence. It also appointed a delegation to discuss constitutional reform with the new Governor of Nyasaland, Sir Robert Armitage.

There are two puzzles presented to the observer by what followed. The first is what role was T.D.T. Banda seen as fulfilling? Was he now simply an interim president, although there had been no formal decision about his presidency? The second puzzle concerns Dunduzu Chisiza. On both visits to Government House for discussions with the Governor, 'Du' was the principal spokesman for the Congress delegation. The delegation on each occasion was led by T.D.T. Banda and included Chiume and Chipembere. Yet although at that point 'Du' did not hold office in the National Executive of the NAC, the official documents as well as Congress sources make clear that he was the primary negotiator with the Governor.

At these meetings 'T.D.T.' confirmed in the eyes of his comrades his lack of ability in negotiation, even in the limited role he had in the proceedings dominated by 'Du'. Chipembere is quite clear that it was at the first meeting with Armitage that he and the other young men decided that Kamuzu's position would have to be that of President of the NAC and not as the principal 'advisor' to the movement. The letters sent to Dr Banda could certainly be interpreted as asking him to fulfil that latter role. Nothing Chip wrote in his biography, however, sheds any light on how it was that 'Du' was in the position to be the star of these meetings. After all the first meeting with Armitage was in September and it was only the previous month at the Annual Conference that Du had been turned down for the post of General

141 W. M. Chiume, *Kwacha*, pp. 89-90.

Secretary of Congress. No memoirs or reminiscences of those days have, as yet, provided an answer to this question.

Be that as it may, Armitage, Colby's successor, courteously went through the motions of discussing the issues of constitutional reform of the government of the Protectorate with the delegation but consistently insisted their proposals were impracticable at that time. (Soon after the second frustrating meeting with Armitage on November 21, 1957, 'Du' left for the United Kingdom to pursue his further education at Fircroft College in Birmingham.) These negotiations were the continuation of Congress's long-term anti-Federation strategy. If the British could be pressed to move forward rapidly towards an elected African majority in the Legislative Council, or even if a substantial number of elected African members were allowed and if the African members were united in a vote for secession, the British public opinion would surely listen and respond favourably to this unambiguous and unchallengeable appeal from the Nyasa people.

Despite the frustrating outcome of the meetings with Armitage, Congress continued to pursue this goal of constitutional reform of the Legislative Council. Congress leaders had no alternative, driven, as they were, by feelings that were close to despair. They had come to see that they faced a crisis through the growing realisation of what an agreement between the Governments of the Federation and the United Kingdom in April of 1957 meant for the future of Nyasaland.

In April 1957, Sir Roy Welensky who had only recently become the Prime Minister of the Federation, visited London and had a series of meetings with British ministers. They came to an agreement which had three main elements of enormous significance. The first was that the UK Parliament "would not initiate any legislation to amend or repeal any Federal Act." This was a dreadful betrayal, as Griff Jones so bitterly insists, of one of the original safeguards much used to persuade the people of Nyasaland that the London Government would always be able to step in and protect them from discriminatory Federal legislation.[142] The second was the declaration that the civil service of the three constituent territories "would become locally based". This would, in effect, bring to end the Colonial Office influence in Nyasaland. When this is taken together with the third decision, which was to agree that the Conference to review the Constitution of the Federation would be convened in 1960, the earliest allowable under the Act setting up the Federation, it appeared to Congress that the granting of Dominion status for the Federation was on the way.

---

[142] Griff Jones, *Britain and Nyasaland*, p. 152.

Both London and Salisbury wanted this review at the earliest possible time so that independence would be achieved by the settler-ruled state before any more effective anti-federation trouble made it appear that the federal experiment was failing. After the review, if all went to plan, the Colonial Office presence in the two northern territories would be removed and the government of the new autonomous Dominion would then also be to arrange its own internal affairs, free from the threat of interference from London.

Thus the dramatic reform of the Nyasaland Legco was now urgently necessary if the voice of the Nyasa people was to be heard at the Federal Constitutional Review in 1960, now less than three years away. In response to this new understanding of the urgency of the situation, the Congress Executive decided to go over Armitage's head and seek an interview with the Secretary of State for the Colonies. A visit to London by a Congress delegation would be good publicity in Nyasaland and also an opportunity to freshen Congress's relations with the various groups in the UK who were critical of Federation. Somewhat to their surprise, the Secretary of State, Alan Lennox-Boyd, who had so recently signed the April agreement with Welensky, readily agreed to meet a delegation from the Nyasaland African Congress in London.

Since in the negotiations with the Governor, T.D.T. Banda had shown his inadequacy as a negotiator in that kind of situation, it was clear that he would be even more exposed as inadequate in any London negotiations. The 'young men' had already agreed that he had to be removed from his position as President of Congress before any such negotiations were undertaken. As Chipembere admits, however, in his autobiography, at the beginning of 1958 T.D.T. was still very popular with ordinary supporters of Congress; he had great ability as a crowd-pleasing orator. Getting him to stand aside for Kamuzu on the latter's return was going to be very difficult, let alone getting him to stand down before the London meeting.[143]

The young men were then presented with an unforeseen opportunity to clear the way for Kamuzu. After a visit to India, 'T.D.T.' was unable to explain what had happened to a generous donation which Congress had received to help with the trip. Because of this problem, in March 1958 the Central Executive Committee suspended him. He immediately attempted to begin a new political movement, the Congress Liberation Party, so the Central Executive Committee formally dismissed him and appointed the Vice-President, Matthews Phiri, as interim President. The next Annual Conference of Congress would be in August 1958 at Nkhata Bay, at which Chip and the others hoped Kamuzu would be installed as the new leader.

---

[143] Chipembere. *Hero.* p. 310.

Whether 'T.D.T.' had misused the money or not was never really investigated; the situation was a chance to get rid of him. The young leaders grasped this opportunity to clear the way for Kamuzu. It was a manoeuvre, however, which left many in Nkhata Bay, T.D.T. Banda's home area, very angry indeed.

The next problem facing Congress was who was to go to London to meet the Colonial Secretary face to face, and also who would best exploit this opportunity to maximise publicity for the cause in the United Kingdom?

As ever in the history of Congress from its very foundation in 1944, this opportunity was in danger of being missed through lack of funds. Congress had decided to send a delegation of three; a member of the Executive, a member of Legco and a chief. This decision was taken in March 1958 when it was also decided that the visit should take place in May, only a few weeks later.

This drastic time constraint on the raising of funds for the trip was imposed by the decision of the Congress Executive that Dr Banda should lead the delegation. He was to be in London in May, sorting out his affairs in preparation for his return to Malawi. Since Banda insisted that May was the only time he was going to be in London, the meeting was fixed for that month, with Lennox-Boyd's agreement.

The rushed fund-raising was also seriously handicapped by the fact that so many individuals who had in the past contributed generously to Congress were still loyal to Manoah. These Manoah loyalists also included the rich Mashonaland branch of Congress. As a result, the fund-raising exercise produced enough cash for one return ticket only.

Chipembere then turned to Mwalimu Julius Nyerere and his Tanganyika African National Union for help. Whether or not the idea of turning to this new source of help came from the Chisiza family - Du's older brother, Yatuta, having only recently returned from Tanganyika - is not clear. It was, certainly, a new departure for Congress whose external connections had always been with the Nyasa diaspora in the two Rhodesias and South Africa.

Mwalimu Nyerere and TANU produced money for one more return ticket to London so only two Congress delegates could go from Nyasaland. It was decided that Chipembere and Chief Kuntaja should be the two to go to join Dr Banda. However, in order to bring the delegation up to full strength it was also decided that Dunduzu Chisiza should be called away from his studies and go to London to complete the delegation to meet Mr Lennox-Boyd.[144]

Meanwhile the whole effort of Nyasaland African Congress was to be centred on preparing the people of Nyasaland for the return of the great man, whom Chipembere was already unblushingly referring to as a 'Messiah coming to free his people'. It was a massive and extraordinarily successful campaign bringing back to the fold many who had been supporting Manoah. To twenty-first century eyes it is somewhat ironic that Chip warned Kamuzu about the nature of this campaign and asked him not to be upset by its extravagance of its language.

It was on this visit to London that Masauko Chipembere and Dunduzu Chisiza would meet Dr Banda for the first time. Just who was this elder statesman, this saviour of the nation, whose return was deemed so essential to the cause, is the question we now need to consider in more detail.

---

[144] Colin Baker in his *State of Emergency* states mistakenly on p. 3 that Chiume was th fourth member of the delegation.

Chapter 4

Dr Hastings Kamuzu Banda

Of the numerous studies of Hastings Kamuzu Banda and the impact he had on Malawi, there are three that are the most notable. The only straightforward biography is by Philip Short entitled simply *Banda*. It is a clear, well-written and well researched study, sympathetic to Banda, by a B.B.C. journalist. One other of the three is intended as a biography, John Lwanda's *Kamuzu Banda of Malawi*, a study of Banda by a fellow Malawian physician. This book, however, is not a straightforward biography but an incisively written, well-informed and determined attack on the 'Banda, saviour and creator of Malawi' legend. The third is not a biography but a study of the nature of Banda's rule in Malawi. It is S.H. Joffe's *Political Culture and Communication in Malawi: the Hortatory Regime of Kamuzu Banda*.

Despite these works and the massive amount of newsprint expended on him during the last four decades of the twentieth century, there is still lack of agreement about Banda's early life. This is partly due to his own reticence and, at times, evasiveness about his early life. This evasiveness was not simply confined to the way in which he tried to conceal his age but refers to a general reluctance to discuss the early years of his life. There are also other blank areas in the official biography promulgated after his return to what was then Nyasaland. The most important and in some ways the most extraordinary omission was created by the deliberate writing out of his life of Mrs French, his mistress, with whom he lived in London and Ghana. Short does include her in his study of Kamuzu but from the time of his return in Nyasaland it was as if Mrs French had never existed.

How dramatically and effectively Banda succeeded in this task of blanking her out of his life is seen in one of Edwin S. Munger's reports in the *American Universities' Field Staff Reports* series entitled *President Kamuzu Banda of Malawi*. In this, Munger wrote

> There have been various rumors that there was a Mrs. Banda, but I have never uncovered any proof and Banda himself would certainly not encourage speculation. In 1966, the Malawi Attorney General wrote to the British publishers, John Murray, successfully requesting deletion from a book on Malawi, then in proof form of material alleging that Dr Banda had been named as correspondent in a divorce action by a Major French.[145]

---

[145] Edwin S. Munger, *President Banda of Malawi*, p. 9.

This is quite extraordinary since everyone who knew Banda at all well before he left Ghana in 1958 knew that Merene French had been his mistress for many years in London and had lived with him as his wife throughout his time in Kumasi. In the campaign against Federation from 1950 through 1953, every Nyasa who went to London as a member of one of the delegations sent there as part of that campaign, met Mrs. French.

Kamuzu's Early Life

Be that as it may, we must begin the story of Hasting Kamuzu Banda's life at the beginning. What do we know about his birth and early life before he embarked on the major journey south to 'Egoli', South Africa, where so many young Nyasas were going in search of work and wealth?

We know from the evidence of his relatives and their friends that he was born in 1898. It was the year, the Kasungu people say, of the conflict which took place not much over fifty miles away between Mpezeni's Ngoni and the British authorities in an area straddling the Nyasaland and Northern Rhodesian border.[146] While he was Life-President of Malawi the government publications always listed 1906 as the year of his birth, which was manifestly untrue since it would have meant that he had started his famous walk to South Africa to seek further education at the age of nine. The issue of his age is further complicated by Banda in the preface to the book of essays *Our African Way of Life*, which he edited along with T. Cullen Young. In it, he writes that he was not more than thirteen years old when the well-known incident when he was accused of cheating took place, which triggered his decision to go south in 1915. The year of that incident, 1915, is agreed by all witnesses as well as by Kamuzu himself and is the fixed point in the various versions of his early life.

Since Banda was recalled to Nyasaland precisely because he was a much older man than the 'boys', Chipembere, Chiume and Dunduzu Chisiza, why was he so concerned about his date of birth and the early years of his life? Concerned he certainly was since, after the publication of Short's biography, Young Pioneers were sent to the house of his uncle the Reverend Hanock Msokela Phiri and all letters between Phiri and Banda in the venerable minister's possession as well as all other letters referring to Banda, were taken away 'for safe keeping'. From 1966, Malawi journalists suffered if they deviated in anyway from official details of the presidential biography. It is not now easy to determine when his desire for secrecy about the early years

---

[146] The three key informants according to Short, *Banda* p. 5 and Rotberg, *Rise of Nationalism in Central Africa*. p. 187, were Banda's uncle the Reverend Hanock Msokela Phiri, and two others of Phiri's generation close to the family, A Msulira and A Chipeta.

of his life developed. It would appear that it was not too long after his return to Nyasaland in 1958 that his age, and indeed, other details of his early life became a no go area by those who interviewed him.

Both Lwanda and Short suggest that this can partly be explained by the fact that Banda was always very image conscious, but an observer must ask why the variation of only four years between 1898 asserted by his uncle and family friends and 1902 to which he had admitted himself should be so important to his image. The 1906 date is so absurd as to be not worth serious discussion yet it was part of the official Presidential biography by the late 1960s. No satisfactory explanation of Kamuzu's obsession with his birth date has yet appeared in the historiography of Malawi, and the discussion of self-image by Short and Lwanda does not help very much in resolving that problem.

Kamuzu was born in a small village, Chiwengo, near Kasungu. His mother was Akupinganyama Phiri and his father was Mphonongo Banda. Kamuzu was Akupinganyama's first child born after a long period when she had appeared to be barren. She bore other children subsequently. Her apparent sterility had been dealt with by a *sing'anga* (a herbal healer) who had prescribed a herbal remedy. This is said to be the reason that the baby boy was called Kamuzu - 'little root' in English. Lwanda however says that the baby was named Kamunkhwala - 'a small dose of medicine' - and that Banda himself later chose the name Kamuzu. Lwanda, unfortunately, does not give us the source of this assertion.[147]

Soon after the birth of her second child, a girl, Kamuzu's mother divorced Mphonongo Banda and later married again. In the Chewa matrilineal and matrilocal form of family organisation, Kamuzu would have remained in the family circle presided over by his maternal grandmother, Chiyendawaka. He did eventually join that family group but only after he had gone initially to live with his father's people, a strange event which has never been explained. What is even more peculiar is that the Kasungu informants of both Short and Lwanda, mainly relations of Kamuzu, have on various occasions denied that this stay with the paternal family ever happened.

Other than a brief reference to this supposed short stay with his father's people, Kamuzu never referred to his father in any other connection, despite many affectionate references to his mother and his sister. The brief stay with Mphonongo's family, for which Kamuzu himself is the source, remains a puzzle. Lwanda has suggested that the almost total lack of reference to his father occurs because Kamuzu deemed his father to have been feckless and lazy, characteristics he abhorred. At other points in his book Lwanda also

---

[147] John Lwanda, *Kamuzu Banda of Malawi*, p. 14.

suggests that Mphonongo was erased from the record because he was a Tonga and not a Chewa, which would have explained his uselessness and laziness in Kamuzu's eyes.[148] However, these suggestions are essentially guesses because there is no substantive evidence at present available to enable anyone to draw a firm conclusion. One could also, however, make another guess based on Kamuzu's stay with his father's people after the death of his mother. If Mphonongo was an Ngoni, who are patrilineal and patrilocal, then that move was not a mystery but something in accord with Ngoni custom.[149] For the adult Kamuzu, however, with his obsessive insistence on his being Chewa and on the Chewa people being the core Malawi stock, an Ngoni father would be an inconvenience to say the least.

What is certain is that Kamuzu grew up among his mother's people. He went through all the traditional ceremonies deemed necessary for a male Chewa as he developed, including initiation into Nyau. As he insisted in the preface to *Our African Way of Life*, '...no Chewa man has the full status of a man if he has not been through the initiation and instructional process.'[150] The various ceremonies that marked the different stages in the traditional pattern of Chewa upbringing for a baby, boy and youth are described by Short in his biography of Banda. In that particular chapter Short includes details of the initiation rituals for a boy becoming a man and a fully initiated member of Nyau, things that are meant to be kept a secret from the world of women and the non-Chewa. These are all described as having been undergone by Kamuzu and Short cites in addition to his Kasungu interviews a number of speeches by Kamuzu and the famous preface to *Our African Way of Life* as authority for this.

When Kamuzu was growing up Kasungu, the headquarters of Chief Mwase, was in the area of activity of the Livingstonia Mission.[151] Kamuzu's uncle, Msokela, had been one of the first local people to be attracted to the mission. He was baptised Hanock by Dr Robert Laws at some point during his school career, which led him to complete Standard VII at the Overtoun Institution at

---

[148] Ibid. p. 86.

[149] [EDITOR'S NOTE: In 1975, during the Livingstonia mission centenary celebrations, I was showing Dr Banda a minute book written in chiNgoni. He told me personally that he knew chiNgoni, adding 'My grandfather taught me chiNgoni'; he then began singing an old Ngoni hymn, '*Dumusan*' uYehova' written by Mawelera Tembo, of which he clearly knew the words. T. Jack Thompson.]

[150] Young, T. Cullen and Banda, H. K. *Our African Way of Life*. p. 25.

[151] The area later was transferred by the Scots mission into the control of the Mkhoma Mission of the Cape Synod of the Nederduits Gereformeerde Kerk, from which the Mkhoma Synod of the CCAP grew. This has led some to suggest, *wrongly*, that Kamuzu was baptised by one of the Afrikaner missionaries of that Synod.

Livingstonia (Khondowe). At that time this was the best education an African could receive anywhere north of the Orange River and it produced men whose command of the English language remained impressive when the present writer met some of these veterans in the 1950s. Msokela went on to be a teacher with the mission; it was much later, in South Africa, that he became a pastor.

Msokela had a powerful influence on Kamuzu's life almost from the beginning. It was he who persuaded the elders of the family to send the boy to school when his parents did not approve. Kamuzu progressed rapidly through the local village school system and in 1915 sat the examinations to select the few who could be admitted to the advanced classes at the Overtoun Institution, where his uncle Msokela had excelled.

The story of what happened then has been repeated many times since Kamuzu first described it in the preface to *Our African Way of Life* in 1946. In those days in the Livingstonia mission there were no printed exam papers; the questions were put up on the blackboard at the front of the examination hall. Kamuzu, small for his age, was at the back of the hall. At one point he stood up so as to see the board more clearly and the missionary, supervising the examination, dismissed him from the room for appearing to have attempted to cheat by looking at the answers of the boy in front of him. The extraordinary coincidence was that the missionary supervising the examination was T. Cullen Young who, in London thirty years later, was to become Kamuzu's close friend.

However righteously indignant the sixteen or seventeen year old youth was at this injustice, he used his emotions positively. The bitter upset did not send him back to the village but it appeared to spur him to find other ways of obtaining further education. Because of the Xhosa missionaries educated at Lovedale who had helped begin the work of the Livingstonia Mission, everyone educated in the Livingstonia school system knew of that famous Scottish educational institution in the Cape Colony.[152] So to South Africa Banda determined to go, following the route already well established by many Nyasas going south to find paid work in Southern Rhodesia and South Africa. This was a journey of at least thirty days of hard walking through Mozambique, crossing the Zambezi at or near Tete and entering Southern Rhodesia close to Shamva.

Kamuzu, on arrival in Southern Rhodesia, went to Hartley where he stayed for two years, working as a sweeper in a hospital, attempting to save enough money to enable him to go on to South Africa. It was proving very difficult

---

[152] See T. Jack Thompson, *Touching the Heart: Xhosa Missionaries to Malawi, 1875-1888*, Pretoria, University of South Africa Press, 2000, *passim*.

to save enough money from his meagre pay to get to Johannesburg when his uncle Msokela arrived in Hartley, who also hoped to be able to get to Lovedale and further his own education. Fresh difficulties were presented to the pair by a new decision of the South African government to allow into South Africa only those 'foreign natives' who had signed a limited term contract to work for one of the mining corporations. Kamuzu and his uncle got into South Africa by signing on as contract workers to serve in a coal mine at Dundee in Natal. The conditions there were so awful that they determined to move on, though that would be illegal since they would be breaking their contract. Nevertheless both men left the mine compound and headed for Johannesburg.

At a railway station on the Natal border they were helped by a Mr MacArthur, an old Scotsman, who introduced himself to them when he heard Scottish usages in the English they spoke. He put them up in his house; this was a pre-apartheid South Africa where, in some areas at least, there was more freedom for Africans than there was in Rhodesia at that time. Mr MacArthur suggested they work their passages on a ship going to the United States and there contact one of the many Black churches where they would receive help to get a good education. The two young Nyasas discovered that the state of the war at sea in 1918 made this impossible and so they decided to go on to Johannesburg. As a final gesture of friendship, MacArthur paid their fares to the Witwatersrand. There they found work at the Rand Deep Mine at Boksburg.

Johannesburg was a lively political scene at that time. Kamuzu met Clements Kadalie, who was in process of creating the first effective Black Trade Union in South Africa, the Industrial Commercial and Workers' Union, which began its fight for workers' rights in 1919. Kadalie had been a classmate of Msokela Phiri's at the Overtoun Institute. Kamuzu also heard speeches by Dr James Kwegyir Aggrey, the famous educationalist from the Gold Coast and Dr A.B. Xuma, who later became President of the ANC and whom he later met in the United States. As important, or maybe more important, in the shaping of Kamuzu's life was the decision both he and his uncle made to join a congregation of an American Black church there in Johannesburg; it was a congregation of the African Methodist Episcopal Church.

During these years on the Rand, Banda also attended evening classes and relentlessly pushed forward his education. 1923, the next year after their joining the AME Church, saw Hanock Msokela Phiri end his search for more education because he was ordained as a minister of the AME and assigned to begin the work of his denomination in the Nyasaland Protectorate.

It was the AME church which now guaranteed support for Banda to enable him to complete his high school education in the United States, so long as he was able to raise his own fare to get there. With his uncle's help, Kamuzu did raise his fare and arrived in the United States in July 1925.

Education in the USA

At the Wilberforce Institute of the AME in Ohio, Kamuzu did so well that he along with three other students, were allowed to receive their High School Diploma after three years instead of the usual four. This success, however, meant that the AME Church funding of his education ceased. It was Dr Aggrey, whom Kamuzu met again by chance, who brought him into contact with a number of rich white American philanthropic families who then helped Kamuzu continue his education. He enrolled at the University of Indiana, Marion Campus, for the pre-medical course and successfully completed the compulsory two years science programme necessary in the United States before entering the medical course proper.

Then, in 1930, in a radical change of direction he transferred to the University of Chicago to study history and politics. This was a period when the University of Chicago was building up its reputation as one of the elite universities in the United States. Kamuzu insisted to Msokela Phiri - the two regularly corresponded - that he did not want to become one of these physicians who knew everything about medicine and nothing about anything else. This new step was all part of being better prepared to return home and serve the people of Nyasaland.

Among some academics at Chicago there was an intense interest in African linguistics at that time and Kamuzu was soon recruited by Mark Hanna Watkins, later to be Professor of Anthropology at Howard University, as an informant. Watkins, as part of his PhD project, was attempting to compile a grammar book of a southern African language. Because he found Banda so knowledgeable and cooperative, Watkins decided to focus on what Kamuzu called Chichewa.[153]

This name chosen for the language and the form of spelling are very significant. In Nyasaland and Northern Rhodesia at that time the same language, though called CiNyanja, was already the *lingua franca* of the administration, the police and the army. In Nyasaland, the Union Nyanja Bible was being used by all the Protestant Churches, not just the CCAP, except in the mainly Tumbuka-speaking Northern Region. Union Nyanja was what was being used in the schools both Catholic and Protestant, again in the Central and

---

[153] Watkins' thesis was published later, in 1937, entitled *A Grammar of Chichewa*.

Southern Regions. In Chicago, however, Kamuzu insisted on the language being called ChiChewa. Even the chosen orthography is an aggressive assertion of difference, refusing to follow the original decision by David Clement Scott of Blantyre Mission to express the sound which designates 'language' by the Italian form 'ci'. Banda insisted on the English form 'chi', the form which he imposed later when President of Malawi.[154]

It is in this connection that remarks made by Mark Hanna Watkins to Professor Shepperson about his relationship with Kamuzu are of great interest. As we saw in Chapter One, by the mid-thirties more and more people were beginning to designate themselves as Nyasas rather than asserting traditional 'tribal' classification as Chewa or Yao, Nyanja or Ngoni. Again we noted in Chapter one that this tendency had become so marked by 1946 that the annual report of the Protectorate Government to the Colonial Office noted this rise of a Nyasa self-consciousness; a nationalism, albeit with a small 'n' at that time. Yet in 1932 Kamuzu is asserting his identity as Chewa, indeed, aggressively so. As Professor Shepperson records

> Because so little material on Banda's reactions to American, particularly black American society was – indeed, alas, still is available – I asked Mark Hanna Watkins what Banda was like when he knew him in Chicago in the 1930s. Watkins' reply came immediately, in a staccato statement which I have never forgotten. Banda, Watkins said quickly, was 'very tribal, very tribal'.[155]

Later in the same paper, Shepperson records how Kamuzu refused to join Watkins in an informal picnic lunch the latter had provided for them both while they worked through the lunch hour, saying sternly 'the Chewa do not eat with strangers'!

At that time distinguished white philanthropists were the source of Banda's financial support, though in Chicago he lodged in the house of Mrs Corinne Saunders, a Black woman who, in an interview reported in the *Chicago Sun*, 12 October 1963, Kamuzu said treated him like a son. Prominent among the white philanthropists giving him help was Mrs Douglas Smith, whose husband was the inventor of Pepsodent, and at whose house Short reports Kamuzu stayed during some of his college vacations.

---

[154] [EDITOR'S NOTE: The question of how the Ci/Chi sound was written is quite complex. Several printed books in CiNyanja, well before Banda was involved, did use the 'Chi' form; see e.g. R. Sutherland Rattray, *Some Folklore Stories and Songs in ChiNyanja*, London, SPCK, 1907 and Meredith Sanderson and W.B. Bithrey, *An Introduction to Chinyanja*, Zomba, Government Printing Office, 1925. By the beginning of the Second World War, most writers had reverted to the older 'Ci' prefix. TJT]

[155] Professor George (Sam) Shepperson, 'Memories of Dr Banda', *Socierty of Malawi Journal*, 51(1), 1998, 74-84.

In this period, when the United States was going through the worst period of the Great Depression with massive unemployment and much social dislocation, Kamuzu was able to 'get by' through living very simply indeed. He corresponded with his uncle Msokela, who was working for the AME in Kasungu. Msokela complained regularly about shortage of funds, and Kamuzu was apologetic about not being able to send him more, though he did send money to his uncle regularly. Msokela's problems were explained, partly at least, when in May 1932 the bishop of the AME responsible for the work in Central and Southern Africa was dismissed for embezzling funds intended for the southern African missions. This, in conjunction with other issues about which we have no definite information, meant that Kamuzu became disillusioned with the AME church and asked his uncle's permission to resign from the denomination. This gesture is remarked on by both Lwanda and Short as an example of Kamuzu's strict adherence to Chewa custom and traditional courtesy. Despite his leaving the denomination, Kamuzu continued to send what he could manage to his uncle to help his work in Kasungu.

When he left Chicago to take up his medical studies in Tennessee, Kamuzu still had vital support from Mrs Douglas Smith and from a new supporter, Dr Walter Stephenson, President of the Delta Electric Company. These sponsors paid his fees and provided maintenance for him at the Meharry Medical College in Tennessee. Banda had wanted to go to Edinburgh to study medicine, British medical qualifications being necessary for someone to practice medicine in a British colony. Presumably his sponsors did not support that idea, but we have no evidence available to confirm or deny that.

It ought to be noted that it was at Meharry that Dr Daniel Malekebu had gained his medical qualifications. Malekebu, later head of John Chilembwe's Providence Industrial Mission in Chiradzulu, was the first Nyasa to complete a modern medical qualification. This achievement by a Nyasa pioneer was conveniently ignored in the campaign in the late 1950s by Congress to build up Kamuzu as the Nyasa 'superman'.

While a student at the Wilberforce Academy and The Universities of Indiana and Chicago, Kamuzu had seen the problems of race relations in the United States but always in a context where there was a significant white community who sought to transcend the barriers that the white racists wished to erect in American society. Things were dramatically different for him at Meharry Medical School. During his five years in Tennessee Kamuzu saw American race relations at their worst. The Ku Klux Klan was a massive presence in the state at a time when the lynching of black men on the flimsiest of pretences occurred only too frequently across the southern States of the United States. Kamuzu witnessed one such terrible incident, which Short reports as remaining fixed indelibly in Banda's mind.[156]

Despite these experiences, and despite his acknowledgment that his political consciousness widened and deepened during these years in the United States (a reference to his contacts with Garveyism[157] and with Dr W.E.B. DuBois[158]) Kamuzu does not make any reference to joining the NAACP or any other Black political organisation. Indeed what appears remarkable to many who have written about Banda is that when he left the United States in 1937 to go to Edinburgh, he went with a very positive take on American society. At a time when many Americans were espousing socialist and indeed communist views on how to reshape society after what many of them felt had been the failure of capitalism in the Great Depression, Kamuzu resolutely saw the American way of life in what many at the time would have considered a flattering light. Lwanda, Short and Rotberg all comment on this. A classic example of his attitude is a speech he made on Communism in the 1960s quoted by Short:

> If in America some people are very rich and others are very poor, it is just that the former have initiative, and work hard too. There are others who are unfortunate and through no fault of their own are poor, but not ... miserably poor ... There is always a chance in America of the poor boy of today becoming the millionaire of tomorrow. Always a hope.[159]

At Meharry Kamuzu worked very hard at his medical studies and achieved his Doctor of Medicine degree in May 1937 with very high marks indeed. Professor Rotberg was able to obtain permission to see Kamuzu's academic record at Meharry and published the high grades he received in *The Rise of Nationalism in Central Africa.*

Kamuzu, however, in 1937 had to leave the United States in order to begin studying medicine in Edinburgh. As we have seen, an American medical qualification would not of itself gain him permission to practice medicine in Nyasaland. This new venture, with fresh heavy costs for travel, fees and maintenance, was possible because of the continuing financial support from Mrs Douglas Smith, as well as a number of Edinburgh ladies who were sup-

---

[156] Short, *Banda*, p. 25.

[157] Marcus Garvey was a Jamaican who began the Universal Negro Improvement Association, a radical Black political movement in the US which had a widespread influence on African intellectuals.

[158] One of the first Black Americans to gain a Harvard degree he was the founder of the still active National Association for the Advancement of Colored People, usually known as the NAACP.

[159] Nyasaland Information Service, 1964, quoted in Short, p. 26.

porters of the Livingstonia and Blantyre missions and possibly from the Moir family.[160]

Studies in Edinburgh

At Edinburgh Kamuzu did not enter the Faculty of Medicine of the University of Edinburgh, which would have entailed him doing the whole medical course again. Instead he registered with the Royal College of Physicians and the Royal College of Surgeons of Edinburgh who had arrangements that allowed medically qualified applicants like Kamuzu to get a fully recognised British qualification in as little as two or three years.

In Edinburgh he made many Scottish friends, most of whom had served the church in Nyasaland or were concerned about African affairs. One of them was T. Cullen Young, to whom Banda did not reveal the latter's role in the Examination Hall at Khondowe until they were working together in 1945-46 on editing *Our African Way of Life*. It was, however, his connection with the Reverend Hector McPherson of the Guthrie Memorial Church in Edinburgh that brought Kamuzu back into active membership of the Church of Scotland. He became a regular attender at the Guthrie Memorial, often being entertained to meals in the manse where Fergus, one of the minister's sons, became Kamuzu's life-long friend despite later disagreements from the 1960s onwards. Fergus McPherson was to serve as Principal of the Overtoun Institution at the time of Operation Sunrise in 1959. Before his transfer to Livingstonia, Fergus worked in Zambia where he became the friend and later the biographer of Kenneth Kaunda, the first President of Zambia.

These very important years in Edinburgh ended in 1940 with Kamuzu's gaining the qualifications necessary for practising medicine in Britain and its colonies from the Royal College of Physicians and the Royal College of Surgeons. These years were also the beginning of a period in Kamuzu's life when he emerged from the very quiet, shy, almost reclusive life-style he had followed in the United States. In the community of the Guthrie Memorial congregation he became so well-known and popular that he was made an elder in the congregation. It was in these Edinburgh years that Banda made lasting friendships; a sharp contrast to the lack of any such lasting friendships made during his years in the United States. Fergus McPherson and T. Cullen Young were probably the most important of these friendships made in Scotland.

---

[160] The family of John and Frederick Moir who had begun the African Lakes Corporation, befriended Kamuzu in Edinburgh, some have suggested that they supported him financially but no definite proof of this is available to the present writer.

It was also in those Edinburgh years that Kamuzu made effective contact with the politics of his homeland and with Nyasas outside his family circle. In Edinburgh the Church of Scotland had strongly supported the stand of the missionaries in Nyasaland who gave evidence to the Bledisloe Commission declaring their belief that the Nyasa people were opposed to any attempt to link the Protectorate in any constitutional way with Southern Rhodesia.[161] Kamuzu discussed the issues with Cullen Young and others and decided to seek the opportunity to appear before the Commissioners after their return from Africa, or at least to present a written submission to them. He was granted permission by the Commissioners to present a written submission. What Kamuzu wrote we do not now know because the submissions to the Commission were lost due to damage to government buildings during the bombing of London in the Second World War. We do know that, in general, his attitude was in support of the position that the Nyasa people were unwilling to accept any closer political or constitutional association with Southern Rhodesia.

Early in 1939 the Colonial Office decided to bring the young chief Mwase to Britain to aid the work being done on the study of CiNyanja in the School of Oriental and African Studies of London University. The church authorities in Scotland suggested to the Colonial Office that Kamuzu be appointed as chief Mwase's adviser during the chief's six month stay in London. In a formal letter of recommendation, Cullen Young referred to Kamuzu as 'a very sound fellow of good judgement and character.'[162] These six months with Mwase added much to Kamuzu's knowledge of political and social developments in his homeland. This was another important step in linking Kamuzu intimately with the new political activity created by the Native Association movement in Nyasaland.

It was also at this time that Kamuzu received two rebuffs which did not seem to trouble him very much. Perhaps this was because the outbreak of the Second World War and its catastrophic early developments made them appear of small consequence in the greater scheme of things. The first rebuff came when the Church of Scotland agreed to send Kamuzu to serve as a doctor with the staff of the Livingstonia Mission, allowing Kamuzu to fulfil his dream of returning to serve his people. To the horror of his church friends in Edinburgh, nursing staff in the mission raised objections to the appointment, insisting they could not serve under the authority of an African doctor. The second rebuff was that his application to join the Colonial medical service in

---

[161] See Chapter one.
[162] T. Cullen Young to Dr Bargery of SOAS, 11 July 1939, quoted in Rotberg, *Rise of Nationalism* p. 189.

Nyasaland made at roughly the same time, received similar objections from hospital staff there. Had the war not developed as disastrously as it did in 1940 the Church of Scotland would have insisted on his going to work in Nyasaland. However there was no point since by then only military personnel were able to travel overseas.

Kamuzu showed no signs of bitterness. He contributed in the July, 1940 edition of the Church of Scotland Magazine, *Other Lands,* a moving tribute to the two brothers Frederick and John Moir, founder of the African Lakes Company.

There is a strange aspect to this episode in Kamuzu's life. This is an accusation of double-dealing by Kamuzu which appears in Edwin S. Munger's *President Kamuzu Banda of Malawi.* In this publication, which otherwise is a panegyric in praise of Banda who is referred to as the 'Bridgebuilder of Africa', Munger says that Kamuzu accepted a grant of £300 from the Colonial Office as a potential Colonial Service doctor while at the same time, without informing either grant-giving body, accepting another £300 grant from the Church of Scotland as a future missionary doctor in training. Munger gives no source for this assertion, saying that whether true or not it rankled with some people in the Church of Scotland. It does seem strange that Munger, who goes out of his way to praise Banda in his pamphlet, should have included this story. As we shall see there are major accusations of ill-doing to be made against Kamuzu Banda, but this little piece of sordid trickery has no factual basis that this writer has been able to discover.

The Move to England

When it was impossible to go to Nyasaland, Kamuzu sought a new beginning. He went to Liverpool where he established a medical practice which flourished so well that he was able to help many poor patients who could not afford to pay the necessary fees demanded in those pre-National Health Service days. Meanwhile he also completed a course in Tropical Medicine at Liverpool University, further adding to his qualifications for medical work in Nyasaland.

He was informed in 1942, however, that he was to be conscripted into the army as a medical officer. Banda refused military service on the grounds of his pacifist beliefs. His plea was accepted and it was ruled that he should then work where the government felt he was most needed in Britain as a civilian, instead of serving in the armed forces. He was sent to Tyneside to work in a Mission to 'coloured seamen'. Quite soon after this he was appointed to the staff of the local hospital in North Shields. After serving there for some time he was released from compulsory national service. He had got to know the area and so set himself up in private practice in North

Shields. There, just as in Liverpool, he became popular in the local community, so much so that when he was detained in March 1959, many of his old patients wrote to the press insisting what a fine man he was.

It was at this time that Kamuzu was able to re-establish contact with his uncle, the Reverend Msokela Phiri. The war had initially disrupted communications with Nyasaland rather badly. However, by 1944 the progress of the war had enabled the restoration of a better mail service between the UK and Nyasaland. Kamuzu was then able also to begin to follow the activities of the newly created Nyasaland African Congress and he established contact with James Sangala, sending 'Pyagusi' regular advice.

As we have seen previously, Kamuzu's attitude towards British colonial policy in Africa north of the Zambezi was the same as that of Sangala, Matinga, Chinula and the other Nyasa leaders at that time. This was a view he had formulated as early as 1935 and he brought it with him as he linked with the NAC leaders in 1944. He made this perception clear in the famous letter he wrote to the British Government in 1949, later published in 1951 as the pamphlet, *Federation in Central Africa*. When Italy in 1935 invaded Ethiopia (Abyssinia as it was called then) Kamuzu wrote a long paper denouncing the invasion, arguing that it was what he called 'retrogressive'. British colonial government north of the Zambezi stood for progress and Italy's policy was the opposite. Still in the same vein, he wrote ten years later to his uncle Msokela insisting that the Colonial Office and the Nyasaland Protectorate Government were trying to help the people; they were friends.[163]

It is this attitude, held in common with most politically aware Nyasas in the 1940s, that would lead to sickening disappointment among those same people when the Conservative Government in 1953 imposed upon Nyasaland membership of the new Federation, despite the protests of the Nyasa people.

Sangala and the other leaders very quickly came to see the need to strengthen their ties with the British Labour Party and other political groups in Britain sympathetic to the cause of African progress. It was decided, as we have seen, to appoint Kamuzu to be the Nyasaland African Congress representative in the United Kingdom so as to facilitate this development.

As soon as the war in Europe ended in 1945, Kamuzu moved his practice to the London borough of Harlesden where in 1947 he enthusiastically joined the newly created National Health Service. Exactly why he moved to London at this point is not clear. It is relevant, however, to point out that he had

---

[163] Short quotes this letter which he says is 'privately held'.

by then made the acquaintance of Mrs Merene French, who had been in South Shields towards the end of the war nursing her mother-in-law.

In any case, in London there began a period in Kamuzu's life in which he seemedmost at ease, most comfortable and most at home. The period when he was a prosperous, confident, respectable, middle-class British family doctor was perhaps the happiest in his adult life and it was the image of that period which he very deliberately preserved with his three-piece dark suit, fawn raincoat and homburg hat, whatever the Malawi climate, almost until his dying day.

In London he became an active member of the Labour Party and the Fabian Bureau.[164] In the Fabian Bureau he got to know and become friends with Arthur Creech-Jones, later Secretary of State for Colonial Affairs, and John Hatch, the writer on African affairs.[165] The Banda of these years in Britain is brought to life so clearly in a passage from Munger's pamphlet, where he describes a journey to Oxford with Banda.

> He was a handsome, well-dressed, alert doctor wearing a homburg …already many of to-day's top African leaders had stayed at his home in Northwest London and many more were to do so before he returned to Africa …We talked on many subjects and occasionally he would lightly tap his rolled umbrella to make a point. He was obviously well adjusted and happy in British society.[166]

His home soon became a meeting place for African students and other African expatriates living in London, the most prominent of whom were Mzee Jomo Kenyatta and Kwame Nkrumah. All three met at the Fifth Pan African Congress in Manchester in 1945, a meeting which was dominated by George Padmore, the West Indian Marxist thinker.

However, although Kamuzu was part of the group and often the host he never accepted the socialist philosophy many of them espoused. Kwame Nkrumah and Kamuzu in particular became very close indeed before Nkrumah returned to the Gold Coast in 1947, which he was to lead into its new being as Ghana. Kamuzu, as the senior partner, used to refer to him as 'my boy Kwame', although it would appear only after Nkrumah returned to Africa.[167]

Meanwhile several of Kamuzu's attempts to encourage the NAC to make its central organisation more efficient, such as establishing a system to control funds centrally rather than leaving the branches with total autonomy as they

---

[164] The Fabian Bureau was a left-wing Socialist think-tank.

[165] Author of among others, *New from Africa*, 1956, *Dilemma of South Africa*, 1965, *A History of Britain in Africa*, 1969.

[166] Munger, *Kamuzu Banda*, p. 1.

[167] Short, *Banda*, p. 47.

had done heretofore, were accepted by Congress. However when Kamuzu suggested that Congress should appoint at least one full time administrator and offered to provide funding for this development, the suggestion although supported by J.D. Sangala and Charles Chinula, was defeated at the annual Conference.

It was the then President of Congress, Charles Matinga, who engineered the defeat of his own Executive's motion to accept Kamuzu's offer. Matinga was seriously concerned that Kamuzu was attempting to run Congress from London and suspected the full-time organiser would be Kamuzu's agent rather than a servant of Congress.

It would be wrong, however, to think of Kamuzu as leading the sort of life in London in the 1940s and early fifties that the young men, Chipembere and the others, led when they were students and first returned to Malawi. Politics, the overthrow of the Federation, and the rapid achievement of self-government was all they thought about. That was not how Dr Hastings K. Banda of Harlesden saw life at all. He had, through incredible determination and discipline, gained a B.Phil. in Politics and History as well as Medical qualifications to allow him to practice in the United States and what was then the British Empire. He had done that so as to serve his people *as a doctor*. When it became impossible to serve in Nyasaland, he continued to pursue what he considered his vocation as a doctor. He was able then and only then to help the NAC with funds and advice and to act as their informal ambassador in Britain.

As we have seen, wherever he had worked as a doctor he inspired a great deal of respect and affection, and so it was in Harlesden. There he was comfortable in the role of a successful doctor with all the dignity and prestige that went with that role. It was from this successful base that he was able to help the Nyasa people. He was a doctor first and foremost; a doctor with genuine political concerns, but not a politician.

This sense of being above all a doctor is attested to from the strangest of sources. In 1945 Banda had met Roy Welensky, later Prime Minister of the Central African Federation, but then a leader of the white skilled workers in Northern Rhodesia. While they were in London, Sir Stewart Gore-Brown, a somewhat eccentric figure who had befriended the young Welensky, but was later an important friend and supporter of Kenneth Kaunda, thought i important for Welensky to meet Kamuzu Banda, this educated, mature Afri can intellectual. Welensky appeared to like this African, who was, at th same time, very British and he noted particularly Banda's insistence that he was primarily a physician.[168]

In Harlesden Kamuzu had a full life, some of which he devoted to helping Nyasaland as well as he could, but it was not the be all and end all of his existence. Even his political life was not exclusively devoted to Nyasaland. He was an active member of the Harlesden Branch of the Labour Party, and he attended regularly a meeting in central London of Africans and West Indians and others interested in the politics of the British Empire in general. The confident, mature Kamuzu Banda was a successful and popular physician with an interest in politics and in the future of the land of his birth.

It is this successful life in London that we need to look at in more detail as it reveals large areas of Banda's life that were understandably ignored when Chipembere, Chiume and the others began their campaign for his return to Malawi as the political Messiah who would lead them out of the Federation and on to the Promised Land of independence. These were also areas of Kamuzu's life which he managed to make disappear from public view once he had returned to Nyasaland. The key figure made to disappear from Kamuzu's life was Mrs Merene French.

Dr Banda and Mrs French

Their situation of cosy conventional domesticity is described by Professor Shepperson who visited Dr Banda at his home twice in 1952. Shepperson says

> Both meetings were very pleasant social occasions as well as opportunities for us to tap each other's brains on the history of Nyasaland. Banda was then living in a substantial and well-kept villa in Harlesden with his friend, Mrs French, and her young son, Peter. The atmosphere was very cosy indeed; and the four of us sat around the table to two excellent high teas prepared by Mrs French.[169]

Kamuzu and Mrs French first got to know each other in South Shields while Mrs French and her little son, Peter, were living with her mother-in-law. Merene French had come to South Shields to care for her mother-in-law who had been unwell. We have already noted how popular Kamuzu was with his patients, so it was not strange that Merene French suggested to her husband that since the well-liked African doctor had arranged to buy a medical practice in Harlesden not far from their home, he might stay with them as a lodger till he was able to buy a house of his own. William French agreed to

---

[168] Roy Welensky, *4,000 Days: The Life and Death of the Federation of the Rhodesias and Nyasaland*, pp. 48-9.

[169] Shepperson, 'Memories of Dr Banda', *Society of Malawi Journal*, 51(1), 1998, pp. 74-84.

this arrangement and in the autumn of 1945 Kamuzu took over his practice in Harlesden while living with William and Merene French as their lodger.

William French asserted in the affidavit he submitted to begin divorce proceedings in 1953 that in July 1946 his wife made clear to him that their marriage was over and that she loved Kamuzu. She then moved into a separate bedroom. Astonishingly French did nothing and they all continued to live in the same house. William French, his wife and Kamuzu each had their own bedroom, but French appeared to accept the fact that Kamuzu and Mrs French were lovers.

Even stranger was the decision that when Dr Banda bought a large house for himself, Mrs French would move in as secretary for his medical practice and housekeeper, having her own bedroom again, while William French would also live in the new house. They continued living in these strange circumstances until 1949. French then left Kamuzu's house, leaving his wife and his son in Dr Banda's care, and still did nothing about a divorce until 1953.

In an interview with the *Daily Mail*, published on December 20th 1997, Peter French insisted that he had fond memories of Dr Banda as a *de facto* stepfather. Their house had been the first in the street with a car in which they took week-end trips into the country and, Peter added, although Kamuzu had been a strict disciplinarian he also lavished many generous gifts on him.

Kamuzu was very popular in his practice and there appeared to be no public concern about his and Mrs French's relationship. As Peter again reported, proprieties were strictly observed; when others were present Merene French always addressed Kamuzu as 'doctor'; only when they were alone did she refer to him by the name he used at that time, Hastings.

Merene French was the hostess when visitors came to the house, as we have seen in the case of Professor Shepperson and so she met many future African leaders as well as important figures in the British Labour Party. In the interview with the *Daily Mail* Peter French recalled Sir Stafford and Lady Cripps coming to lunch. More importantly Merene French met all the Nyasa visitors who came to London in the various delegations sent to meet the Secretary of State at the Colonial Office or to lobby opinion in Britain as part of the fight against the imposition of Federation. Peter French recalled his memories of accompanying his mother when she took some of these visitors to buy warm clothes more suitable for the British climate than those they had brought with them. Despite this public role she played in his life in London and even more in Kumasi, after Kamuzu's return to Nyasaland Mrs French is never mentioned publicly by the many Nyasas who had met her and knew of her previous role in Kamuzu's life. What is even more extraordinary is that later, after Kamuzu's release from Gwelo in 1960, Mrs French was treated as an honoured guest by Kamuzu's companions on the early visits to London to negotiate the future of the Protectorate with the Macmillan Government, but that did not change the fact that in Malawi Mrs French simply did not exist. In the late 1940s and early 1950s, however, Kamuzu was a successful London family doctor, with a concern for his homeland. This concern, though, did not always take a straightforward political form. For example, for over a decade Kamuzu paid the fees of young Nyasas and a few African students from elsewhere enabling them to continue their higher education. Given his own history, that is not surprising. At various times he made it clear to friends that he saw these actions as a way of repaying the generous help he had been given during his struggle for education. He also had other concerns. Soon after the Second World War ended he used his money to start two different enterprises in Nyasaland which were intended as models of African self-help. The first was a co-operative experimental farm project in Kasungu; the second was a business venture, the creation of the Trading and Transport Company, also based in Kasungu.

It would appear that Kamuzu had settled for life in London. There he could use his contacts in British politics and his financial resources to help his home country in a variety of ways. It appeared that the idea of going to Nyasaland as a doctor was no longer part of his plans. He could be of more general use to the development of his country by remaining in London and continuing doing what he was doing. All of this, however, depended on Britain continuing to follow its policy of the paramountcy of native interests in the colonial territories in Africa north of the Zambezi.

Opposition to Federation and the Move to Ghana

The crisis over the possible creation of the Federation of Nyasaland and the two Rhodesias changed everything. Kamuzu was alarmed when the Labour Party, a party of which he was an active member, contemplated the creation of this new state. Politics then moved into the centre of Kamuzu's life and dominated it. From 1950 to 1953 Kamuzu was deeply involved in the massive campaigns in England and Scotland in opposition to the imposition of Federation against the wishes of the African people of the two northern territories. Kamuzu spoke at meetings all over the United Kingdom and was the star speaker at a number of particularly successful public meetings in Edinburgh and Glasgow during this campaign. These massive protest meetings created a very heady atmosphere and he and many others felt that British public opinion was capable of changing Government policy.

It came as a terrible blow to him that, after they were elected, the new Conservative Government carried on regardless and the Federation was inaugurated despite all of these widespread and well supported anti-federation efforts in the UK When this defeat in Britain was followed by the disastrous failure of the Nyasaland African Congress campaign of passive resistance, Kamuzu did plumb the depths of despair. Philip Short asserts that at this time the clear failure of both the farming and transport initiatives he had financed in the Central Region contributed further to his feeling of defeat. It was at this point in 1953 he decided to go to Ghana.

This decision is puzzling, however; he was still a popular and successful family doctor. It is true that he was deeply disappointed by the victory of leaders of the white Rhodesians and the betrayal by the British Government of what before 1952 he had seen as their essentially well-meaning policies in Africa; but why leave London and the very secure existence he had created for himself?

Short asserts that the reasons he gave to the Devlin Commission, were the same as he learned from an interview with someone who at that time felt he could not allow his name to be made public. (When Short published his biography, Kamuzu was still in power and so quite a few other interviews in his book are also 'unattributable'.[170]) Kamuzu explained to Devlin that the reasons for his going to the Gold Coast were that

> although his views about Federation were unaltered, he did not want to continue in active opposition to it, which if he remained in London would inevitably be the case. He wanted, he said, to give it a chance.[171]

Why would he be forced to continue in active opposition to Federation if he stayed in London? If the obligation to oppose federation was so deep within him, then he could oppose the Federation from Accra. In Gold Coast he could still be reached and could still continue his role as opponent of the new state and external adviser to the NAC. Admittedly communications between Nyasaland and London were easier than between Gold Coast and Nyasaland but in Gold Coast he could still have been an active and effective critic of the Federation. This was particularly so since the Prime Minister and Foreign Minister of the new Ghana that Gold Coast was about to become were his old friends, Kwame Nkrumah and Kojo Botsio. Going to live in the Gold Coast by no means necessitated a withdrawal from campaigning for Nyasaland's secession from the Federation. He chose to end the role he had been playing up till then. He was not forced but chose to go into exile from his old life in London and to withdraw from his role as adviser to Nyasaland African Congress.

This desire to withdraw from public view was further emphasized by his decision not to live in Accra, the capital, where he had friends and many

---

[170] Short, *Banda*, p. 75.

[171] *Report of the Nyasaland Commission of Enquiry*, (Cmnd 814) 1959, p. 12.

acquaintances, but instead to live up-country in Kumasi, the old capital of the Ashanti Kingdom. (Ironically, the capture of Kumasi by the British in 1894 is the first battle honour on the colours of the 1st (Nyasaland) Battalion of the King's African Rifles, a flag still honoured in the modern Malawi Army.) Some commentators have asserted that Nkrumah was upset by his old friend's decision to go Kumasi; the annoyance did not last long if it existed at all since the two men remained close. Be that as it may, the decision to go to Kumasi is indicative of a profound need to withdraw from public view.

These actions of Kamuzu can better be explained, perhaps, by the shock he received when, in 1953, William French finally chose to sue for divorce. The exposure of the bizarre nature of the early years of his relationship with Merene French was not only humiliating, the whole affair was also destructive of his public image and his self-image. He loved the idea of himself as the respectable and respected popular family doctor and pillar of polite society, someone who had, through Herculean efforts, reached this pinnacle of success, and could smilingly refer to Kwame Nkrumah as 'my boy' and inform an American academic that he had been the mentor as well as the friend of Mzee Jomo Kenyatta.[172] A bizarre 'ménage à trois' did not fit into that image at all.

Short and Lwanda both view Kamuzu's leaving London for Kumasi as a critical, if not the critical moment in his life: a moment when Kamuzu completely lost confidence in himself. One piece of evidence that neither of these writers uses in asserting this idea is that the divorce proceedings which appeared to upset him so deeply did not appear to have made any impact on the people of Harlesden nor on the political figures, African and British, among whom he moved in London. Kamuzu appears to have been so affected by the exposure of the details of the early bizarre relationship with William and Merene French that he felt he could not face his old world and had to start anew.

Yet his situation had not in fact changed; he was still the well-respected doctor, member of the Labour Party and host to African politicians resident in or visiting London. It would seem that he had not needed to leave; the detailed contents of French's petition for divorce which he felt to be devastatingly humiliating were not known outside a very small circle. When his political activities in 1958 and '59 put his name in the headlines, the people of Harlesden remembered him with affection and respect; nobody mentioned divorce proceedings. It would appear that in 1953 he had so lost his nerve and self-confidence that he could not see that French's petition for divorce

[172] Edwin S. Munger, *President Kamuzu Banda of Malawi*, p. 1.

131

had no real impact upon the respect with which he was held in both local and political circles, in London and in the UK generally.

Kamuzu, depressed about the Conservative Government's imposition of Federation and the collapse of local resistance in Nyasaland, and the supposed exposure of his private life in a humiliating manner, now seemed desperate to drop out of sight. The supreme confidence which had so marked his time in the United Kingdom was gone and a sense of failure had taken its place. If this is a correct reading of his situation in 1953, it gives additional support to the idea propounded by both Short and Lwanda that the events of 1953 had profound, long term results on his personality. These writers feel that these events account for Kamuzu's later furious, at times hysterical, reaction to any disagreement with his views. They see Kamuzu having been struck by a deep sense of insecurity by these events which never again left him.

Despite these changes in her lover's life, Merene French did not change in her devotion to Kamuzu. She followed him to Kumasi and lived there with him as his wife, though without any legal ceremony taking place. Poor Peter, aged thirteen, was left behind and was very upset when, after staying with his mother's sister for some time, he had to go to live with his father with whom he did not get on.

Life in Ghana and Renewed Interest in Nyasaland Politics

In Kumasi Dr Banda lived quietly with his partner, practising medicine and staying away from the limelight. He took no part, initially, in the affairs of Nyasaland and the Federation. Despite it being widely asserted that Dr Banda remained aloof from his old friends Nkrumah and Kojo Botsio in Accra, that is not so. He was in touch with Nkrumah and the Botsio family throughout his time in Ghana. Their continued intimacy is clear in a letter of the 8th February 1956. Kamuzu wrote to Nkrumah

> This is my usual periodic letter to you ... I was very glad to hear from Mrs French on her recent visit to you and Mr Botsio, that in spite of everything, you looked much better than the last time she came to Accra.[173]

At the end of the year, as part of their continuing correspondence Nkrumah wrote to Dr Banda asking him for the names of suitable people to invite from Nyasaland and Northern Rhodesia to attend the Independence celebrations in March that year. The letter went astray and since he had had no reply Nkrumah sent a visiting Nyasaland Trades Unionist, a Mr Mussah, up to Kumasi to see that Kamuzu was well and get the names from Banda, whose

---

[173] HKB to Nkrumah. 8th February 1956. Banda-Nkrumah Collection of letters in possession of David Rubadiri.

judgement he clearly depended upon.[174] It is important to note the Nyasa leaders whom Kamuzu recommended. They were

1. Mr J. Chinyama, Senior Member of the Legislative Council.

2. Mr W.M. Chirwa, M.P., one of the two African members of the Federal Parliament representing Africans, though later you will hear more of this.

3. Mr T.D.T. Banda, recently elected President-General of Nyasaland African Congress.[175]

Kamuzu went on to say that Congress was in a mess in Northern Rhodesia, being in the process of great change and so he recommended D. Yamba, a Federal M.P., and the most senior member of the Northern Rhodesian Legco, Mr P. Sokoto. He went on to say that if Dr Nkrumah felt he had to make a gesture towards Congress then he should invite Harry Nkumbula.

This letter ends with a paragraph which confirms Dr Banda's intimacy with both Nkrumah and Botsio during his time in Ghana and puts in question the various assertions about the split between them that have been published in the literature. It also shows the central part in his life that Mrs French was continuing to play.

> Mrs French has not been very well, though she is somewhat better now. As soon as she is well, she is coming over to see you all, and, as usual, will be staying with the Botsios.

Much has been made by some commentators of the brief difficulty Kamuzu had with the Gold Coast Medical Council. The details of this difficulty are still not clear. Some have suggested it was over Kamuzu allowing members of the staff of his clinic to carry out medical procedures they were not formally qualified to do. Others have suggested that it was a matter of Kamuzu having carried out a number of abortions. What little hard evidence there is points to the first suggestion as the more likely cause of his temporary suspension. The Medical Council published a notice suspending Kamuzu without explanation on 7 December 1957; in May 1958, however, the Council formally restored his status as a medical practitioner. By that time, as we shall see, Kamuzu was again on the move.

Most commentators on this period of Banda's life suggest that he showed the first signs of coming out of his withdrawal from public affairs in November 1956 when he chose, somewhat reluctantly, to reply to a letter from Chipembere. 'Chip', as we saw, wanted Banda's endorsement of his demand that Manoah and Kumbikano resign from the Federal Parliament or face expulsion from Congress. Kamuzu recommended instead that they be allowed to finish their term, a very moderate answer and not one that

---

[174] HKB to Nkrumah, 21 January 1957, Banda-Nkrumah Letters.
[175] Ibid.

Chipembere wanted to hear. However, it was an answer: the first serious correspondence with a politician in Nyasaland or anywhere else of which we know. Kamuzu was beginning to be active again and emerge from 'hiding', although it was still a very tentative emergence. This was very clear when, in March, 1957, T.D.T. Banda visited Gold Coast for the Independence Celebrations of the birth of Ghana. Kamuzu did agree to a meeting with the President of the NAC, but his reply to T.D.T.'s invitation for him to return home to Nyasaland was very vague indeed. Back in Nyasaland all that T.D.T. could announce was that Kamuzu would return 'in the next few years' and Short suggests that even this was perhaps uncertain.[176]

The above paragraph represents what we might call 'the accepted account' of these events. However, letters between Kamuzu and the Reverend Tom Colvin of the Blantyre Mission, deposited in Edinburgh University, cast a very different light on the situation.[177] These letters show that T.D.T. Banda was only able to go to Ghana for the Independence Celebrations with the aid of money loaned by Colvin to 'T.D.T.' on the strength of Dr Banda cabling to Colvin, guaranteeing re-imbursement of £50, a massive sum for someone on a missionary salary in the 1950s.

Clearly Kamuzu was already heavily involved with Nyasaland affairs. Chipembere, Chiume and the other Congress leaders in Nyasaland appear to have been unaware of Banda helping with T.D.T.'s expenses. They were also unaware that, as the Colvin letters show, Banda had his own group of correspondents who had been keeping him in touch with events in Nyasaland for some time.

In the letter thanking Colvin, Banda showed that his old pro-British stance was still alive and well:

> Among other things Mr [T.D.T.] Banda has told me everything about you. It is very encouraging to me to know that we still have your type of European among us in Nyasaland. Rev. Andrew Doig is another. I can assure you that it is you, Rev. Doig, and a few others, who realise that we, too, are human beings, who are the real builders of a lasting British Commonwealth.[178]

What is even more revealing is that Kamuzu has clearly already made up his mind to return to Nyasaland to practise as a physician and to fight the Federation. In this letter of 9 March, 1957, he asks Colvin to look out for a plot in Chichiri where he might build a house and clinic. He is planning, he says, to start transferring money to a Building Society in Nyasaland so that funds

---

[176] Short, *Banda*, p. 83.

[177] Three letters from H.K.Banda to Rev Tom Colvin dated March 9, 1957, March 12, 1957 and 25 May 1957, Centre for the Study of Christianity in the Non-Western World Archives, University of Edinburgh.

[178] H.K.Banda to Tom Colvin, 9 March 1957, CSCNWW Archives.

will be built up to allow him to purchase a plot of land and build a house and clinic in late 1959 or 1960. He asks Colvin to recommend a building firm that can be relied upon.

In the next letter of 12 March, Kamuzu asked Colvin to keep him in touch with how things are going in Nyasaland, and, in passing, says that Manoah Chirwa had been writing to him and keeping him up to date on Nyasa affairs. These letters give a clear picture of someone who has firmly decided to return to Nyasaland and who is well informed about Nyasaland affairs. In the letter to Colvin of 25th May 1957, written ten days after the Ghana Medical Council had restored his licence to practise medicine, he makes his position very clear. Kamuzu confirms to Colvin that he wants him to go ahead to investigate the two plots of land which Colvin had deemed suitable in the Chichiri area. They must, he insists, be near a good road and have water and electricity, because he needs to have an effective medical practice in order to make a living. He also asks Colvin to look out for any small estate that might come on the market in the Blantyre-Limbe area which he thinks might be a good alternative to the two sites already found by Colvin. Kamuzu, or Hastings as he still signs his letters at that time, also explains why he is coming home now and had not done so earlier:

> If I have kept quiet since the settlers and the British Government imposed their Federation in 1953, it is only for the reason that I wanted to give everybody a fair chance. I wanted to give my own people a chance to have a full taste of what it means to live under a government of European settlers of Southern Rhodesia. I wanted to give the European settlers a chance to prove it to us, the Africans, that when they say they want partnership, they mean it. And finally, I wanted to give the Colonial Office a chance to prove it to us, that Federation would not mean any change in the life of the Africans of Nyasaland, as it claimed in 1952-1953.
>
> Now, after three years of Federation, I know what my people feel about it. ... So, I have decided to return home within the next two or three years, to begin the battle again, where I left off in 1953.[179]

T.D.T. Banda's promise to the people on his return to Nyasaland that Banda was returning in two or three years was not, then, a product of dissimulation by Kamuzu but an accurate report of Kamuzu's firm intention. Chipembere's task was not, as Short and Lwanda suggest, persuading Kamuzu to return, but rather it was to persuade him to change his time-table for that return. This is also what Chipembere records in his autobiography. To the young men it was impossible to wait until 1959 or 1960 for his return. They were already building up a momentum in revitalising dormant branches of Congress and in popularising their campaign for an African majority in Legco and the secession of Nyasaland from the Federation. All of this was focussed around the promise of a new day that would come with the return of the leg-

---

[179] H.K. Banda to Tom Colvin, 25 May 1957, CSCNWW Archives, University of Edinburgh.

endary *mchona*, Dr Banda. That momentum, however, could not be sustained for very much longer without Banda's return or some other dramatic event. There was no way they could wait till 1960. In any case, 1960 would almost certainly be too late. The existing Colonial Office stake in Nyasaland, which was the legal avenue by which the Nyasa people could achieve secession from the hated Federation, would disappear with the creation of the new self-governing Dominion which Welensky in Salisbury and Lennox-Boyd in London planned as the outcome of the Constitutional Review of that year.

Pressure on Banda to Return to Nyasaland

Chipembere and others continued to press Kamuzu hard to return as soon as possible. It is, however, important to note that they knew nothing about Manoah and others keeping Kamuzu up to date on Nyasaland affairs. We know from the Colvin letters that already in March 1957 Kamuzu had come to a firm decision; he had accepted that the politics of Nyasaland needed his active concern. His careful planning of a purpose built house and a clinic makes that clear; he also, however, had decided on a timetable which was hopelessly awry as far as the young men were concerned and appeared to misunderstand the political reality of the situation in Nyasaland created by the coming Federal Review Conference in 1960.

Short has suggested that the decision of the British Government to give way to Welensky's pressure to bring forward in time the Constitutional Conference, at which Welensky hoped to gain Dominion status for the Federation, played a large part in this re-awakening of Banda's political commitment. Lennox-Boyd, the Colonial Secretary, made public that the conference would meet in 1960, the earliest time permitted by the constitutional arrangements made in 1953, and would consider full membership of the Commonwealth' for the Federation. In the minds of Congress veterans and the new young generation alike, this meant that permanent white settler rule was to be entrenched. The 'amalgamation' fought against since the 1920s was to come in via the backdoor of Federation, as the opponents of Federation, including Kamuzu, had forecast.

That this was the key to Banda's return to political activity appears far from the case. The announcement of Lennox-Boyd's decision was not made until April 1957 by which time Kamuzu had already made up his mind to return. Given the great pressure Chipembere and the others had to put on him to return in 1958 rather than later, Lennox-Boyd's announcement appears not to have made much of an impact on his thinking.

Both Lwanda and Short suggest that without the problems that arose with the Medical Council of Ghana, Kamuzu might not have accepted the pressing invitations from Chipembere and the others.[180] Certainly, after his suspension from pursuing his medical practice there was no work for him in Ghana unless and until his name was cleared. It was cleared, as we have seen, and he appeared never to have doubted the outcome of the case, since already on March 7th 1957, before the result was announced, he was confidently planning to return to Nyasaland *to work as a physician.*

What had made him decide to return to Nyasaland, a decision clearly made before 12 March, 1957 is not completely clear, but the Colvin letters seem to indicate that the problems with the Ghana Medical Council were not very important, if important at all. The real issue is why he dropped the time-table set out in the letters to Colvin and decided to return to Nyasaland in the summer of 1958. It certainly was not the reason he gave to the Devlin Commission, where he said it was the Welensky – Lennox-Boyd deal about constitutional change. We have seen that even after Lennox-Boyd's decision was made public Kamuzu's timetable continued to be the leisurely carefully planned one of the letters to Colvin. Was it the continuing pressure from Chipembere, or perhaps it was what he was learning from his chosen informants in Nyasaland, about which Chipembere knew nothing.

These letters from his informants were clearly unknown to Short, Lwanda and other writers about this period, though they recognize that by 1957 Kamuzu was receiving from Nyasaland many appeals to return; but these were the appeals promoted by Chipembere and Chiume's campaign for him to return as a messianic leader. The letters from his special correspondents were a different matter. The existence of these correspondents, one of whom was Manoah Chirwa, was unknown to most people and their existence has only come to light through the availability now of the Colvin letters. The existence of this group of informants may very well explain the two visits paid to him by Nyasaland Europeans in the summer of 1957. The two visitors were the Reverend Andrew Doig and Major Peter Moxon.

Doig was a minister who had served the Blantyre Mission and the Blantyre Synod of the CCAP since 1938. He had represented African Interests in the Nyasaland Legco with Congress support and, more recently, had just decided to resign from his position as a member of the Federal Parliament. Having 'given Federation a chance', he became certain that the Federation meant settler rule and not partnership; so he resigned. This was triggered in particular by the failure of the British Government to support the African Affairs Board, leaving it exposed as toothless facade.

---

[180] Short, *Banda.* p. 85, Lwanda, *Kamuzu Banda*, p. 19.

Major Peter Moxon was a farmer in the Southern Region, married to an African woman, and a supporter of Nyasaland's withdrawal from the Federation. Clyde Sanger in his *Central African Emergency* says they had a great influence on Banda's decision but doesn't produce any hard evidence for this assertion.[181] If they were part of Kamuzu's group of correspondents who had been keeping him informed of Nyasaland affairs then Sanger's suggestion would carry more weight than it has often been given. But Sanger, like Short, Lwanda and other commentators did not know that the decision Banda had to make was not whether or not to return - he had already made the decision to return - but rather when to return.

Peter Moxon, in a later interview with Robert Rotberg, said that he thought that all Kamuzu wanted from him was reassurance that his returning to Nyasaland would be a good thing. Moxon explained the visit to Kamuzu was added on to his visit to his brother, who had a senior appointment with the Ghanaian Government. He had apparently not gone to Ghana primarily to talk to Kamuzu, which is what Andrew Doig had done.

What inspired Andrew Doig to make that journey has puzzled a number of observers but it now appears he was one of the hitherto unknown group of Banda informants and it would appear the visit was made in that connection. Although serving as a member of the Federal Parliament, Doig had continued to have good relations with the NAC. Short and others have suggested that he went to persuade Banda to return and control the wild young men. That is not impossible but it is just as likely that he went to point out the urgency of the situation which made nonsense of the timetable Kamuzu had set out in the letters to Colvin, about which Doig knew.

Welensky, whom Doig knew well, never hid his aim to remove 'the dead hand of the Colonial Office from Nyasaland' and insisted that this would be achieved at the Constitutional Conference timed for 1960. Doig, with his close contacts in Salisbury, knew that 1960 would see Nyasaland incorporated into the kind of autonomous settler-dominated state the Nyasa people had feared and resisted for thirty years. He saw clearly that if Banda was going to be of any help in the struggle, he had to come to Nyasaland as soon as possible, just as Chip and Chiume had been begging him to do.

What does take a little explaining is how Doig's visit was financed. There is no record of the Church of Scotland authorities having anything to do with it. It was a long and expensive journey even on a Federal MP's salary: Salisbury to London, London to Accra, and then the long overland trek to Kumasi, which had no airport at that time. It would appear unlikely that Doig suddenly decided to embark on this trip entirely on his own initiative.

---

[181] Clyde Sanger. *Central African Emergency*, pp. 198-99.

Whatever the answer is to the problems surrounding Doig's visit, it was very soon after it that Kamuzu made up his mind to change the timetable of his return to Nyasaland.

Congress Delegation to Meet the Colonial Secretary

Kamuzu informed Chipembere that he was making arrangements that would bring him back to Nyasaland by the end of July 1958. He needed some time, he said, to clear up affairs in Ghana and in London where among other assets he still owned a substantial house. Kamuzu's return to London enabled him to accept Congress's invitation to head the delegation it was sending to meet the Colonial Secretary. Thus it was that in London during the last few days of May 1958, Masauko Chipembere and Dunduzu Chisiza met for the very first time the man whose return to Nyasaland they had already built up among the people to a giddy high point of almost messianic expectation.

Chipembere has left a vivid account of the weeks the delegation spent in the United Kingdom where, after the meetings with Lennox-Boyd the Nyasa group spent the rest of the time campaigning to raise popular British support for their cause.[182] In his autobiography and various essays he makes no reference to the interview Dr Banda requested with Robert Armitage, the Governor of Nyasaland who was on leave in London at the time. The meeting took place in Armitage's flat in St James' Court on the 10th June. Armitage makes no reference to any other Nyasa being present.[183] When one adds this to the absence of any notice of the meeting by Chipembere, one has to wonder if the Congress delegates from Nyasaland knew about the meeting.

Before we look at Chip's thoughts on these first encounters with Kamuzu, we need to look briefly at the meeting with Lennox-Boyd on the 13th of June. At the meeting with the Secretary of State, the Congress delegation again presented their plans for constitutional reform which the Governor already informed Lennox-Boyd privately he judged utterly impracticable, while giving a non-committal response to the Congress delegation at their meeting in Zomba. Their plan for a Legislative Council elected by universal adult suffrage, though with six seats reserved for non-Africans, and the Governor's Executive Council elected by the Legislature, was unacceptable to the British Government. The Secretary of State did assure the delegation, however, that the British Government fully appreciated the need Congress felt for Nyasa opinion to be effectively expressed at the Federal Constitutional Conference in 1960. Lennox Boyd went on to assert that he expected the

[182] Robert I. Rotberg (ed.) *Hero of the Nation*, pp. 320-24.
[183] Colin Baker, *State of Emergency: Crisis in Central Africa, Nyasaland, 1959-1960*, I.B. Tauris, London and New York, 1997, p. 3.

Governor to make suggestions for constitutional change in the Protectorate as soon as he, the Governor, returned to the Protectorate early in August.

During these few weeks of campaigning in the UK, Chipembere was particularly impressed by the support Nyasaland received in Wales. He had gone there to further the anti-Federation campaign with Andrew Doig, confirming the latter's role in what might be called the Banda entourage at that time. Chipembere also reports on some events which cast a shadow on Kamuzu's personality, but he admits in his autobiography that he cast these aside at the time because he had committed himself so completely to the campaign portraying Kamuzu as 'Saviour of the Nation'.

The first of the two more important doubts that were raised was that the politically important African student group in London were very critical of Congress's choice of Kamuzu as leader. Many of these students were experienced and mature men, like Oscar Kambona of Tanganyika, already picked by Mwalimu Julius Nyerere to be a cabinet minister, and Fred Ginwala, a leading South African exile. Since, however, Kamuzu had been away from London for nearly five years, they were basing their opinions on a short acquaintance of few weeks after his return from Kumasi. It was clear, however, that he had made an unfavourable impression on them. This is in contrast with what appeared to be his leading role in such Pan-African circles in London before he had left for Kumasi, when he had seen himself as mentor to Kwame Nkrumah and Mzee Jomo Kenyatta.

What was perhaps more worrying was Kamuzu's behaviour towards the delegates from Nyasaland and some of his other friends helping with the campaign they were waging during the visit to Britain. Chipembere remembers Kamuzu angrily and unnecessarily rebuking Clyde Sanger, a reporter sympathetic to Congress, which produced from Sanger the response, "But what have I done? Why are you angry with me?" Chipembere reports that later that same day in the middle of an informal conversation with, among others, the Reverend Michael Scott, Kamuzu quite unfairly rebuked Andrew Doig in very angry terms. Chipembere goes on

> What disturbed me about some of these rebukes was that they were intended for the Malawians present ... It was clear that he wanted us to see how "strong" and "courageous" he could be and how he didn't regard whites as superiors, a lesson we did not need to learn so late in our nationalist careers.[184]

Chip was also distressed when he discovered that Kamuzu appeared to think that Nyasas from the homeland were in some way backward. He records how, when he hesitated for a moment to gather his thoughts before answering a question which included the word 'portfolio', Kamuzu whispered to

---

[184] Ibid. p. 323.

him 'By portfolio he means a ministry or a department; do you under-stand?'[185]

Their financial resources coming to an end, Chief Kuntaja and Chipembere had to return to Nyasaland before Kamuzu was ready to accompany them, despite the wish of the Central Committee of Congress for all three to return together. (Dunduzu had, meanwhile, gone back to his studies at Fircroft College in Birmingham.) However Kamuzu insisted he could not return at that time and that, in any case, he wanted Kuntaja and Chipembere to return before him 'to prepare the way'. 'Chip' comments 'Little did he realize that there had already been more than enough preparation'.

---

[185] Ibid. p. 322.

Chapter 5

Towards the Emergency

In the history of Malawi according to Kamuzu, his arrival began a new era in the history of African nationalism in the Nyasaland Protectorate. At last the real fight to secede from Federation and to achieve independence began. A helpless people were energised and inspired to new activity, a hitherto dormant people came to life.

The reality of the situation was dramatically different as we have seen. While they were still trying to persuade Dr Banda to return, the new young leadership of Congress were leading a re-energised, growing and increasingly powerful movement of opposition to Federation. The almost universal opposition of the Nyasa people to Federation did not abate after the defeat of 1953. What was crushed by the defeat was the formally structured Congress movement. Opposition to Federation and bitter disillusion with London over what Nyasas saw as the betrayal of Nyasaland was widespread in 1953. It would take time, however, before this anger and resentment could be channelled effectively by a revitalised Congress.

Building on the restored foundations created by Sangala, and exploiting the widespread disillusion with Britain, the new leadership of Congress set out to achieve their aims with total dedication to the cause. They rapidly made secession from the Federation and the achievement of self-government the central issue, day in and day out, for the politically conscious people of the Protectorate. Dr Banda's agreement to return home simply enabled the young Congress leaders to add a new theme to their propaganda so effectively propagated through the Legco Hansard. Chipembere and the others used the promise of Banda's return to create a wide-spread sense among Nyasas that they were on the edge of a new beginning. The new beginning would be marked by the arrival of the Doctor at Chileka airport they insisted. This image of the new beginning was created and fostered by the young men and women who were leading Congress.

Not only did the promise of the return of this experienced mature man help deflect the attention of more conservative and traditional groups away from the youthfulness of Chipembere, Chisiza, Chiume and the others but also Dr Banda was someone respected by the older generation of Congress leaders. He had advised these pre-1953 leaders, he had welcomed them to London and provided them with generous hospitality there and, before his self imposed exile in Kumasi had regularly sent them money to help the cause. He, like them, could never be attacked as a mere *mtumbidwa*.

While preparing people for the return of the hero, Congress continued to pursue vigorously the campaign for the UK government to grant a major constitutional reform of the Legislative Council of Nyasaland. Congress sought a Legislative Council which would have an over-all African majority. The Legislative Council would then represent the anti-Federation opinion of the African people of the Protectorate.[186] This reform had to be carried through urgently, however, if the Nyasa case for secession was to be put effectively at the expected Review of the Federal Constitution.

However, both the Colonial Office in London and the new Governor, Sir Robert Armitage, felt that since Legco had been restructured only two years earlier, to ask for such a major change so soon was unreasonable. Despite this, as we have seen, the Secretary of State for the Colonies, Alan Lennox-Boyd, had assured the Congress delegation to London that the British Government appreciated Congress's desire for effective representation at the 1960 Federal Review. He had also affirmed the Colonial Office's willingness to continue discussions on possible reforms of Legco leading to greater African representation.

What the officials in Zomba and the politicians in London were willing to contemplate and what Congress sought were very far apart. The British Government continued to say that Federation was here to stay while Congress wanted these reforms in order to secede from the Federation. Despite this, however, Lennox-Boyd's assurances had roused hopes in the leadership of Congress. These were quickly dashed. On his return from leave in August, the Governor, Sir Robert Armitage, did not announce any further plan for constitutional reform.

Date of the Constitutional Review Conference sets the Agenda

The 1960 date for this crucial review of the Federal Constitution was a key factor in all the planning done by the Congress leadership. When the 1960 Federal Review Conference took place, if it went as was planned by the Conservative Government in London and Welensky's Federal administration, then Nyasaland's links with Britain would be cut off. Nyasaland would become a province of a white ruled independent Commonwealth country, where guarantees about race discrimination or land apportionment, made before the take-over 'would not be worth the paper they were written on'.

Throughout the 1950s and on into the early 1960s British ministers would insist that Federation was not a step towards the old amalgamation. They

---

[186] This potential legitimization of secession was the result of the peculiar nature of the Federal Constitution which had left London with power at the Territorial level north of the Zambezi. This was precisely what Welensky wanted to end as soon as possible.

asserted, and some modern commentators have agreed with them, that the aims of the Federal Government under Roy Welensky were not inimical to aspirations of the African people of the two northern territories. Their view was that a move towards Dominion status was not intended as a means of setting the ruling white minority of the Federations population free from the constraints imposed on it by the original 1953 Constitution.

As we have asked before, how could British ministers go on saying this kind of thing when they could read in the Rhodesian and South African press what Rhodesian politicians were saying to their home constituents? There is no doubt that many British ministers and officials were able to go on believing in the policy of 'partnership' as a reality, because of the impact Sir Roy Welensky's personality had on them. Sir Roy convinced them that he meant what he said about a middle way between the permanent White supremacy of the Republic of South Africa and African nationalism, which was held by senior British Ministers and officials of the time to be equally racist. It would appear that Welensky honestly believed in 'partnership' but it was a partnership where the majority of Africans would not be accepted as equal members for 'generations', as one of his allies put it.[187] This position of asking African people to be patient and wait for 'several generations', while being treated as dependents to be guided and looked after meanwhile, was a totally untenable political position in the 1950s. It was, however, the basis of Welensky's claim to be what he called 'a liberal'.

Again and again in the years leading up to the 1960 review, Welensky would insist that a fundamental flaw in the constitution of the Federation was the continuing Colonial Office administration of the territorial affairs of the two northern territories within the Federal structure. This meant, he insisted, that the Africans there constantly looked to London not Salisbury as the focus of their political activity. He was correct. As we have seen, exploiting this situation created by the 1953 constitution was the deliberate policy which J.F Sangala had embarked on immediately after the debacle of 1953. His policy was to concentrate on London and ignore Salisbury. The Federal Government, Welensky complained, was cut off from the very people it wanted to reach in order to show them the advantages Federation was bringing and how they had a future in the Federation.[188] This was a principal reason, Welensky asserted, that the Federal Government wanted the role of the Colonial Office in the administration of the two Northern territories ended.

---

[187] Joelson to Welensky, 26 November 1958, The Papers of Sir Roy Welensky, Coffin 24 File 151.

[188] Ibid. Welensky to Joelson, 3 January 1957.

Only with Dominion status and virtual independence could the experiment of racial partnership be made to work.

Yet even in Welensky's own correspondence we can see that he knew that he had very little support among whites in either of the Rhodesias for even his very weak 'equality after some generations' type liberalism. Indeed in this correspondence one is left in doubt as to how far he believed it himself. In his letters to Joelson, the editor of *East Africa and Rhodesia*, there is unambiguous confirmation of the fears of the Nyasa people that Federation was always a cover for amalgamation and white supremacy. On 16 July, 1956 Welensky wrote

> You know, Joelson, we have been able to keep the European quiet here for a long time and have got him to accept a number of things which have not been very palatable, but if this position carries on very much longer and he sees no sign of us *becoming masters in our own house* then I think you can expect a change of outlook here.[189]

At that point in 1956 the effectiveness of Congress protest in Nyasaland was already such that Welensky was insisting to friends privately that the Federal Government needed to be granted Dominion status as soon as possible, if not immediately.[190] This would enable him to deal with the problems in Nyasaland effectively which he believed the British were incapable of doing. Friends persuaded him to wait. They were sure the Federation would gain Dominion status at the Federal Review Conference which Welensky should persuade the British to call at the earliest legal opportunity. As we have seen this new timetable was achieved the next year in April, 1957 by the famous agreement with Lennox-Boyd setting the date of the Review at the earliest possible date under the terms of the 1953 constitution.

In his letter persuading Welensky to calm down and wait for the Review Conference Joelson confirmed all the fears of the Nyasa people had they been able to read it. He reminds Welensky that he must wait for the Review Conference, since the 1953 constitution could not be altered before that Conference met. He insisted "*unitary government must come,*" and the granting of Dominion status at the Review Conference would open the way for it.[191]

Welensky's correspondence with Joelson and others confirms what the Nyasa people had asserted all along, that Federation was a step towards a 'unitary state' what used to be called amalgamation, where 'we can be masters in our own house'. In this context Welensky appears to have thought if he got Dominion status in 1960, he could create a political situation that

---

[189] Ibid. Welensky to Joelson, 16 July 1956, the emphasis is the present author's.

[190] Ibid. File 151.

[191] Loc. cit. Joelson to Welensky, 20-24 July. 1956 (one letter); emphasis in the original.

would allow, after several generations, some sort of equality for Africans. However, he also knew that the overwhelming majority of Rhodesians wanted 'to be masters in their own house' without any belief whatever even in his feeble brand of liberalism. How well he knew this appears in his re-iterated fears that unless he could get Dominion status at the earliest opportunity, white Rhodesians would reject Federation and retreat into a radically white supremacist state in Southern Rhodesia.[192]

The Congress Campaign Forces the British to Act

For the Nyasaland African Congress in 1958 time was of the essence. Real change had to be achieved in the composition of the Nyasaland legislature before the Review Conference. Only then could the long term opposition of the people of Nyasaland to any close political association with the 'white' south be effectively presented at the Conference. If that could not be achieved and increasingly that looked to be the case, then the drastic alternative of creating a major political crisis by making Nyasaland ungovernable was their other option. The crisis thus created would be a crisis in London as well as in Africa. Hopefully the pro-Nyasaland lobby in Scotland and elsewhere in the UK would be able to take advantage of the crisis to make the headlines. The popular pressure in the UK and the impasse in Nyasaland would then lead the British Government, it was hoped, to conclude that the secession of Nyasaland from the Federation was the best way forward.

Whether the new leader came or not, Congress was exerting already an enormously powerful challenge to the Boma by presenting itself to the people as an alternative government. How effective this was we have seen confirmed by Welensky's desire, as early as mid 1956, to obtain the powers to deal with Nyasaland's affairs directly because he judged the Nyasaland administration as failing to cope effectively with the challenge from Congress. Welensky was correct in his judgement. By the middle of 1958 Nyasaland African Congress had created a situation where the growing popular unrest in the Southern Province and the situation in the Northern Province where the Boma was struggling to maintain even token authority, had combined to create what in physics would be called a 'critical point'. Very soon the Protectorate government would have to act to suppress Congress or make major concessions to it.

In the Legislative Council which was, it must be remembered, only advisory to the essentially authoritarian, if paternal, power of the Governor, the Congress members behaved as if they were the Opposition in a democratic leg-

---

[192] Welensky Papers, Coffin 24, files 151 and 152, *passim*.

islature. In the country at large, through their constituency meetings, they behaved in the same way.

The Congress Members of the Legco were not, however, in a democratic situation. They could not overturn the Government as in a democracy because they did not have a majority in the Council. Even more important, the constitution of the Protectorate did not give them the means to obtain one. The Legislative Council was only advisory to the Governor whose authority was entirely independent of that body and independent of the will of the people of the Protectorate.

This was an essentially frustrating situation and if the constitutional changes for which Congress was pressing were not met, the situation could not go on as it was. Because of popular unrest in many parts of the country and the frustration created by the constitutional impasse, some sort of explosive confrontation was inevitable whether Dr Banda arrived or not. An autocracy cannot go on for long co-existing with a nationwide, popular opposition, particularly when, as in this case, the two have diametrically opposed aims on something as fundamental as secession from the Federation.

The old colonial regime in Nyasaland had gone along well enough before 1953 because, although an autocracy, its benevolence and good intentions were taken for granted, as we have seen.[193] The imposition of Federation had terminally damaged that trust of the Boma in the hearts and minds of the Nyasa people. In the past District Commissioners had run their district in cooperation with the chiefs in a system that depended on the people's trust and willing cooperation for it to work. It could not continue when many people openly opposed the system as they were doing in the Northern Region and in parts of the Southern. When many began to see the DC as a political opponent, instead of, if not as a friend exactly, at least as a fair referee, the old system was on the edge of complete breakdown.

This threatened breakdown of the system of government in Nyasaland existed before Kamuzu's return. This is also the judgement of the *Nyasaland Commission of Enquiry*, usually referred to as the Devlin Report. Devlin wrote of Banda's arrival in the Protectorate

> It speeded up the tempo but it did not decisively alter the character of events thereafter. Already a clash between the Government and Congress was highly probable. The differences between them had got almost beyond discussion. It was not simply that the two sides were far apart: each had an attitude of mind which the other was beginning to find exasperating.[194]

---

[193] Banda and Nkumbula. *Federation in Central Africa*. passim.
[194] *Report of the Nyasaland Commission of Enquiry*. Cmnd 814. Par. 31.

Could Congress Channel and Control the Popular Excitement it was Creating?

The growing unrest, when it was further stimulated by the build up of expectations that something was really going to happen when Dr Banda came home, created a situation that was constantly hovering on the edge of going beyond the control of the leaders of Congress. Chipembere himself testifies to this sense of uncontrollable excitement in describing the turmoil that erupted at Chileka Airport on the 29th June 1958 when, with all Nyasaland waiting for him, Dr Banda failed to arrive.

Many writers, when dealing with this period in the history of Malawi, pass over the Chileka incident with only the briefest of reference to it, which is to misunderstand its significance. In his biography of Banda, Short relegates mention of Banda's failure to appear on the 29th June to a mere footnote. The Devlin Commission itself gave it one brief paragraph. This misunderstanding of the import of the events of that day means we must look at those events in some detail.

People had already been very disappointed when Dr Banda had not accompanied Chief Kuntaja and Chipembere on their return from the meeting with the Secretary of State in the UK. In his autobiography Chipembere wrote that Dr Banda had insisted that he would arrive on Sunday, 29th June and that they were to make appropriate preparations to welcome him at Chileka on that day. Congress dutifully sent out word that there should be a mass welcome for the returning hero at Chileka on Sunday 29th June. All over the Southern Province people had begun organising how to get to Chileka to welcome their new leader.

According both to Chipembere and Chiume in their autobiographies, Congress had not received even the slightest hint from Banda that his arrival on the 29th was in any way in doubt. Thus, when the day of the promised return of the hero arrived, a large crowd gathered at Chileka. They were watched over by a substantial force of police and observed by many more pressmen than usually attended political events in the Protectorate. The official police report stated the crowd was around 2,500, while Congress suggested 10,000 people had gathered; the real number was certainly larger than that stated by the police but less than Congress suggested. Though if one counted the thousands lining the road from Chileka into Blantyre then ten thousand is undoubtedly an underestimate. Those lining the highway, however, were not directly involved in the events at Chileka, though they did contribute to the extraordinary sense of excitement and tension that Sunday.

While waiting at Chileka, Chipembere and other prominent Congress leaders were taken aback when, some time before the plane was due to arrive pressmen told them that Banda was not on the plane. The reporters informed the stunned Congress leaders that Government officials had told them this and that the control tower had radioed the plane and the captain had confirmed that Banda was not on board.

When Chipembere, Chiume and Orton[195] tried to tell other leading congressmen this dismaying news, they were rebuffed. The main body of the Congress leadership insisted that this story was a trick to get the crowd to disperse and then it could be reported that Banda had returned to his homeland to a very poor reception. These Congress veterans insisted that everyone had to wait until the plane arrived and the passengers disembarked. Their suspicions are understandable since, as we have seen, Banda had been so adamant that the 29th was the date for his return.

In his autobiography Chipembere asks the very relevant question, 'why did the Protectorate Government not inform him or one of the other African Members of the Legislative Council that Banda was not going to be on the plane?' They had, after all, known for at least twenty-four hours that this was the case?

The senior British officials running the Protectorate in the absence of Armitage who was on leave, were clearly unsympathetic to Congress. However surely they were not so childish as to withhold this information in order to have the ordinary members of Congress waste so much of their meagre resources to no purpose, which is what Chipembere suggests?[196]

Because of the unwillingness of the bulk of the Congress leadership to accept the story given to 'Chip' and Chiume by the pressmen, the massive crowd did not receive even a hint that there was a problem. They stayed excitedly awaiting the moment when the greatest of all the Nyasa *machona* would set foot on the soil of the motherland.

At Chileka, in those days, spectators had easy access to the tarmac and so a large number of the huge crowd were able to gather on the edge of the runway to watch the passengers disembarking from the aircraft, eagerly anticipating the appearance of the returning hero. Then the cry went up 'where is he?' as consternation and then alarm spread through the excited onlookers.

The press reports at the time, said that the people surged forward towards the plane and, as their leader and spokesman, Chipembere demanded that he be allowed to search the aircraft. The reality was something much more disturbing because it revealed that feelings were running so high that the leadership of Congress could not control the crowd.

---

[195] By this time Orton Ching'oli Chirwa was back in the Congress again.

[196] Chipembere, *Hero of the Nation*, p. 328.

Chipembere and Chiume went forward after the last passenger had disembarked and asked for the captain's confirmation that Kamuzu was not on the flight. 'Chip' then announced to the crowd that Dr Banda had not travelled on the plane. They would not believe him and people yelled that they must be allowed to search the aircraft. In the midst of the hubbub, the captain of the flight said that he would be happy if someone delegated by the crowd should search it. Some people called out for Chipembere to do it and he went through what he knew to be a mere formality.

After searching the plane Chipembere was then profoundly shaken when, on announcing that Kamuzu was not hidden inside the aircraft, he was greeted by jeers and calls of "liar". Chipembere describes what happened next,

> ... someone shouted. "Perhaps they killed him and threw his body out from the plane during flight!" Others responded: "yes they've killed him: they've killed him! Murderers! Burn their plane! Set their plane on fire!" The crowd got closer to the plane and was going to surround it, ready to burn it or smash it to pieces. At this point, we the leaders appealed to the crowd to do no damage to the plane and to keep away from it. No damage was done, but the crowd refused to move away from the plane. After persistent pleading from us most of them moved, but a group of about thirty or forty men, mostly youths, refused to move.[197]

It was Orton Chirwa who finally got that last stubbornly dangerous group to leave the vicinity of the aircraft. He suggested that the next move needed careful planning and that they were within earshot of too many whites to plan safely. He pointed to a spot well away from the plane and said they should go there and plan the next move. The young men moved where Orton had directed them and many of the crowd joined them.

Everyone was pacified eventually when Chipembere and Chiume promised to phone London and get confirmation that Kamuzu was there, alive and well. In his autobiography, Chipembere insists that they were not allowed to use any phone at the airport. They had to dash back into Blantyre to telephone London from there, return to Chileka and only then were they able to reassure the many people who were still waiting. The people then dispersed quietly; consoled with the promise that Dr Banda would arrive the next Sunday.

The press in the Federation made an enormous fuss about the disturbances the airport. In the Nyasaland Legco there was a heated debate about the chaos at Chileka, of which Chiume and Chip took full advantage to praise Banda and to attack the Federal authorities. The press and the eagerly read copies of Hansard all fed into the general excitement about Kamuzu's return and there seemed to be an even greater sense of expectation growing than there had been the week before. More people than ever appeared to be pla

---

[197] Chipembere, Ibid. p. 330.

ning to turn up at Chileka. An important factor affecting attendance on 6th July was that for most workers the monthly payday came between the two Sundays. As a result many had money to pay for travel that they had not had the previous Sunday.

When we consider the events of Sunday 29 June 1958, the first important thing to note is that they illustrated the extent and depth of the political excitement surrounding Banda's return that the young leaders of Congress had created. The events of Sunday also showed that these same young leaders had difficulty in controlling the people so aroused, and that this surge of excitement and desire for action needed to be guided carefully or it might end in chaos.

Did the party have the organisation to guide and control the excitement and the impact of the sense of impending change that they had created among the people? This was a vital question because this level of passion among the Congress supporters could not go on very much longer without their being given some sense of having achieved some tangible success.

The second important thing revealed by the events of that day was how completely out of touch Dr Banda was with the realities of the situation in Nyasaland. The leaders of Congress had not received even a hint from Kamuzu that he might not be on the plane that Sunday. When Chipembere and Chiume had phoned London to contact him they had, in fact, not been able to reach Dr Banda. They were, however, assured by whoever received their call that Kamuzu was alive and well. The Devlin Commission reported that he was addressing a meeting that day. What 'Chip' was told, when he phoned that afternoon, was that Banda was visiting friends. What is very revealing, however, is that, when finally Chipembere was able to speak to Dr Banda later that evening, Kamuzu had found the whole story amusing. Chipembere was stunned because Kamuzu "did not appear to appreciate the seriousness of the tragedy he had nearly caused."[198]

There is also a major puzzle about that afternoon, a puzzle Devlin touches on but makes no real attempt to resolve. During all the excitement and turmoil that afternoon, with the crowd threatening to burn the aircraft and Orton saving the day – what were the police doing? Devlin deals quite briefly with the events of that Sunday in one paragraph of the Report. He ends the paragraph thus

> The incident illustrates the sort of difficulties that were in store for the police. On this occasion they did not attempt to restrain the crowd by force; and Congress lead-

---

[198] Rotberg, op. cit. p. 330.

ers thereafter used it to point out the advantages of being allowed to handle the crowd themselves.[199]

Neither Devlin nor Chipembere ask why did the police remain so quiet and leave it to the Congress leaders? They were taking a terrible risk; if Orton Chirwa had not persuaded the hardcore group to move away, could the police have intervened in time to stop the plane being set alight if that group had suddenly decided to act? After all aviation fuel is highly volatile. Did whoever was in control of the police at Chileka misjudge the seriousness of the risk or did he want a serious incident to occur which would justify widespread arrests and banning orders?

Kamuzu Arrives at Last

Whatever the reason for their risky tactics on the 29th, the police were out in force the next Sunday, as were the people, in bigger numbers than ever. What is somewhat surprising, after the tension of the previous Sunday, was that the mood of the crowd on Sunday the 6th July was a happy one. Clyde Sanger of the *Manchester Guardian* reported that the people were full of what he called 'naïve cheerfulness'.[200] Without any sense of incongruity many waved the British Union Flags that had been given out at the time of the Queen Mother's visit to Nyasaland and hoarded for future use. Choirs sang and dancers danced in a fine party spirit.

Eventually the plane arrived. After all the other passengers had disembarked Kamuzu appeared at the door of the aircraft. As always he was dressed in a dark, three-piece business suit and homburg hat. He stood there and shouted the Congress slogan '*kwacha*' (dawn, the time for waking up). Descending the steps from the plane he was surrounded by leaders of Congress and the many invited guests. He was invested with a chief's cloak of civet cat skins by Mai Inkhosi Gomani, the widow of Inkosi Gomani - he who had been the most effective protester in 1953. Kamuzu's uncle, the Reverend Hanock Phiri, the same uncle who had guided him in both Southern Rhodesia and South Africa, presented him with a broom with which to sweep away the Federation.

Dr Banda, having received all the necessary formal greetings from the various dignitaries there to meet him, spoke at a short press conference. He was introduced by Chiume as a 'symbol of our desire for independence'. The Doctor spoke very briefly insisting on his mission being a peaceful one. He was then whisked off to Blantyre along the Chileka road thronged with

---

[199] Cmnd 8-14, Para 46.
[200] Clyde Sanger, *Central African Emergency*, p. 8. *The Manchester Guardian* is now *The Guardian*.

crowds of people eager to see him. He spoke again later at a rally in Soche where he was again introduced by Chiume. As at Chileka, Kamuzu emphasized he had not brought secession in his medical bag, it would have to be worked for, and again he emphasized strongly that in the struggle ahead the spear was not the weapon to be used.

Dr Banda's Relations with the Young Leaders

It is difficult to know now the details of exactly how, in those first few weeks after his arrival, Dr Banda and the leadership of Congress came to terms with each other. We do have in bare outline the activities Dr Hastings K. Banda - as most still referred to him at that time - embarked on. He paid a large number of courtesy visits to European officials. He also embarked on a rapid nation-wide speaking tour. All of this was a preparation for his 'coronation' as President General of Congress at the Nkata Bay Conference of Congress in August. He appeared at the public meetings as 'the symbol of Nyasa nationalism' as Chiume called him, the supreme leader who was going make the break through and free the people from the hated Federation.

An historian who has written much on this period presents us with a major problem about our understanding of what was going on. In his *State of Emergency*, Colin Baker writes

> Chiume made the introductory speech at Chileka in which he said Banda had come to lead them but he had come to carry out the wishes of the people, and he, like anyone else who did not follow the wishes of the people, would have to go if he did not do so. Chiume repeated the point the same day at Soche: 'Dr Banda should be our leader so long as he toes the party line.' On the evening of Banda's arrival Chiume, Chipembere, Chisiza and other Congress leaders met in secret and agreed that Banda would remain their leaders as long as he accepted their policy, but no longer.[201]

If Chiume issued this bold warning at two different public gatherings on Banda's first day in Nyasaland we would have to conclude that the leadership of Congress were publicly setting limits to the authority they were willing to grant Dr Banda. It would also appear that the master publicist, Kanyama Chiume, was altering radically the whole thrust of what hitherto had been Congress propaganda about Dr Banda and his role as the Messianic Saviour of the nation.

There is no record of any other speeches setting out such limitations on Banda's leadership being made at that time. More importantly, everyone whom I have interviewed who was present at Chileka or Soche or both has

---

[201] Colin Baker, *State of Emergency: Crisis in Central Africa, Nyasaland 1959-1960.* London, Taurus Academic Studies. 1997. p. 4.

denied that Chiume said any such thing at either place.[202] That careful reporter from what was then the *Manchester Guardian*, Clyde Sanger does not mention these remarks, neither in his book nor in the reports he filed.[203] Baker's authority for his assertion consists of a letter to him from R. Mushet, an officer of the Nyasaland Special Branch, together with the evidence that Finney, the head of Special Branch, gave to the Devlin Commission.

Baker's report raises questions, not about Chiume's attitude at the time, but about the reliability of Special Branch information. Further to the reliability of Special Branch as a source, we see that Baker's informants insist that Dunduzu Chisiza was at that evening meeting but how could he have been there when he was in Birmingham at the time? This is hardly a casual slip and further casts doubt on the accuracy of the information that the Nyasaland Special Branch was gathering.[204]

The autobiographies of Chiume and Chipembere contribute to the difficulties of knowing what went on in those first few weeks of Banda's return. They each give somewhat contradictory pictures of Dr Banda and their reactions to him in this period.

In his autobiography Kanyama Chiume insists that he and others were both amazed and depressed by some of Kamuzu's actions in those first days after his return. Chiume writes

> We had allocated him a house which had belonged to a coloured man. It was a perfectly good house and at that time one of the best that an African could occupy. But as soon as he saw it he scolded us smartly for not putting him in a white area ... he was adamant and insisted that the house *selected* was beneath his dignity. He would not eat *nsima* (stiff porridge) and he was, to all intents and purposes, a white man.[205]

Calling Dr Banda a 'white man' was not a baseless political jibe by Kanyama. In many ways Kamuzu had been so profoundly distanced from ordinary African life for so long that there was a great deal of truth in it. This was not just a matter of his inability to eat *nsima*. It can be seen in his treatment of even the brightest and most sophisticated Nyasa as if still a boy to be guided and led and not as a colleague as in his whispered coaching of Chipembere at press conferences on the latter's visit to the UK. At a less serious but still revealing level he often told European friends how, when he had to accept hospitality on those early trips into the countryside, he detested having to bathe in the usual village way, that is standing on a flat stone in a

---

[202] Interviews with Colin Cameron, Mrs Rose Chibambo, Mrs Molly Dzabala and members of the Chokani and Kahumbe families.

[203] Clyde Sanger, *Central African Emergency*, London, Heinemann, 1960.

[204] Baker makes clear that he consistently refers to Dunduzu in ways that allow no confusion with his brother Yatuta.

[205] M.W. Kanyama Chiume, *Kwacha: an Autobiography*. pp. 90-91.

tiny reed enclosure and pouring hot water over himself from a basin. In other similar stories, he suggested to European friends that these trips were part of the sacrifice he was prepared to make for the struggle![206] Strangely, after these complaints about his being a white man, Chiume goes on to say "in fairness to him, however, he was very extreme in his statements right from the first meeting."

Chipembere, in his autobiography, makes no mention of the issue of housing or of Kamuzu's refusal to eat *nsima* and so on, although he does complain of Kamuzu's too friendly relations with Europeans officials. Elsewhere in essays and interviews published in the late 1960s and early 1970s Chipembere did, however, complain about Dr Banda in similar terms to those of Chiume, indeed some of his accusations are more damning than Kanyama's.[207] More important, however, is that Chipembere specifically contradicts Chiume's assertion of the radicalism of Dr Banda's early speeches.

Initial Disappointment with Dr Banda's Message

In contrast with Chiume's assertion, Chipembere describes, in his autobiography, the prolonged struggle he and other leaders had to undertake to wean Dr Banda away from the very moderate tone and content of his early speeches. They also felt that they had to persuade him to drop what in their view was his far too conciliatory and friendly attitude to the Protectorate's administrators and to Europeans in general. 'Chip' devotes several pages in his autobiography describing this campaign in some detail.

Far from being 'radical from the beginning', Chiume's words, a moderate 'British gentleman and physician' was certainly the image that Banda presented on arriving in Nyasaland. This is reflected in reports by many observers other than Chipembere. For example, soon after Kamuzu's arrival, his presence in Nyasaland was welcomed by the *Nyasaland Times* as well as by many senior members of the Protectorate administration. The *Nyasaland Times* gleefully trumpeted of Kamuzu that "It seems the extremists have got it all wrong".

Until the eve of the Nkhata Bay conference, it would appear that Kamuzu's relations with many in the administration were very cordial. Indeed there is evidence that Dr Banda was more able to express his feelings openly to some European administrators than he was to any of his colleagues in Congress. A classic example is his remarks to M. Harris, the District Commissioner at Kasungu when dining at the DC's house during his first nation-wide tour.

---

[206] Conversations with the late Fergus Macpherson, a close friend of Dr Banda's from 1938.
[207] For example, Chipembere, 'Malawi in Crisis' in *Ufahamu*, Vol. I, No 2, 1970.

That evening Kamuzu confided to Harris that he was dismayed by the low level of development in Nyasaland and went on to exclaim "what am I to do?"[208] This story is in keeping with his completely unnecessary whispered coaching of Chipembere in the meeting with Lennox-Boyd we have already noted.

The first thing that had to be changed in Chip's view, was the large number of courtesy calls Dr Banda was paying on a wide circle of European officials. This was vital because, in the eyes of many, in particular Mikeka Mkandawire, J. (Stenning) Msiska and the well-organised youth movement in Blantyre, this behaviour was utterly bewildering. It also gave some credence to those, and they were not just a few, who had questioned the decision to invite Kamuzu to return.

Chipembere and Kumtumanji met formally with Kamuzu over this issue and insisted that, for the dignity of Congress, he should only pay such formal calls on really senior and important British officials. Chip comments

> Banda exploded and made thinly-veiled remarks indicating that what I said was a sign that I was uncivilized, a type of remark which those of us who were close to him quickly found to be his favourite way of embarrassing into silence any African who criticized him.[209]

Banda took the point, however, and from then only met with senior officials when serious business demanded it.

The next task that Chip set about was the essential one of changing the tone and content of Kamuzu's speeches. At the first few formal rallies on the Protectorate-wide speaking tour, Kamuzu spoke first and was then followed by others who were to support what he had said. Early on this tour Kamuzu made a speech at Chief Kuntaja's similar to that which he had made at Chileka. In the speech he again emphasized his coming to build bridges between the races. When he finished to comparatively tepid applause, Chipembere then spoke. He first called on all Nyasas to drop all loyalties except that to Kamuzu as 'Leader of the Nation' and then launched into a very fiery speech. He fiercely attacked the administration, the settlers and African stooges. He sat down to massive applause. Kamuzu then significantly broke with the arranged programme and decided to speak again and this time his radical challenge to white rule brought enthusiastic response from his audience. In his autobiography Chip goes on

> This sort of occurrence took place at several meetings and rallies thereafter. ...
> Banda, in his craving for popularity and to avoid our stealing the show from him, as

---

[208] Colin Baker, *The Revolt of the Ministers*, London, I.B. Tauris, 2001, pp. 4-5.
[209] Chipembere, *Hero of the Nation*, p. 335.

well as to gain the support he needed to fulfil his mission of leading us to self-rule, found himself steadily and increasingly following the line of the radicals.[210]

Chipembere also insists that criticisms of Kamuzu by white Federal politicians and by conservative Africans drew angry reactions from Banda and helped speed the process of change. The result was that again and again Kamuzu would re-iterate and re-emphasize the very points to which his critics objected. Thus Kamuzu's bitter reaction to criticism shaped what he said and how he said it rather than his having a clear planned style and content for his speeches at that time.

These experiences did soon shape a clear style and firm pattern of content to his speeches however. It was a very rigid pattern covering a limited range of ideas that were repeated again and again, almost like a liturgy. Indeed Kamuzu himself later admitted that in the period before he was arrested, he only made four speeches or rather he declaimed one or other of only four speeches depending on the situation. In many ways the content of his four alternative speeches was not so very extreme but increasingly his style of oratory was – witness his famous remarks in a speech in Blantyre three months after his return – "When I die, remember my words - carry on my work - when I am dead my spirit will carry on the fight from hell or from heaven". This was potent stuff to an audience the overwhelming majority of whom were Christians but for whom the ancestors were a living part of reality.

However, in those first weeks Banda did not speak only at rallies. Whenever he travelled, if people had gathered at a roadside to see him pass he would stop and speak with them for a few minutes even if this led to his being late for appointments. Indeed this became a striking feature of these first months in Nyasaland.[211] It not only confirmed the special popular status he had been given and was now fulfilling but fed into it and developed it further. At the end of those first four months Chipembere rightly judged that their campaign to create a new level of popular political activity around Banda as national hero had succeeded beyond their hopes and expectations.

The Nkhata Bay Conference

The Nkhata Bay Conference of Congress was like a coronation. There was a real change in the authority of the President of Congress. Not only was Kamuzu elected as President by acclamation, but Congress decided that the President General should have new authority over the membership of the

---

[210] Ibid. pp. 337-38.

[211] These spontaneous chats with people at the roadside ceased to be a feature of his behaviour even before 'Operation Sunrise'.

Congress Executive. We have seen that previously when each member of the Congress executive was individually elected this had led to whoever was elected President being saddled with an executive containing some of his most bitter rivals. At the time of T.D.T. Banda's election, he had been given the right to co-opt additional members of his own choice to the Executive. This was done to help give the President more power and authority within the Executive and help it have the kind of central direction it had so often lacked in the past.

At Nkhata Bay it was decided that the new President should choose all the new members of the Executive committee himself and simply have his choices confirmed by Conference. This dramatically increased the power of the President and meant that Kamuzu had effective power over the movement that no previous president had had.

The Devlin Commission Report, Short in his biography of Dr Banda and Colin Baker in his *State of Emergency* and in his *Revolt of the Ministers*, all list the new office-bearers chosen by Banda as Chipembere, Treasurer; Chiume, Publicity Secretary; Dunduzu Chisiza, Secretary; Lali Lubani and Lawrence Makata as members of the executive together with a new initiative, the appointment of Mrs Rose Chibambo as the first woman member of the Executive. Mrs Chibambo was appointed to create and lead the new Women's League of the Nyasaland African Congress.[212]

These writers, along with most other commentators writing about that conference, have not noted the significant error in this listing. Dunduzu Chisiza was not appointed Secretary General at the conference, Kamuzu forbade the appointment.[213] Initially Kamuzu had agreed to Du's appointment, but withdrew his approval when some European friends had written to him saying that Dunduzu was too stubborn and conceited 'to be a loyal assistant'!

Chip, in his biography, emphasizes the story of Dunduzu's rejection and writes that Chiume 'was inclined' to agree with Banda. It was only some weeks after the Conference, when Chiume was out of the country, that Chip worked on Banda, pleading that the central office of Congress was in serious need of an effective leader.[214] Kamuzu gave way to Chipembere's plea and only then was Dunduzu recalled from the UK to become Secretary-General of Congress.

---

212 As we have seen she was already head of a women's movement she had begun five years earlier.

213 Chipembere, *Hero of the Nation*, pp. 354-55.

214 Chipembere, *Hero of the Nation*, pp. 354-55.

It is only in Chipembere's autobiography that we have a full exploration of the serious difficulties and tensions that erupted at Nkhata Bay at the time of the Conference and almost caused it to break up. Afterwards in the general euphoria of that time no one wanted to recall the crisis that had erupted at the conference.

At the 1957 Conference in Blantyre, the arrangements for feeding and housing delegates had not been the best and Chiume and the Nkhata Bay delegates offered to house the 1958 Conference and promised to do a better job than had been done in Blantyre. By the time August 1958 came round, however, things had changed. Nkhata Bay district, as Kamuzu himself said 'had the reputation of being the most politically conscious in Nyasaland'.[215] Their local hero was, however, T.D.T. Banda and by August 1958 the people of Nkhata Bay were furious with the leadership of Congress about the way they had treated 'T.D.T.'. They decided to boycott the conference. So instead of receiving the promised outstanding care, the majority of the delegates had to live on *phala* (thin porridge) and little else during the conference.

What happened was that Chiume had kept the people of Usisya and Chikwina on side, but the rest of the district, about 80% of the population, were solid in their boycott of the Conference despite the excitement about Kamuzu's return. Chipembere reports what happened thus:

> Many delegates felt that it might be wise to adopt a conciliatory attitude to the dissidents, but Chiume and his supporters regarded this as a confrontation. Any attempt at reconciliation was unacceptable humiliation. He was able to convince Dr Banda that the dissidents were irrational and hostile and to arrange for Dr Banda to refuse to meet Chief Mankhambira and other prominent Nkhata Bay men who had come to greet Dr Banda in order to explain why they were boycotting the conference and to assure him of their support for him as an individual. [*It was the young leaders with whom they were furious because of their conduct towards T.D.T.*][216]

'Chip' went on to insist that, unfortunately, Kamuzu was easily convinced by Chiume that the dissidents were being tribalists, conveniently omitting the whole issue of the treatment that had been handed out to T.D.T. Banda. Living at Chikwina, Chiume's home several miles to the north-west of Nkhata Bay, Banda was cut of from the membership of the Conference.

The delegates, who were constantly hungry, came to know that the possibility of reconciliation with the Nkhata Bay folk had been blocked by Chiume and their anger then focussed on him. Chipembere describes what happened in great detail because he believed that it explains why, from that time, Kanyama Chiume became unpopular among top and 'medium level' leaders

[215] Donald Brody *Conversations with Kamuzu*, Part 11, put on web December 2000.

[216] Chipembere, *Hero of the Nation*, pp. 351-52. Comment in italics is the present writer's.

in Congress in all three Regions. Kanyama's notorious brusqueness with people, hitherto overlooked because of his outstanding abilities, now began to annoy many.

Dr Banda's Attempts to Pursue his Medical Practice

After returning from the Nkhata Bay conference, Dr Banda worked hard at getting his medical practice going. He had both found a suitable building and also engaged staff before he left for the conference. Among those recruits was Cecilia Kadzamira, later to become first his secretary, then his 'official hostess' and eventually Mama Tamanda Kadzamira, whose name Kamuzu would join with his own as if his wife. An outstanding example of this way of speaking of Amai Kadzamira occurred when the *Daily Times* reported Kamuzu saying, on the occasion of Orton Chirwa's death, 'Mama and I were very sad'.[217]

Cecilia Kadzamira was the maternal niece of John Tembo. Tembo was one of the graduates recently returned to Nyasaland, but he was a fringe player at that time, not one of the inner circles around Chipembere, Chiume or the Chisizas.

Kamuzu began to work hard at his practice and restricted his public speaking engagements to the week-ends only. It is not clear how he came to think his practice could make him much money. What could be called the African middle-class was tiny at that time and in the situation of Nyasaland in the last months of 1958 who else, who could afford fees, was going to use his in practice?

Dr Banda did, however, persevere with his practice and continued to restrict his speaking engagements to the week-ends. He only accepted engagements during the week if these were necessary meetings with the Governor or other senior officials in Zomba. Clearly in this period the day to day running of Congress was in the hands of the Executive and not the week-ends only leader.

The Clock Tower Incident

It was, however, the aftermath of one of these Sunday engagements which provoked the *Nyasaland Times* and the settler politicians into an extreme, almost hysterical reaction. For them and many other Europeans the events surrounding a Sunday speech by Banda was a turning-point and the political atmosphere in Nyasaland was dramatically and decisively changed.

---

[217] *Daily Times*, 6 Dec. 1992.

On 26th October 1958 the Blantyre branch of the NAC called what Chipembere refers to as 'a routine district public meeting'[218] at the market. Dr Banda was not able to address it because he was suffering his first attack of malaria since his return. When Chipembere, who was to stand in for the Doctor, saw the enormous crowd that had gathered, he decided that Banda had to be there, he believed that he was not up to carrying off the meeting by himself. He writes in his autobiography that he told Chester Katsonga, the District chairman

> I would go and ask Banda to come, at least to say a few words. Banda was happy at this frank admission on my part that there were situations which he alone could handle adequately.[219]

Banda agreed and came to the market. He was unwell and even more emotional than usual. The content of his speech was not itself unusual, his denunciation of the Federation and of colonial rule was routine enough, the speech was delivered, however, with such emotion and passion that the crowd was wild with excitement. Despite the high state of excitement, however, the meeting itself passed off without incident.

Afterwards a number of people gathered at the Blantyre clock tower to get their buses home. As Devlin later commented, it was Sunday and no special transport arrangements had been made so many had to wait a long time. There was some jeering of passing European motorists, then for a period of about ten minutes stones were thrown at passing cars driven by Europeans. Two European women were slightly injured as a result.

The reaction in the main European community was astonishingly powerful. The *Nyasaland Times* launched a sustained attack on the Nyasaland Government. This has been well summed up by Lord Devlin

> The Nyasaland Times reported the incident in lurid language. It referred to "mob law", to "two hours of threatening violence when no European or Asian was safe to walk the streets or drive past in a car", and to Africans "stretching across the road like a black tidal wave". The editorial described the incident as "a raw display of racial hatred without parallel in this country" and demanded to know why the Riot Act had not been read.[220]

A series of bitter editorials followed in the next couple of weeks continuing the attack on the government of the Protectorate over its inaction. These editorials pitched things in desperately emotional terms

---

[218] Chipembere, *Hero of the Nation*, p. 341
[219] Ibid.
[220] Cmnd. 314, p. 29.

> If women, of any race, cannot travel around Nyasaland without harm, then we will descend into savagery. The despicable act of injuring those two women deserved swift retaliation, without second thought.[221]

There were even calls for the federalisation of the police which only confirmed the suspicions and fear of the Nyasa people about the intentions of the Federal Government.

The reason for this reaction was that for some weeks across the Southern Region many Europeans had felt a surge of anger from among the Nyasa people that upset them and threatened their sense of the proper order of things. The comparatively minor incident that Sunday at the clock tower in Blantyre served to focus their growing sense of unease and recognition that Congress had created a critical situation in Nyasaland in terms of who ruled the country.

The complaints by the *Nyasaland Times* and settler politicians about lack of concern and action by the Administration were nonsense because the Intelligence Committee of the Nyasaland Government, in conjunction with the Federal government, was already making preparations for action. Obviously the general public white and black could not be informed of this. Already, three weeks before the clock tower incident took place, after a meeting of the Intelligence Committee on October 7th 1958, T.R. Wade, the Federal liaison officer present reported to his boss in Salisbury

> Government considered it advisable to hit Congress with all possible provocative measures in order to force Banda into taking some unconstitutional action.[222]

In the same letter, Wade reported that the Nyasaland Government was contemplating deposing all pro-Congress chiefs in the Southern and Central Regions but would take no action in the NorthernRegion, since all the chiefs there were anti-Federation and pro-Congress.[223]

How Strong was Congress in October 1958?

It is at this point when senior officials of the Nyasaland Administration admitted that they were no longer confident about the effectiveness of their authority in the Northern Region, that it is convenient to review the situation in each of the three regions of Nyasaland.

Much of the writing about this conflict as it developed in the second half of 1958 reflects what is going on in the Southern Province rather than the whole country. Because the Congress members of the Legislative Council

---

[221] Ibid.

[222] Quoted in Colin Baker, *State of Emergency.* p. 6.

[223] Ibid.

had created such a stir in Zomba and in front of the eyes of the settler population, the overwhelming majority of whom were in the south, the history of what went on in the South has been seen, too often, as the history of the country. This tendency has been encouraged by the concentration on the South by the Nyasaland Administration which is illustrated starkly by the pattern of the deployment of their security forces. It is astonishing to note that in 1953 there were only seventy members of the Nyasaland Police in the whole of the Northern Region and even in February 1959, on the eve of the Declaration of a State of Emergency there were only 128, less than a tenth of the establishment of the Nyasaland Police.

In contrast with the Administration's concentration on the South, it was in the Northern Region that the most startling growth of Congress had taken place in the years of revival after 1953. By October 1958 the growth in the number of new branches of Congress founded in the North had outstripped the number of branches in the other two regions combined. 48 branches had registered in the North compared with only fifteen in the rest of the country

It was also in the North that the vast majority of acts of open opposition to the Government took place. Acts of defiance of government authority had not disappeared in the North after 1953 as they had done in the South and Centre. The implementation of the agricultural rules had always been unpopular in the North and provided ample opportunity for creating disorder. This had been sporadic and unorganised until the return of Flaxon Musopole to Nyasaland from South Africa in 1955. Unlike the other young men returning to Nyasaland at this time, Musopole had not attended university but had been deeply involved in the Defiance Campaign in South Africa. He had also been influenced by the South African Communist Party which had played such an important role in that campaign.[224]

On his return Musopole soon began to organise acts of deliberate disobedience to the Government across the whole Region and he also deeply influenced the attitudes of the new branches of Congress that were springing up. It has to be noted, however, that most of these branches were founded by either Kanyama Chiume or Dunduzu Chisiza. These two, however, had to spend a great deal of time in Blantyre and Zomba. In contrast Musopole concentrated his activities in the North, rarely leaving the Region. His popularity grew considerably both within Congress branches and among the people of the North in general. His Defiance Campaign experience in South

---

[224] Flaxon Musopole's importance was ignored or unknown to most students of the period until the publication of John McCracken's seminal article 'The Ambiguities of Nationalism: Flaxon Musopole and the Northern Factor in Malawi Politics, c. 1956-1966' in *Journal of Southern African History*, Vol. 28, No 1, March 2002.

Africa when brought to bear on the problems of his homeland created a harder edge to the rural disobedience in the North than the Boma experienced elsewhere.

In the Southern Region the growth of the influence of Congress in this period was strong and consistent, though the leaders were still unable to translate this influence into as many formal branches of the organisation as they would have liked. However, the growing influence of Congress upon the people at large was already causing apprehension, as the columns of the *Nyasaland Times* showed. It was in the urban areas of Blantyre/Limbe and of Zomba that Congress was at its strongest in the Region. In Blantyre the long established 'Youth Wing' and Rose Chibambo's 'Women's Wing', established several years before Dr Banda appointed her to create a national movement, had strength not only in numbers but also in the quality of the members of these organisations. Formal Congress organisation, however, was still almost completely lacking in the Fort Johnston area and in the Lower Shire.

As in the past, however, outside Ntcheu and Lilongwe where Congress was strong and to a lesser degree Kasungu, it was the absence rather than the presence or the influence of Congress in the Central Region that was to be noted. A greater degree of rural prosperity in some parts of the Region compared with conditions in the South and North was perhaps a factor in this situation. As we shall see, people in the Central Region could be roused to active opposition to government, but until 1959, these incidents only occurred when one of the national leaders was speaking on a visit to a particular district in the region.

The Inevitability of a Showdown between Boma and Congress

The Nyasaland Government began to prepare for decisive action against Congress soon after Kamuzu's return when it became clear that he was not going to 'tame the Young Turks' but rather continue to lead Congress along the path the young men had already laid out. Senior officials in government anticipated that the critical time might well be in the middle weeks of 1959. The new head of the Nyasaland Police Special Branch, Philip Finney, who had arrived in Nyasaland only in September, had, as one of his first jobs, to revise the lists of those who were to be arrested in the event of the declaration of a State of Emergency. At the same time a review was undertaken on what preparations were required to accommodate a large number of prisoners should it become necessary to declare a State of Emergency. It is interesting to note that a preliminary review of those needs had been carried out as early as July of 1958

These were confidential matters. What was public and deliberately so, was the arrival in Nyasaland in the middle of September, 1958, of a 500 strong detachment of the all-white Royal Rhodesia Regiment. The visit was stated to be one of those routine exercises that troops must go through to be ready for any of the many tasks they might be called on to perform. Commentators at the time saw it as a gesture to the white voters in Nyasaland before the upcoming Federal elections scheduled for 12 November that year.

It was also intended by Welensky to say something to Nyasas. It did - confirming their worst suspicions of the Federal Government. These fears were further confirmed by a Nyasaland Government statement of 10th November stating that the Nyasaland Government was determined

> To maintain law and order throughout the Protectorate and to deal firmly and effectively with those who disturb the public tranquillity ... in addition to its own police force the Government has, as the Federal Prime Minister recently observed, the resources of the Federation behind it. It would make full use of those forces should the need arise.[225]

Meanwhile Congress continued to prosecute its policy of challenging the authority of the Nyasaland Government. Dr Banda did not in any speech call on people to disobey the Government agricultural or forestry rules, but the high pitch of excitement his rhetoric produced needed an outlet. Since the pattern of disobedience challenging the authority of both Government and those chiefs who supported it in this area was already going on, Kamuzu's speeches, where the administration of the agricultural and forestry rules were regularly condemned, stimulated an expansion of these conflicts.

The campaign of disobedience also began to take on an added urban dimension. In Zomba and Blantyre crowds gathered to greet Dr Banda as he passed by, usually in connection with his meetings with senior officials. While still waiting to see the Doctor pass by, if ordered to disperse, they refused and conflicts with the police ensued. Groups of women deliberately challenged the police on a regular basis in those situations.

The aim of the leadership of Congress was to bring about one or other of two alternative situations. One was to force the Nyasaland Government to concede to the demand for an African majority in the Legislative Council and perhaps even the Executive Council although Dr Banda, at least, hinted at flexibility on that issue. How far Chipembere, Chiume and Chisiza were aware of that willingness is not clear. It did not matter because a clear African majority in the Legislative Council alone would enable a vote for secession from the Federation to be passed. At that point the Federation issue would be re-opened in British politics.

---

225 *Nyasaland Times* 11 November, 1958.

If these changes were not forthcoming in time for the Review Conference, then the intention was to force the Boma to take such repressive action against Congress as would cause a crisis for all three governments, Federal, Nyasaland and British. At that point, as in the first instance, the strong lobby in Britain which had consistently insisted that Nyasaland should never have been included in the Federation against the wishes of its people, would then go into action. Federation and the possibility of secession from it would be a major issue in British politics whichever way things went.

It was, after all, only through the action of the British government that Nyasaland's secession from the Federation could be achieved. The British Government had to be brought to the point that it saw Nyasaland's secession from the Federation as a solution to its problems.

All African People's Conference

On the 1st of December Dr Banda went off to Accra to attend the All African People's Conference hosted by his old friend, Kwame Nkrumah. Kamuzu had not wanted to go. It is not clear why, but it was not because relations between Nkrumah and Dr Banda were bad as many have suggested. As we have seen relations between the two while Kamuzu had been living at Kumasi had been close.[226] It was decided that Kanyama Chiume should go as the Nyasaland delegate. However, entreaties from Kojo Botsio, the Ghanaian Foreign Minister finally persuaded Dr Banda to attend as well.

At the Conference Dr Banda in no way courted publicity and let Chiume hold centre stage as far as Nyasaland was concerned. When asked to join the Conference Steering Committee he refused saying that he had far too much to do at home to have the time to do the work that membership of the committee required. Neither did he attend many of the sessions of the conference, saying to friends that the routine bored him. Some have said rather that he was upset by not being given his due as an important leader by the delegates. This can hardly be so among the leaders at least, since they asked him to join the Conference Steering Committee

One thing he did pick up on at the Conference was the widespread assertion by so many speakers that the way ahead was along the path of non-violent resistance, of going to prison as non-violent martyrs. It was being widely discussed and touted as the most effective revolutionary technique. Dr Kiano of Kenya made a powerful speech extolling the ideological rightness, the moral value and the effectiveness of non-violent but radical resistance to colonial authorities. Kenneth Kaunda and Joshua Nkomo were both at the

---

[226] See Chapter 4.

Conference and they insisted that their parties were going to adopt this policy. Short, in his biography of Dr Banda, asserts that it was at the Conference that Kamuzu, reflecting on the situation in Nyasaland, decided that negotiations alone would not be enough to achieve his aims. The Governor and the Secretary of State for the Colonies in London would not agree to an African majority in the Legislative Council and the Executive so that secession from the Federation would become possible. More direct action would have to be taken, non-violent of course, but on a scale to threaten the Boma's ability to rule. It would appear also according to Baker's analysis of the thinking of Armitage's senior officials that they, like Philip Short, appeared also to think that Banda's return from Accra marked the major shift to direct action on the part of Congress.[227]

It is more accurate, rather, to see it as decisive change in Dr Banda's thinking, though as we shall consider shortly, his experience in Salisbury on his return journey possibly had more to do with this change than any pondering he might have done in Accra. As far as the young leaders of Congress and the membership of Congress across the country were concerned the direct challenge to the Boma's authority was something they had already undertaken and in the North particularly, had been pursuing for some time.

Dr Banda's Return from Accra

On his way back from Accra, Dr Banda had to change planes in Salisbury. There he discovered that the Nyasaland Government had made arrangements to prevent him flying to Blantyre until Monday. This was to prevent crowds gathering to receive him as they would have done had he arrived on the Sunday. His displeasure turned to furious anger when, at the airport, he was treated like a criminal. His person as well as his luggage were searched while he was detained in the terminal building for over an hour.

The next day, Sunday, he gave a speech in Highlands, one of the Salisbury townships. This was an extraordinary affair which had a wide impact on the African population of the Federal capital, not just the Nyasa *machona* of whom there were many but local people also, maShona and amaNdebele.[228] Clyde Sanger, a British newspaper reporter, who was at the meeting commented that his speech "was a more virile rallying-call than the Mashona and Matabele [*sic*] had heard in sixty years" - a reference to the first Chimurenga. In some ways this was Dr Banda's most famous speech and one that aroused African nationalist feelings to a high level of excitement in the Federal capital itself. It certainly hit the headlines in the local press and

[227]   Baker, *State of Emergency*, pp. 11-12.
[228]   Sanger, *Central African Emergency*, pp. 243-44.

annoyed intensely the Southern Rhodesian and Federal Prime Ministers. Banda's rhetoric was passionate

> To Hell with Federation ... They can do what they like to me. They can send me to prison. They can kill me. I will never give up the fight for freedom. If I die, my ghost will fight it from the grave ... We have to be prepared to go to prison, let us fill their prisons with our thousands, singing Hallelujah ... If they send me to prison, I do not mind. They can put me on the Seychelles like Makarios, or on St Helena like Napoleon. I am prepared for anything even death.

He went on to warn his audience that unless they followed his lead they would end up sharing the fate of their brothers and sisters in South Africa. Part of his peroration was to insist that 'throughout the history of the world there is no incident where a so-called moderate has achieved anything'. Where now was the man who had come 'to bridge the gulf between the races' of whom Chipembere complained?

This exciting experience in Highlands continued into the next day. Enormous crowds gathered in the township to see him leave for the airport. That morning he appeared to receive adulation surpassing the enthusiastic reception that he received regularly in Nyasaland. Young women, as he was leaving, were said to have hurled themselves onto his car to kiss it. The 'high' that Kamuzu had created during that week-end survived the journey north. In a number of speeches in the next few weeks, he re-iterated his call to people to be ready to march into prison in their thousands singing Hallelujah. He again and again emphasized his readiness to go to gaol.

At this very same time, the last week of December 1958 and the first couple of weeks of January 1959, a deadline, the 28th February, was set by the Governor for the completion of detailed planning of the facilities to hold hundreds of detainees, for the stockpiling of barbed wire and poles and the completion of basic non-secret work needed to prepare for the construction of the camps.

Dr Banda and senior Boma officials continued to meet to discuss constitutional advance. These meetings were, as they had been for some time, an almost meaningless charade. The Colonial Office and the Governor were determined not to make changes that would enable a Nyasaland Legislative Assembly to pass a vote of secession from the Federation, and the Nyasaland African Congress could settle for nothing less. An African majority in Legco was the unshakeable bedrock of Kamuzu's proposals and was never negotiable. An African majority in the Legislative Council is exactly what the Governor could not concede because 'we might vote ourselves out of [the] Federation.'[229]

---

[229] Baker, *State of Emergency*, p. 14

In the literature discussing these few months of the history of Nyasaland there is much detailed analysis of the possibilities of compromise. Pages have been written discussing what hints of concession Banda might have given at this meeting or that, and what the Governor, or his senior officials thought what deal could be agreed to. At times Armitage appears to believe that some kind of constitutional compromise could be reached and was disappointed when Lennox-Boyd failed to come to the Protectorate for further discussions on the topic. He then appeared to lay much store on a projected visit by Lord Perth, Minister of State in the Colonial Office.

All of this appears, in retrospect, to have been little more than a game. Armitage was clear that no constitutional arrangement that would enable a vote for secession to pass could be allowed; but this was the very least that Congress wanted. What the various meetings and discussions achieved was time for Armitage to press on with the preparations for the declaration of a State of Emergency.

Federation-wide support for this course of action was worked out at a Conference beginning on 20th February. The day before Armitage decided to ask for the 1st Battalion of the King's African Rifles plus platoons of the Northern Rhodesian Police Mobile Force to be sent to the Northern Region to restore the authority of the Boma there. On the 20th February Armitage met with Dalhousie, the Governor-General of the Federation, Roy Welensky and Malcolm Barrow, the Prime Minister and Deputy Prime Minister of the Federation, the Governor of Northern Rhodesia, Arthur Benson and Edgar Whitehead, Prime Minister of Southern Rhodesia. As Armitage informed the Colonial Office he left the meeting assured of their support in terms of troops and police.

We have seen that Dr Banda, after his initial nationwide speaking tour, settled into a rather strange routine for the leader of a national movement. He worked at his medical practice during the week, allowing no Congress work to intervene apart from his visits to Zomba to continue these fruitless discussions with the Governor or his deputy on constitutional reform. He conducted these negotiations on his own, for the most part. He travelled to address Congress rallies and make major speeches only at the week-end. It is clear then that the day-to-day administration of the activities of the Nyasaland African Congress was something he left to others.

Again and again in books like Short's biography, *Banda*, Baker's *State of Emergency*, Wood's *The Welensky Papers* and others, the writers refer to Dr Banda's reorganisation of the Congress; the implication is that he worked at reorganising the structure, policy and workings of the Congress and its branches across the country. He did not do any such thing. He appointed the new executive after the Nkhata Bay Conference and it was these men and Rose Chibambo who ran Congress and oversaw its growth and its activities.

They continued their propaganda blitz promising that a new day was about to dawn because of the return of the Doctor. The impact of Kamuzu's speeches was a very important element in keeping the people on a high level of excitement but it was they, not he, who ran the party on a day to day, week to week basis. Dr Banda made no attempt to hide this reality at the time. His life-style made it self-evident who was running the machinery of Congress.

New Pressures on the Governor

In response to the continued and growing public disorder, the Governor had by mid January decided on his course of action. While getting the preliminary planning for the declaration of a State of Emergency underway, Armitage had reviewed the various options open to him including deportations and the use of criminal charges brought through the courts. At the beginning of the year he finally decided on the declaration of a State of Emergency as the most effective way of dealing with Congress. As we have seen, he had on the 20th February confirmed that the necessary reinforcements of troops and police would be available to him from the other three governments within the Federation. All that was left was to decide when everything could be got ready to house the numbers of people that would be arrested. The Governor had set the 28th February as the deadline for the basic preparations for detention centres to be completed. The day set for the sweep up and into detention of the core membership of Congress could only then come in March at the earliest.

Meanwhile, since he appeared to be negotiating seriously with Kamuzu, there was increasing pressure from within the European community in Nyasaland on the Government to act decisively. This had started after the so-called 'Clock Tower' incident and had gained in intensity as a result of the increase in confrontation between the Nyasa people and the Boma. We have seen that active challenges to the Boma had been going on for months before Kamuzu's return, particularly in the North. The tempo of these challenges to authority increased rapidly in the first two months of 1959.

The usual pattern was for people to be arrested for breaking agricultural, forestry or veterinary rules and then for more people to gather and threaten the chief's courts where the protesters were being tried or even the police stations where they were held. The police had had, on a few occasions, to bring in the army who felt they had no recourse but to open fire.

Typical of these occasions was what took place at Chief Chigaru's Court. The District Commissioner, who had read the Riot Act to no avail, would have preferred to use a police baton charge to disperse the crowd but the police had no riot type batons. As a result the DC had had to hand over the problem to the Army who had opened fire briefly and one person died as a result. This incident is a classic example of how the past traditions of policing in Nyasaland were completely unprepared for the new relationship between the people and the Boma that the imposition of the Federation on the country had created. In keeping with Nyasaland's traditions the police at Chigaru's court had no riot gear!

So many Europeans in Nyasaland felt that the Government was not doing enough that real pressure was put on the Governor and his administration. Alarmed Europeans wanted immediate and drastic action not just to crush the anti-Boma actions of people but to do something to contain the fundamental change in African attitudes towards European rule and Europeans of which they were becoming increasingly aware.

The Forgotten Leader

This pattern of regular local challenges to the authority of the Boma increased in number and frequency in all three Regions in January and February of 1959. In the Northern Region where the majority of such incidents had taken place over the previous three years, this increased activity was the continuation of a planned process, not planned by the executive of Congress but by Flax Musopole. The effectiveness of his activities in the North is exemplified by the way he had already pushed the growth of Congress membership in Karonga from a mere 200 at the end of 1957 to 2,200 by the time of Dr Banda's return to Nyasaland. Across the Region he had organised such a pattern of confrontations with the Boma that, as we have seen, officials in Zomba recognized that they were barely holding on to a semblance of ruling the Northern Region. In the light of this it is extraordinary that it has been suggested that it was only in 1959 as a result of a message from Dunduzu Chisiza that trouble broke out in Karonga district.[230]

In February 1959 under Musopole's leadership the level of the already widespread opposition to the Boma was raised dramatically. Serious rioting took place in many areas of the North from the 8th February onwards. There were two particularly startling actions taken at Musopole's instigation - first Karonga and its airfield were temporarily taken over by a crowd of about six hundred people on 19th February and the next day the airfield at Fort Hill was also removed from Government control. These dramatic events were the

---

Baker, *Emergency*, pp. 24-5.

next stage in the plan to make the North ungovernable. A programme which had been dramatically signalled by Musopole's brilliant show of defiance of the Boma when Dr Banda came to speak in the Misuku Hills at the end of 1958. In a deliberate and very specific gesture of rejection of Government authority Musopole had all the hills surrounding Banda's meeting ablaze with bush fires. In many ways it was Musopole that was 'setting Nyasaland on fire'; Dr Banda's favourite description of what he was doing at that time. Certainly by the end of February 1959 the Government of Nyasaland had either to accept it no longer ruled the Northern Region or take drastic action to restore its authority there.

The 'Bush' Conference and the 'Massacre Plot'

As the Governor was finishing his preparations to declare a State of Emergency, he and his senior officials began to receive reports from the Special Branch of a plot to systematically murder the European population of Nyasaland. This plot had been said to have been hatched at the January emergency meeting of Congress. Information about this plot was being pieced together from scattered pieces of intelligence that had been collected about what had gone on at the 'Bush' conference. The story of this 'Massacre Plot' then became a very highly effective propaganda justification of the declaration of the State of Emergency. It was so used though the State of Emergency had been planned to take place weeks before any word of a massacre plot reached agents of the Nyasaland Government.

The one matter agreed by all sides in any discussion of the Massacre plot is that Congress did call an extraordinary National Conference to meet in Blantyre/Limbe on the week-end of the 24th and 25th January 1959. What is in dispute is why it was called and what was decided at the various sessions of the Conference.

In the weeks that followed the Conference the Nyasaland Police Special Branch pieced together fragments of information from a number of informants. It is important to note that none of these informants had been at the meetings so that their reports were already second-hand. However, the reports were sufficient for the senior security officials to conclude that Congress had planned a campaign of violence against Europeans and Asians on a large scale in the event of the assassination or arrest of Dr Banda. By 18th of February the Commissioner of Police reported to the Governor that:

> The Nyasaland African Congress has prepared plans for the mass murder throughout the Protectorate of all ... Europeans and Asians, men, women and children, to take place in the event of Dr. Banda being killed, arrested or abducted.[231]

---

[231] Quoted in Baker. *State of Emergency*. p. 19.

A much more detailed version of the plot can be found in Sir Roy Welensky's *4000 Days*.[232] He gives there the full-blown version that was much publicised in the British press and elsewhere after the State of Emergency was declared. In this version it was said that after Banda was assassinated or arrested the leadership would be taken over by a committee consisting of Chipembere, Chiume, Dunduzu Chisiza and Rose Chibambo.[233] They were to fix a day – R Day – when the violence was to begin which was to be a fortnight or so after Banda's death or arrest. In the interval the leadership were to recruit murderers and other thugs to do much of the killing. The district chairman of each district of Congress was to be responsible for organising the murders of the white officials in the district. The Zomba committee of Congress was to organize the murder of the Governor and senior officials there. European and Asian women and children were to be killed, their bodies mutilated ... on and on the details went.[234]

It would appear that the atmosphere of almost hysterical complaint in the European community in the Southern Region about the threat from Congress had communicated itself to the Congress leadership. Chipembere in *Hero of the Nation* suggests that the loose talk among some Europeans led the Congress leaders to fear a possible attempt to assassinate Dr Banda. More seriously they feared that Kamuzu might be suddenly snatched by Nyasaland or Federal authorities; they had to plan so that they were clear about what action to take and have preparations ready for this eventuality.[235] These would have to be confidential so the only way to proceed was to call a meeting of representatives of all the branches of Congress to meet in an emergency conference. Dunduzu Chisiza called an urgent meeting of the Executive which agreed with his calling the conference. Neither Chipembere nor Chiume attended that meeting of the Executive.

Dunduzu at the Executive meeting also insisted that there were other urgent matters that needed to be dealt with. These were first that the main source of Congress funds, its branches in Southern Rhodesia, appeared to be under

---

[232] Roy Welensky, *4000 Days*, Collins, London, 1964, pp. 118-119.

[233] It seems strange that no one has chosen to comment on the fact that at the time of the Conference when apparently planning all this violence Mrs Chibambo was eight months pregnant.

[234] After Operation Sunrise my wife and I visited Mrs Chibambo where she and her new baby daughter were held in a hut on the barbed-wire fenced Zomba Prison football field. After we had all hugged each other, Rose, with our daughter in her arms, turned to the young Rhodesian officer who was supervising our visit and said "These two were the first on my list for killing, you know." The young man was clearly deeply embarrassed by this incident which contradicted what he had been told.

[235] Chipembere, *Hero of the Nation*, pp. 372-73.

threat of being banned, second there had been some wavering of loyalty to Dr Banda in some branches in the Central and Northern Regions. This was the result of a whispering campaign about his apparent disdain for things African and complaints about his suitability as a leader by men who had known him in the old days in South Africa.

A few days before the conference convened, the Executive met again to draw up a plan of action on the event of Dr Banda's death or arrest. This was to be presented for discussion at the Conference. Dr Banda excused himself from that meeting since it affected him personally. Chiume was also not present at the meeting since he was abroad fundraising. Those who drew up the tentative action plan were Chipembere, Rose Chibambo, Dunduzu Chisiza, Lali Lubani, Lawrence Makata and F.M.B. Chaluluka.

It is very important to note that initially Dunduzu applied for permission to use the Ramsey Hall in the middle of Blantyre as the venue for the conference. This was turned down by the District Commissioner Blantyre. Such a large gathering of Congress militants in the middle of Blantyre, he judged, would have been seen as further provocation by those Europeans already upset and seeking stronger action from the Boma against Congress.

On Saturday 25th January 1959 220 delegates gathered in conference at the alternative venue for the meetings. This was the hotel owned by Mikeka Mkandawire in Ndirande. Loudspeakers were laid on to relay proceedings to the crowds of people gathered outside. Dr Banda's safety was one of the first things discussed and Yatuta was appointed as his bodyguard though he was called 'secretary'. The facilities at Mikeka's hotel were far too small and it was decided that there was no alternative but to have an open-air venue for the second day of the conference. A site was found near the Kanjedza forest project, the site of a village from which people had been moved as part of the urban planning against which Mikeka Mkandawire had been campaigning for the previous seven years.

The delegates gathered on the Sunday morning at Congress headquarters in Ndirande. Singing and shouting slogans the delegates were then driven in lorries to the site which was about two hundred yards from the main road. The whole operation was noisy, boisterous and hardly secret. What was secretive was that no note-taking was allowed and this rule was very strictly enforced.

Certainly people were tense and excited as Chipembere points out in his autobiography. When was something really going to happen? Nothing had changed, there was no promise of constitutional change and many knew that in 1960, they might be locked into a completely independent state ruled by the Rhodesian whites.

In the sessions held that Sunday what appears to have been agreed was an acceleration of the number of incidents of direct conflict with the Boma so as to make the country ungovernable and create sooner rather than later a crisis. That this might involve what Chipembere insisted would be retaliatory violence was discussed and the possible use of this tactic was accepted. One of the things that would merit what was deemed retaliatory violence was the arrest or assassination of Dr Banda. In a series of, at times, heated discussions, it is also clear that some hotheads talked the nonsense that enabled the 'murder plot' to be pieced together by the Nyasaland Intelligence officers. These suggestions of killing all Europeans and Asians were never deemed a serious issue by the conference. As Chipembere pointed out in his autobiography the leaders knew full well any such actions would result in disastrous consequences for the Nyasa people.[236] Also most officials of Congress were well aware any such action would have fatally undercut their support in the UK from the Church of Scotland and the Labour Party - support which was vital if they were to be able to secede from the Federation.

Operation Sunrise[237]

In February clashes between the people and the Boma increased, notably these began to occur on a large scale in the Central Region for the first time. In the North actions taken under the leadership of Musopole had already made the Region ungovernable by the beginning of February. During the month army and police reinforcements were moved into the Protectorate from both Rhodesias and the Tanganyikan police re-opened Fort Hill airfield. On the 26th of February the Southern Rhodesian Government proscribed Congress and detained 495 leading members of Congress. As the Prime Minister of Southern Rhodesia had said at the meeting of heads of government conference in Salisbury on 18th February,

> The right thing ... was for him to clear up all the subversives in Southern Rhodesia first and get them inside, at which time he would then be able to agree to further reinforcements going to Nyasaland.[238]

After that Sir Robert Armitage was ready to activate his planned State of Emergency.

At midnight of March 2-3 1959 a State of Emergency was declared and the various 'snatch squads' moved out to arrest what the Special Branch judged

---

[236] Ibid., pp. 383-4.

[237] 'Operation Sunrise' was the code-name given to the Declaration of the State of Emergency, and the military action which followed it.

[238] Quoted in Baker, *State of Emergency*, p. 27.

to be the élite leadership of Nyasaland African Congress, two hundred in number. In the next few weeks further sweeps were made and eventually something close to fifteen hundred Nyasas were detained including three outstanding women and a baby, Rose Chibambo (and her newly born baby girl Kaidi), Vera Chirwa and Gertrude Rubadiri.

Somewhat to the surprise of the Security Forces no opposition was offered to the arrests. Two platoons of the Army and the Police Mobile Force accompanied the squad sent to arrest Dr Banda. There was no fighting, the Doctor was sound asleep in bed until rudely awakened and bundled off to Chileka in his pyjamas and dressing gown. Yatuta Chisiza accompanied him and at Chileka they were joined by Dunduzu Chisiza and Chipembere and all four flown to Southern Rhodesia.

Dr Banda was clearly expecting the arrest. His actions on the day before his arrest make it appear he even knew when his arrest was going to take place. That day, March 2nd, Kamuzu called a Church of Scotland missionary, Albert McAdam, to his house. He gave Albert all the cash he had in the house. Kamuzu also entrusted him with all the papers and files he had there other than his medical files. McAdam took these away in Kamuzu's Landrover which was also entrusted to the Scot for safe keeping. I never knew the amount of the cash but it was not so great as to cause comment when Albert paid it into his bank account. The confidential papers Jenny McAdam sewed into cushions and mattresses for safe-keeping.

Throughout the country when people awoke and discovered what had happened, however, there was a massive popular reaction. The Nyasa people were bewildered and angry. As the Devlin Report commented, the declaration of a State of Emergency had never been used before in Nyasaland and it bewildered people as well as angering them. Griff Jones, in his *Britain and Nyasaland* confirms this.[239] There was an outburst of confrontations with the authorities and in the North, where Flax Musopole was still at large and directing affairs; many well organised acts of sabotage were carried out. Culverts, for example, were expertly diverted so that sections of roads were swept away and bridges were set on fire.

There was more violence in the Protectorate after the 3rd of March than there had been before. The most appalling incident took place at Nkhata Bay where twenty local people were killed and twenty-eight wounded when a very large crowd of unarmed but angry and bewildered people appeared to threaten the three soldiers and a sergeant guarding the pier where the *M.V. Mpasa* was tied up and taking on board detainees to be transported south.

---

[239] *Britain and Nyasaland*, p. 241.

A second cadre of leaders were arrested in a sweep on March 7th. Those detained included almost every university graduate in the country, including some who had been disappointed that they had not been picked up in the first sweep four days earlier. This was not the end as the authorities felt it necessary to detain more and more people. One of the most important leaders of Congress, Kanyama Chiume, was out of the country and decided to go to the United Kingdom to help the massive effort mounted by the Labour Party and the Church of Scotland to challenge the British Government to explain and justify what had happened in Nyasaland.

Dr Banda, Chipembere, Dunduzu and Yatuta Chisiza were housed in the European section of Gwelo prison; the other Nyasa leaders taken to Southern Rhodesia were housed in either Khami Prison, near Bulawayo or at Marandellas. The majority of ordinary detainees were kept in Nyasaland in the emergency detention centre at Kanjedza, a subdivision of Limbe.

There then followed a series of actions by troops and police across the country to quell any further disturbances, weed out troublemakers and in the words of one DC 'make Congress unpopular', presumably for bringing this trouble about? Colin Baker described the pattern of these actions succinctly:

> The broad pattern used in this campaign ... was one of 'cordoning and searching' villages. Security forces would surround a village at night and then police or soldiers would go into the village, knock on doors – breaking them if necessary – and order all the men into the centre of the village. They would then be questioned under guard while the houses were searched – often in a rough manner – and documents and weapons, including agricultural implements, seized. In a number of cases Congress activists gave themselves up rather than risk further damage to their relatives' and their own property.[240]

The Northern Region was a different matter. It took significantly longer for the authority of the government to be restored. Indeed the lack of government authority there combined with the belief in the 'Murder Plot' created an attitude of mind among some senior officers verging on panic. A classic example was the request to use aircraft against 'rioters'. One specific example was the request of the officer commanding troops in the Northern Region for an air strike on crowds in Mzimba. This was sensibly turned down but further discussion taken as far as the British cabinet about the possible use of aircraft did include references to possible use if needed to avert a massacre![241]

In addition to the action on the ground in the pacification process, the Government Information Service began a campaign of publicity against Congress and in a particularly stupid move distributed a circular encouraging

---

[240] Baker, *State of Emergency*, p. 63.
[241] Ibid., pp. 57-8.

people to name troublemakers while promising that their anonymity would be preserved.

> You can either report personally to a Government Officer or, if you prefer to remain anonymous, send an unsigned letter to your District Commissioner giving the name and address of any Congress member still at large. (There is no need to put a stamp on the envelope).[242]

It was this kind of action that led the Devlin Commission to declare that Nyasaland had become a 'police state'.

Amidst all the anger over the actions of the Nyasaland Government what no one at the time noticed was that Nyasaland African Congress had won. They had created a crisis for the Nyasaland Government, the Federal Government and, most importantly, the British Government. Public opinion in Britain could now be focussed effectively on the Nyasa people's persistent opposition to inclusion in the Federation because the Federation and its future were again an issue in British politics - exactly what Welensky had wanted to avoid.

---

[242] *Nyasaland Government Information Bulletin.* No 10. 6 May 1959.

Chapter 6

From the Devlin Commission to Kamuzu's Release

Almost every book on this period of Malawi history concentrates on what the various white governments in Zomba, Salisbury and London were doing at this time. The deliberations in and communications between the three capitals over the need to declare a State of Emergency, the work of the Devlin Commission, its report and the need to answer it, the negotiations over the creation of the Monckton Commission, its work and final report, these are the issues that occupy the writers of the period. The result is that it appears as if the people of the Protectorate were simply passive onlookers, crushed by the battering they had taken in the 'pacification process' immediately following Operation Sunrise. This was decidedly not so. There was the beginning of a rebuilding of Congress activity in the Blantyre/Limbe area and to a lesser extent in Zomba that began only a few weeks after Operation Sunrise had ended. Perhaps even more important, though it was not so recognized at the time, was the awakening of political activity where it had previously hardly existed at all in the large Chewa Central Region outside the long term active areas of Lilongwe and Ntcheu. This new activity and political activism was also awakened in the Lower Shire area of the Southern Region. Again this was a product of the vigorous activity of the security forces carrying out the various security sweeps that followed Operation Sunrise. As people were released from detention lively unofficial activity came to exist where none had existed before. The result is that careful consideration will have to be given to a Nyasaland which is being transformed into Malawi by a Congress more widely supported than ever.

The news of Operation Sunrise and the accusation that Congress had plotted a massacre of Europeans and Asians produced a massive reaction in Britain. The Labour Party and the Church of Scotland each began a vociferous campaign challenging the need for the creation of a State of Emergency in Nyasaland. They refused to accept that the Massacre Plot was real. Senior figures in both the Labour Party and the Church of Scotland insisted that they knew personally some of the most prominent leaders of Congress and argued that these friends were incapable of supporting such a plan. Some Labour Party figures, notably Fenner Brockway, asserted that the plot was fiction, a deliberate lie concocted to justify the declaration of a State of Emergency.

It should be noted in fairness to Robert Armitage that the Governor certainly did not use the 'plot' to justify the declaration of a State of Emergency and, indeed, pressmen noticed his subsequent reluctance to make any use of it at all.[243] He was later to recall his surprise at the massive use made of the 'Massacre Plot' by British Ministers.

> When I read that Lennox-Boyd had said in the House of Commons that a massacre was being planned and that was the main reason for the declaration of the State of Emergency I was staggered. In my broadcast earlier that morning I had made no reference to any massacre or murder plan or anything of the sort.[244]

British Government Reactions to the State of Emergency

In London, however, as in Welensky's Salisbury, it was the planned massacre of Europeans and Asians that was the central focus of what was said. In their statements to the House of Commons on the situation in Nyasaland both Lennox-Boyd, the Secretary of State and his Deputy, Julian Amery, focussed on the awful threat created by the planning of a massacre of Europeans and Asians by Congress. Amery even talked of killing of Europeans in terms of the Mau-Mau atrocities in Kenya. It would appear that the ministers in London did not want to admit that the crushing of Congress and mass arrests of the Congress leaders had been agreed upon before there had been any word of a 'Murder Plot'. By the end of 1958 Dr Banda and the Congress leadership had either to be granted significant concessions or Congress had to be crushed and it had been decided that Congress had to be crushed.

The repeated insistence on the 'Murder Plot' by the British Government, a focus on the threat from the Nyasaland Congress in statements by Welensky on the situation did not help the government's cause in Church and Labour circles in the United Kingdom. On the contrary it provoked an even higher level of indignation. Indeed the anger felt in Scotland overflowed party lines and a powerful majority in the Kirk were so upset that one of Welensky's colleagues insisted that the Federation had two main opponents in the United Kingdom, 'the Church of Scotland and Labour extremists.'[245]

Barely a week after the declaration of a State of Emergency and the confident assertion about avoiding a massacre in Nyasaland, Lennox-Boyd's communications with Lord Perth indicated that, astonishingly, the British Cabinet did not appear to know what was going on in Nyasaland in any detail or with any certainty. Lord Perth was visiting the East African colonies when Lennox-Boyd telephoned him on the 9th March saying "David you have no idea how much trouble we are having over Nyasaland. Go there

---

[243] It was noted in newspapers as far apart politically as the *Observer* and *The Daily Mail*.

[244] Quoted in Brian Lapping, *End of Empire*, p. 486.

[245] W. P. Coffin 11, File PM 60/12 Ellis to Welensky June 4 1959.

and find out what is going on."[246] Needing to know and letting the people of the United Kingdom know had already led the Cabinet to decide on the 5th March, in the absence of Macmillan who was in the Soviet Union, to set up a Commission of Inquiry into the situation in Nyasaland.

In response to Lennox-Boyd's request, Perth went to Nyasaland arriving on the 12th of March and staying until the 17th. In that short time Perth attempted to be as thorough as was possible in attempting to 'find out what was going on'. He then went on to consult Roy Welensky and the Federal Cabinet and the Governments of Northern and Southern Rhodesia.

Perth returned from the Federation on March 21st. In his official report on the visit and in the additional notes specifically on his visit to Nyasaland which he recorded formally as a separate official document, there are four things noted of particular importance.[247] The first is the conclusion that ninety-nine per cent of the African civil servants in Nyasaland were committed to Congress and that they were keeping the "flames of Congress alive". The second is the insistence on the need for legislation to be passed in Nyasaland to allow the Governor to keep people in detention beyond the end of the State of Emergency. Thirdly Perth laid particular emphasis on the evidence showing the persistent fomenting of opposition to the Federation by the Church of Scotland missionaries and the African church members whom, he insisted, the missionaries had misled. (After the consistent reporting by the previous Governor, Sir Geoffrey Colby, of the genuine, long term and widespread African opposition to Federation, for a Secretary of State to believe this opposition stemmed from Scottish missionaries misleading the people is astonishing.) Fourthly Perth notes that when he informed the Federal cabinet that the British Government intended to appoint a Royal Commission of Inquiry into the future of the Federation they rejected vehemently the setting up of any such inquiry. It was after all in their eyes a revolutionary new idea that was suddenly being foisted upon them by Macmillan.

It is interesting to note that only five days after Perth left the Federation, the Secretariat of the Nyasaland Government, having dealt with Congress, turned its attention on Congress's missionary allies and put out a Confidential Report entitled 'The Church of Central Africa Presbyterian'. This was a report which, unusually for the time, used the correct name of the African church in Nyasaland that had grown out of the Church of Scotland Missions and the Mission of the Cape Synod of the Nederduits

---

[246] Baker, *State of Emergency*, p. 71.
[247] Perth's main Report is CO 1015/1977 and his Nyasaland Notes are CO 1015/1976.

Gereformeerde Kerk van Suid Afrika. The confidential report ended with the following paragraph

> 66. The Church of Scotland and the Foreign Mission Committee in the United Kingdom are directly responsible for the attitude and actions of members of their Church with regard to the Federation issue in that
>
> > (a) They have sent into the mission field in Nyasaland persons with extreme left-wing political views who have had the effect of greatly exacerbating African opposition to Government, and of impairing race-relations generally.
> >
> > (b) The Moderator of the General Assembly; of the Church of Scotland in 1958 openly advocated participation in politics as a Christian duty.
> >
> > (c) By promising to consider the views on the Federation issue of the Christian Action Group in Blantyre before the General Assembly of the Church of Scotland they have actively encouraged those opposing Federation to look to the Church of Scotland in the United Kingdom for assistance.

By the beginning of May, so as to be in time for the meeting of the General Assembly of the Church of Scotland, there was circulating in Scotland a pamphlet published under the aegis of the Federal Government's publicity organisation in the United Kingdom, entitled 'The New Face of the Kirk in Nyasaland'. This pamphlet was little more than an edited and scaled down version of the Nyasaland Government's 'Confidential Report'.

Macmillan Decides to Review the Future of the Federation

On the 11th March Macmillan returned to the United Kingdom and recorded in his diary that the wider problems of 'whether the Federation can continue in its present form' had to be studied before the constitutional conference promised for 1960 could take place. That the British Prime Minister had decided that it was necessary to have an Inquiry into whether the Federation could continue in its present form, let alone gain Commonwealth status was a dramatic and sudden reversal of British policy. Welensky had every right to be astonished. In 1957 the declaration by the British Government on what they expected to happen in 1960 had ended with this paragraph.

> The purpose of this conference is to review the Constitution in the light of the experience gained since the inception of the Federation and in addition to agree on the constitutional advances which may be made. In the latter context the conference will consider a programme for the attainment of such a status as would enable the Federation to become eligible for full membership of the Commonwealth.[248]

The decision that it was now necessary to review whether the Federation could continue in its present form was a revolutionary decision taken by Macmillan. He insisted that it was a necessary response to a new situation. In the recent past there had been a massive increase in the political

---

[248] Ibid. p. 77.

consciousness and political activism among the African people north of the Zambezi. This was a situation that he and other British leaders had only become aware for the first time.

> Had I then realised, or had indeed any of us realised, the almost revolutionary way in which the situation would develop and the rapid growth of African Nationalism throughout the whole African continent, I think I should have opposed the putting together of three countries so opposite in their character and so different in their history.[249]

This really was a very weak excuse for British policy vis-à-vis Nyasaland in the past. The previous Governor, Sir Geoffrey Colby, had known the situation very well and had made it clear to London in his reports over his time as Governor including his farewell communication with London. On this issue he had simply and consistently been ignored despite the respect in which he was held by colleagues in London and Africa. When opinion from someone as distinguished as Colby was ignored then it is not surprising that the British Government consistently disregarded African opinion in Nyasaland, even when this led to violence as it had done in 1953.

As recently as January of 1959 at a meeting with his officials and the three Governors of the three East African territories, Lennox-Boyd had sketched out what was agreed as a suitable future for their territories. It was agreed that Tanganyika would gain independence by 1970, to be followed by Uganda and then Kenya in 1975. By the time the situation of these territories is reviewed by the British Government in the new post General Election world the situation was viewed profoundly differently.

The Federation had been held up to both black and white as an example of living together. This was no longer seen to be true. The people in Southern Rhodesia lived together in relations that were little different from the apartheid of South Africa. The Federal Constitution made a marginal difference to a small number of people but if Federation led to Dominion status in 1960 what was the rate of African progress going to be. This was a situation that Macmillan could no longer accept.

Macmillan's later insistence to Welensky and the Federal Cabinet that the British Government was committed to the Federation did not hide the fact that a new situation had been created. Welensky and his colleagues had come to realise that Macmillan was now moving them into uncharted waters and they had to try to hold fast to what they thought had been promised them.

The British Government was upset by Welensky's refusal to cooperate over the setting up of the Royal Commission as ministers felt that they needed the

---

[249] Harold Macmillan, *Pointing the Way*, p. 131.

Nyasaland Inquiry and the Royal Commission to be announced at the same time. This would enable them to restrict the remit of the Nyasaland Inquiry to the immediate events that had necessitated the declaration of a State of Emergency. Welensky and his ministers were agreed with the support of Whitehead and the Southern Rhodesian Cabinet in total opposition to the creation of any Royal Commission that could be construed as an investigation of the Federation.

> We told Lord Perth that there were many forces then working within the Federation and from various motives, for its dismemberment. A Royal Commission would be fatal to our position, as a Government and as a party, because we were the only party really determined to preserve federation.[250]

What particularly incensed Welensky was that the crisis which, in the minds of the British, necessitated the setting up of a Royal Commission was created by happenings in Nyasaland over which the Federal Government had no control. It was a British mess in their view, to get out of which the British had had to call in Federal help, yet now a Royal Commission was to investigate the future of the Federation.

Adopting this attitude was to go on ignoring, as the British had been doing until this revolutionary decision by Macmillan, the almost universal opposition of the people of Nyasaland to any form of political association with Southern Rhodesia, be it amalgamation or federation. This opposition had been clearly and consistently articulated since the late 1930s, and it was this opposition, which had at last, because of the Nyasaland Emergency, made such an impact on Macmillan that he had become convinced of the need for the Royal Commission.

The British Government in response to Welensky's refusal to countenance a Royal Commission sent Lord Home to Salisbury to attempt to persuade him change his mind. Home had always got on well with Welensky and it was hoped he could persuade the Federal Prime Minster to accept the creation of the Royal Commission in time for the two bodies to be able to operate together. Surely, Home argued, Welensky could appreciate that the last thing that the British Government or they wanted was for the Nyasaland Inquiry to get involved in the fundamental, long term opposition of the Nyasaland people to the Federation. Not only would it raise big problems for the Royal Commission on the Federation, it would also raise major problems for the working of the Constitutional Review of 1960 - so important to the Federal leaders.

---

[250] Welensky, *4000 Days*, p. 119.

The Appointment of the Devlin Commission

The British Government needed an answer quickly. They had, after all, announced the setting up of the Nyasaland Inquiry as long ago as the 5th of March.[251] The selection of its membership and its beginning work simply could not be delayed much longer.

Meanwhile Kanyama Chiume, abroad at the time of the declaration of the State of Emergency, had astutely decided to stay in Britain and take full advantage of the massive popular interest in Nyasaland that the Church of Scotland and the Labour Party were encouraging. Just how effective the line taken by the Church of Scotland was can be seen by the re-alignment of what was then the principal Tory quality newspaper in Scotland, *The Scotsman*. Within a week of the declaration of the State of Emergency, *The Scotsman* had become a severe critic of government policy with regard to Nyasaland. Its Letters to the Editor page was expanded and became a vehicle for widely based criticism of Government policy in the Protectorate.

Kanyama's decision, though criticised by many back home, had its wisdom further confirmed when, within a few days of the declaration of the State of Emergency, he was interviewed sympathetically on British television. This was noted with some bitterness by the Special Committee to Supervise Federal Propaganda which Welensky had set up on 3rd March and which met almost daily afterwards.[252] At the time of Chiume's triumph Welensky's committee had achieved nothing in the British media. Worse was to follow when, having arranged for a face to face debate on British television between Chiume and a spokesman chosen by the Federation's friends in London, most viewers felt that Chiume had made a better impression on the TV audience.[253]

Meanwhile the continued and bitter resistance to the idea of a Royal Commission on the part of Welensky and his colleagues meant that the British Government simply had to go ahead and appoint the members of the Inquiry into the Nyasaland 'disturbances' and set it in motion without any further delay. The decision killed stone dead any plan to announce the Inquiry and the Royal Commission at the same time and thus enable the

---

[51] The twists and turns of the discussion of this problem in London and Salisbury are well covered in Baker, *State of Emergency*, pp. 75-9 and from a Rhodesian point of view in Welensky, *4000 Days* where Welensky sees the whole affair as a plot against him engineered by Macmillan.

[52] Minutes of the Committee can be found in Welensky Papers, Coffin 6.File P.M. 5/4. Bitter disappointment over Chiume's coup over television coverage appears in Minutes of 6th meeting, Tuesday, 19 March.

[3] W.P. Coffin 24, File 151, Joelson to Welensky 18 March 1959.

United Kingdom Government to limit the remit of the Inquiry as they had hoped they might.

Although later Macmillan would insist that the Inquiry was clearly defined as a narrowly restricted one, it in fact took a long time to set up and such a variety of forms and membership were discussed that the original narrow restriction disappeared. It was only after much toing and froing over the composition, aims and membership, including at one point the idea that the membership might consist of British Members of Parliament, was its membership finally agreed. The team to carry out the Inquiry was agreed should consist of a senior judge and two other members who should be experienced senior public figures.

This did not bring the problems to an end. There were further delays as a number of names were considered and Lennox-Boyd pressed a very senior judge, Lord Morton, to accept the chairmanship but he turned the appointment down as did a number of other senior figures who were approached. Finally it was the choice of Lord Kilmuir, the Lord Chancellor, of another distinguished High Court judge, Sir Patrick Devlin, a life-long friend of Lord Perth's, which broke the impasse. Devlin accepted the appointment and Macmillan agreed to the appointment without comment. The two other members selected were E.T. Williams, Warden of Rhodes House, Oxford, who had been a senior Intelligence Officer during the Second World War and Sir Percy Wynn-Harris, the Governor of the Gambia, who had previously served in East Africa.

It would appear that no safer 'establishment' team could have been put together to keep things under control and deliver a 'safe' report. On the eve of the Commission's appointment being publicly announced on 24th March, one significant change was made. It was announced that one further member had been added to the team specifically in response to Scottish concerns. The new member was Sir John Ure Primrose, a prominent Scottish Tory. Primrose had also served with British Intelligence during the war. The appointment, warmly supported by Lord Home, appeared to be an additional 'safe pair of hands' to the team.

In the various discussions that took place with Devlin as he prepared for his task, a number of things were said that allowed the Inquiry wider scope than the British Government had originally wished it to have. Rather, by the time Devlin was appointed a narrow focused understanding of the task of the team had been significantly modified. Colin Baker quotes Devlin as saying of a meeting with Lord Kilmuir:

> He [Kilmuir] said it might involve finding to what extent Federation was a cause of the disturbances. He was perfectly frank about what the Government policy was. He said 'We believe in Federation. But of course it is open to you to find that the

186

ordinary African does not. We hope you won't make that finding, but if you do, we shall have to accept it.[254]

Baker adds this comment:

> The real position, of course, was not simply that the government hoped Devlin would not find a cause of the disturbances but that he would not inquire into the Federation and its effects at all.[255]

Baker says this and it is clear that he is reporting accurately what had been the initial attitude of key figure in the British Government. By the time Lord Kilmuir was briefing Patrick Devlin things had changed. Baker's 'real position' appears to have been forgotten as the delays and the refusal after refusal to take part in the operation were recorded. Certainly what Baker calls the 'real position' was never put to Devlin and is an indication of the disarray in Macmillan's cabinet at that time. The result was that Devlin and his colleagues set off to begin work in Nyasaland without any sense that their task was a narrowly restricted one and that they had misunderstood 'the real position'.

The Devlin Commission in Nyasaland

The Commissioners arrived in Nyasaland on the 11th April and for the next five weeks took evidence at venues scattered from the north to the south of the Protectorate. They then heard further evidence in Bulawayo from Nyasas detained in Federal prisons in Southern Rhodesia and also from Federal officials, notably from General Long, Commander of the Federal army, who had to be warned by Williams, an old acquaintance from the War, not to adopt 'old boy attitude' when describing his troops 'roughing up' Africans in Nyasaland. The Commission then finished the weeks of hearing evidence in London on 26th of June.

While the Commissioners were in Bulawayo the General Assembly of the Church of Scotland then at the height of its influence and with its largest active membership in the twentieth century, debated the Nyasaland Emergency. The measure of how seriously the Government took this debate was the presence of three British Cabinet Ministers, Rab Butler, Alex Douglas-Home and Lord Perth in the Visitors' Gallery throughout the long day. Meanwhile, people in Nyasaland were deeply concerned and that morning, the 25th of May, the Moderator of the General Assembly had received the following telegram from Kanyama Chiume.

> In this perilous time in the history of my country when the civil liberties and freedom of my people are shamefully scorned and suppressed, may I, as a member

---

[254] Baker. *State of Emergency*. p. 81.

[255] Ibid.

of the church, assure you of the unfailing friendship and brotherhood between the peoples of Scotland and Nyasaland.

Butler and his two colleagues were deeply disappointed but hardly surprised when, at the end of a long and at times emotional debate, the Assembly voted overwhelmingly to receive the Report and Supplementary Report of the Assembly's Special Committee on Central Africa. These Reports included a four page statement made by the Blantyre Synod of the CCAP which was highly critical of the situation in Nyasaland.

There were three specific recommendations to government in the motion passed by the Assembly which, if followed, would render it impossible for the Federation to achieve Dominion status and would necessitate major changes in the constitution of the Federation if it were to continue at all.[256] In summary the Assembly requested that there should be no Dominion status granted without the agreement of the majority of the Federation's inhabitants, the territorial constitution of Nyasaland should be amended so as to allow an African majority in the Legco, and all detainees should be brought to trial or released forthwith.[257]

Mention of the Church of Scotland, the Kirk, at the beginning of a discussion of the Devlin Commission is far from inappropriate, though it might appear so to some. It was pressure from the Kirk that led to Ure-Primrose's addition to the membership of the Inquiry. Its impact was even greater as Baker asserts in his *State of Emergency*

> As things worked out, the Church of Scotland was able, in many respects, to turn the Devlin commission into a referendum on the Federation. It is clear that large numbers of African members of the Church thought that this was indeed the purpose of the inquiry.[258]

The only African member of the Church of Scotland in Nyasaland and later Malawi was Dr Banda who never formally joined the CCAP. Baker is quite correct when he reports that the members of the CCAP came to see the Devlin Commission as an inquiry into the working of the Federation insofar as it affected Nyasaland.

The encouragement of Nyasas by the Scottish and Irish missionaries working with the CCAP to give evidence to the Devlin Commission undoubtedly helped this. More than anything it was, however, the efforts

---

[256] *Reports to the General Assembly of the Church of Scotland, 1959.* p. 683.

[257] Ibid.

[258] Baker, *State of Emergency*, p. 85. The African Christians were members of the CCAP not of the Church of Scotland. The CCAP came into being in 1924, the church which during 1959 and 1960 the Church of Scotland missionaries working in Nyasaland joined, relinquishing their membership of the Church of Scotland.

made by Patrick Devlin and his colleagues to establish clearly their independence of Government that impressed the people of the Protectorate. Except when it was absolutely impossible to avoid it, the Devlin team did not stay with or socialize either with the Colonial Office civil servants or with the European population. This was puzzling behaviour in the eyes of most Europeans in the Protectorate and was noted by the African population.[259] In the eyes of the members of Patrick Devlin's team it was only logical behaviour. How could they be an unbiased, fair-minded, investigative team and behave as if they were part and parcel of the British Government organisation in the Protectorate. The African people saw this and drew their own conclusions that the Federal and Nyasaland Governments were under scrutiny – which they were, as was the behaviour of Congress. The important point was that the Commission appeared to be one that the people could trust and with which they could cooperate.

Of course the strong encouragement of the missionaries serving the Livingstonia and Blantyre Synods of the CCAP helped but on its own it would not have been enough to produce the massive African demand to be heard. Missionaries working in the Livingstonia Synod undoubtedly did help to organize the crowds of people who wished to give evidence to the Commission, notably in the Deep Bay (Chilumba) area where a CCAP elder, Mr. Mafumbanya and Bill Henry, a Scottish missionary had helped organise a petition with 1800 signatures to be presented to the Commission.[260] Again at Livingstonia, or Khondowe as it was also often called, missionaries typed up the many written submissions that people wished to submit to Devlin.

The Commission decided that they could actually stay at Khondowe with the mission staff African, Scots and Irish. The visit to Livingstonia and the acceptance of the hospitality of the Mission caused a lot of unhappiness in official circles. The commissioners noted how enjoyable their visit had been yet the Governor and senior officials saw the Livingstonia staff as allies of, if not formal members of Congress. In fact the visit to Khondowe was such a social success because the Commissioners were able to experience living in a community as near to ignoring racial difference as was possible in Central Africa in the 1950s. As Anthony Fairclough, secretary to the Commission, put it to one of the Livingstonia Synod officials, Mr Mtawali, it was only at Livingstonia that the Commission had found any real fellowship between Europeans and Africans.[261]

---

[59] Baker, *State of Emergency*, in Chapter 4 Baker cites many examples of how this behaviour disconcerted so many Colonial Service officials and their spouses.
[60] Bill Jackson, *Send us Friends*, p. 126.
[61] Bill Jackson, *Send Us Friends*, p. 127.

There is no doubt that in the warm and friendly atmosphere, the members of the Commission were very relaxed but there was only one incident when a member of the Commission could be seen as letting his guard down about his attitude to the Governor and his administration. This was a dismissive grunt by Ure-Primrose when the Reverend Bill Jackson and the Reverend Fergus Macpherson had put in a good word for the Governor.[262] Ure-Primrose's attitude rather carelessly shown was not made public until Jackson, many years later, recorded it in his book *Send Us Friends*.

The contrast between the genial acceptance of the hospitality of the Mission at Livingstonia and the strict avoidance of any apparent intimacy with anyone connected with Government aroused angry comment in Government circles. It helped the case of those like Kettlewell, who insisted from the beginning that the Commission was hostile to the Government, though, interestingly, Kettlewell was one of the few senior Government officers who impressed the Commission favourably. The other senior officials who gained the approval of the Commission were Hasgard, Brock and Roberts.[263]

Kettlewell was not alone in his judgement of the Commission's attitude; from early on many officials began to feel that the Report was going to be critical of Armitage and the government of Nyasaland. How far this perception was encouraged by some officials in London is open to discussion since it was only ten days after Devlin had begun his work in Nyasaland when a senior official in the Colonial Office in London sent the Governor a copy of a circular composed by the Secretary of State that dealt with 'the principles to be followed when a Governor wishes to dissent from the findings or opinions contained in the report of a Commission of Inquiry'. The same official also suggested to Armitage that he was now free to proceed along the guidelines suggested in the circular.[264]

The climax of this developing understanding among officials of what the Commission might say was the decision by the Governor to ask the three Provincial Commissioners to compile an assessment of what they thought might emerge in Devlin's Report. The three officials prepared their attempt to second guess Devlin which reached London on 5th July. In this they stated, after outlining various possibilities, that the best outcome from the Devlin

---

262 Macpherson had been a friend of Dr Banda's since student days in Edinburgh, when Banda had been made a Church Elder in Macpherson's father's congregation. They remained friends even when they differed politically from the time of the 'Cabinet Crisis'. Macpherson was also a friend and biographer of Kenneth Kaunda, first President of Zambia.

263 Baker, *Emergency*, pp., 113-14.

264 The circular and Gorrell Barnes' letter of 21 April, 1959 to Armitage can be found in CO 1015/1535.

190

Commission for which the Governor could hope was a Report which generally vindicated the Government's actions but which strongly condemned the detailed handling of the Emergency particularly the use of unnecessary force. This assessment confirmed the fears of many officials in Zomba and London about the outcome of Devlin's work. From this time onwards there was panic in London and the decision that a rebuttal needed to be prepared and that Devlin's report could not be made public until it could be accompanied by an answer.

One can look back today and ask with some puzzlement why this was deemed necessary and why the officials in Zomba and London were so upset. After all Devlin vindicated the Governor's decision to declare a State of Emergency though highly critical of the use of unnecessary violence. The problem seems to have lain with the state of mind of Lennox-Boyd, the Colonial Secretary, and his colleagues at that time. They saw Devlin's Report as a threat to the continued existence of the Conservative Government. This is a dramatic contrast with how it was viewed a few months later by Iain Macleod, Macmillan's choice as Colonial Secretary. Almost immediately on appointment Macleod had private talks with Patrick Devlin, and certainly did not see the judgements as threatening the security of the state; Macleod found Devlin's Report technically true if somewhat overwritten.[265] In any case from the outset Macleod felt that the future of Nyasaland lay with Banda and although it might take time "I was really determined to release him from the moment I became Colonial Secretary".

The contrast between this cool confident approach with the attitude of Lennox-Boyd and his colleagues which can only described as one approaching panic is remarkable. Lennox-Boyd was particularly alarmed at the possibility that Devlin's Report might be published before he had read it. He was convinced that the Report was one that was potentially disastrous for the Government. He therefore decided that Devlin's Report should be made available to his office in time for a rebuttal to be prepared. Then both Devlin's Report and the official rebuttal could then be published at the same time, a procedure which was approved by Macmillan.

British Reactions to the Devlin Report

When Devlin's Report was finally made available to the Prime Minister and his cabinet, the fury directed towards Devlin and his team was vitriolic. Macmillan's sympathetic biographer, Alistair Horne, says that the Prime Minister was appalled at the content of the Report "and furious with the

---

[265] N. Fisher, *Iain Macleod*, pp. 187-88.

author"[266] In his private diary Macmillan wrote the quite bizarre comments that leave him sounding like a demented Orangeman.

> The poor Lord Chancellor - the sweetest and most naïve of men - chose him. He was able, a Conservative, runner- up or nearly so for the Lord Chief Justice. I have since discovered that he is (a) Irish - no doubt with the Fenian blood that makes Irishmen anti-Government on principle, (b) a *lapsed* Roman Catholic. His brother is a Jesuit priest; his sister a nun.[267]

This comment was being made about a senior British Judge, born in England of an Ulster Catholic father and a Scottish Protestant mother, brought up in Aberdeen, who was a life-long member of Macmillan's own Conservative Party. This extraordinary insistence on Devlin being an Irishman is repeated in Anthony Sampson's *Macmillan*.

The Government's response was prepared at Chequers over the week-end of the 18th and 19th of July. A powerful team was assembled that week-end, the Lord Chancellor, the Attorney-General, the Secretaries of State for the Colonies and for Commonwealth Relations as well as a cohort of senior civil servants. The Governor of Nyasaland joined the gathering accompanied by Finney, the head of the Nyasaland Special Branch and Roberts, the Solicitor-General of the Protectorate. Both teams came to the meeting with a considerable body of material already prepared but they worked over the next 48 hours to create an effective rebuttal of their own Commission's Report. On the Monday, Armitage spent the whole day in the Colonial Office helping to finalise the draft. The draft was then transformed into a White Paper, formally approved by the Cabinet as Cmnd 815, *Despatch from the Governor of Nyasaland commenting on the Devlin Commission's Report*.

On the 28th July the Report of the Devlin Commission was debated in the House of Commons on a Government motion, which, in the strange jargon of British Parliamentary procedure noted it and thanked the members of the Commission for their work. In effect it was a rejection of the Devlin Commission's findings. As a result of this and what Macmillan insisted was the sympathetic response to the debate on the part of the press the Prime Minister felt that he could relax and enjoy what amounted to a victory.

This was a mark of what Macmillan could talk himself into believing since a significant segment of the press took the Devlin Report very seriously. Not surprisingly the *Observer* praised the Report very highly but notably two leading conservative journals, the *Daily Telegraph* and the *Economist* praised Devlin's report in major articles and insisted on its long term importance.

---

[266] Alistair Horne, *Macmillan, 1957-1986*, p. 181.
[267] Ibid.

Macmillan's happy relief that they had won a victory and effectively killed off what they saw as the threat from Devlin does not alter the fact that the United Kingdom Government had believed itself to have been facing a major crisis. We have noted already Macmillan's extraordinary comments in his diary on first reading the Report. The various members of the Cabinet were agreed that the Report threatened their hold on office, in Macmillan's own words, the Report "was dynamite and may well blow this government out of the water."[268]

The seriousness of the threat in Macmillan's judgement necessitated the calling of a special meeting of the cabinet. This took place on the 20th July. Macmillan believed that this was a decisive moment for the Government, it either stood together or he would resign, though he did not tell his colleagues so beforehand. Each member of the Cabinet having been given adequate time to read Devlin's Report was asked to declare his position. Each in turn said that the British Government must back the Nyasaland Government and the Colonial Secretary. Of this outcome Macmillan wrote:

> This was a fine performance and most impressive. Mr Gladstone used to call his last cabinet the 'Blubbering Cabinet'. This is a 'Manly Cabinet'. I told them, *after* the decision had been taken, that had it gone otherwise, I should *not* have continued as Prime Minister.[269]

This meeting of the Cabinet was not made public at the time. It is a witness to the incredible feeling of vulnerability through which the Macmillan administration was passing at this time. The members of the Cabinet took heart from that meeting and appeared to proceed with confidence to the debate in the House of Commons and as we have seen, once that vote was won Macmillan appeared to be full of confidence.

It was certainly a confident Macmillan who announced on September 8th that he had obtained from the Queen formal permission to dissolve Parliament and call a General Election. Polling Day was set for the 8th October 1959. The election resulted in a resounding victory for Macmillan and the Conservative Party which placed the Prime Minister in a new position in the party as well as in the country. This allowed Macmillan choice in making appointments which he had not had before.

From Nyasaland African Congress to Malawi Congress Party

In Nyasaland, or rather in Malawi, for that was what the leadership of Congress had left instructions that the country was now to be called, there

---

[268] Ibid.

[269] Quotation from his private diary inserted on page 738 of Volume 4 of his autobography. *Riding the Storm.*

was stirring of renewed Congress activity despite the massive clamp down by the security forces unprecedented in the history of the country.

Shadrak Khonje and Augustine Mtambala, two graduate schoolteachers in Blantyre, who had both been surprised and disappointed to find themselves still free after the many waves of arrest had swept so many into detention, had begun to take action. They felt it was their duty to keep the flame of Congress alive. The leadership of Congress had expected arrests and had already decided who should step into their shoes when they were arrested. Those they had chosen had already received letters of authority signed by Lawrence Makata, Lali Lubani, Masauko Chipembere and Dunduzu Chisiza. Their instructions included the decision that from then on the country should be referred to as Malawi. These instructions were hopelessly inadequate since wave after wave of the members of Congress were arrested. Congress had simply not anticipated the scale of arrests and suppression that was to take place. In the end the total of men and women arrested reached one thousand three hundred and twenty-two, a number way beyond any idea the Congress leadership had entertained when planning their challenge to the authorities. Thus there was no third or fourth, let alone a fifth or sixth layer of nominated leadership. Khonje and Mtambala simply took up the task themselves to try to keep Congress alive by holding informal meetings in people's houses initially in the Blantyre/Limbe area.

Khonje was engaged to a young woman, Ceciwa Bwanausi, a younger sister of Augustine Bwanausi and Dr Harry Bwanausi who had both been arrested on the 7th of March. Mtambala, Khonje and Bwanausi, who soon added others to their number in the midst of the severe repressive actions of the security forces, slowly spread their activities beyond simply the Blantyre/Limbe area. The kind of situation in which they were operating initially is vividly etched in Ceciwa's memory of having to dive into a ditch while on the way to a house meeting to escape being caught in the searchlight of a police Land Rover enforcing the curfew.[270]

The effort of those young people was greatly helped by the mass of the African civil servants as they gradually recovered their nerve. They were judged by Lord Perth, as we have seen, as already a vehicle of keeping the flame of Congress alive. This small but growing network gained fresh strength as people started being released from detention. The name Malawi

---

[270] Ceciwa Bwanausi Khonje. 'Malawi History ... and Political Expediency', unpublished personal memoir, held by the present author.

194

was now used for the nation inside the detention centres and from them spread out into the country at large.[271]

What the authorities did not realise was that bringing so very many people into detention created new activists and revived the commitment of others. Veterans and youngsters only recently recruited into the Youth Wing were brought together with people who had simply been swept up in the effort to crush all Congress activity. What was created was the kind of training camp which Congress had never been able to afford to create. Many people who had only been names became real to men brought into detention from all over Malawi. People who had been only on the fringe of active commitment to the cause were, by the experience of detention, made activists.

This is not to minimize the fierce toughness with which initially the detainees were treated at Kanjedza, which interestingly was in marked contrast with the treatment of the leadership who were taken south and detained at Khami, Marandellas and Gwelo. Nor is it to pretend that detention camp life was a pleasant experience even when the original brutality at Kanjedza was ended. It is, however, to recognise that Kanjedza Detention Centre did create a new commitment and a new understanding for many. It also created new determined cadres of activists among those arrested in areas like the Lower Shire and the major part of the Central Region where committed activists had hitherto been few.

In the midst of all this activity a lively new addition to the movement arrived at Blantyre Mission of the CCAP in mid-July. This was Aleke Banda, a nineteen years old high school student who had been arrested in Southern Rhodesia where he lived with his parents. After a brief period in detention in Southern Rhodesia he was deported to his parents' homeland, Malawi – a country he had never seen. Arriving at Limbe Railway Station he had made his way to the Blantyre Mission. There he found a temporary home with Albert and Jenny McAdam, the caretakers of Kamuzu's car and private belongings while he was detained. He was clearly very bright and so Phil Howard, the managing Director of Booker-McConnell gave him a job. This was a more or less nominal post invented by Howard to sustain the young activist. Aleke very quickly got in touch with the nascent trades union movement in Malawi. This enabled him to legally produce a political newssheet, nominally an organ of trade union propaganda. This newssheet, called *Ntendere pa Ncito*[272] was duplicated on Blantyre Mission for Aleke by Stewart McCullough, an Irish missionary with the CCAP.

---

[271] The first written record of a modern use of the name Malawi was in Cullen Young and Kamuzu's edited volume. *Our African Way of Life* in 1946.

[272] Literally 'Peace at Work' in English.

Meanwhile, as people were released from detention, Congress, in the form of the new Malawi Congress Party came into being across the country. The Party did not yet exist officially but it had come into being again and groups were meeting unofficially across the country. This was the result of the initiative that had been taken by Shadrak Khonje and his friends and then was nursed along by Aleke Banda and the journal *Ntendere pa Ncito*.

In July 1959 Orton Chirwa was transferred from Khami prison in Southern Rhodesia, where with a number of other graduates like Augustine Bwanausi, Willie Chokhani and David Rubadiri, he had set up an informal school to further the education of their fellow detainees. Orton was brought to Zomba Prison where he was held in extraordinarily relaxed conditions. I visited him there and was allowed to talk to him freely and unsupervised as we sat with our backs against a wall in the red dust of the prison yard. This freedom to talk privately was in stark contrast with Kanjedza where for many months after that date I was allowed weekly visits to detainees. I was, however, at all times supervised strictly and was never allowed any kind of unsupervised visit with a detainee, even with one who was very sick.

Orton was a little puzzled by the dramatic change in his circumstances and the hints which he had received of an early release. On that day when I visited him he was somewhat evasive about what he thought was going to happen. That some of the Governor's advisers felt that he might be persuaded to lead an alternative political organisation almost certainly lay behind the move. Certainly later Orton would joke about offers having been made to him. Any such move was, however, forestalled by the organisation set up by Shadrak and company.

On August 8th Orton was released from Zomba Prison. Shadrak, Augustine Mtambala and others involved in the organisation of the unofficial MCP went to see him at Colin Cameron's[273] house very soon after his release. They were certainly afraid that Orton was going to be used by Government to set up an alternative Party to anything representing the old or new Congress. They sought to remove him from temptation's way by inviting him to become acting President of the Malawi Congress Party and to explore with the Colonial Government the possibility of making the Party a legal body. Orton agreed instantly without any apparent hesitation.

The delegation and Orton were clear that together they were undertaking a holding operation and that Kamuzu would automatically assume the leadership of the Party as soon as he was released. This had been arranged by the leadership on the eve of the first sweep of arrests. It has to be noted

---

[273] Cameron was a young Scottish lawyer and member of the CCAP who was very sympathetic to Congress. He became the only European member of Banda's first Cabinet.

however, that in the pre-arrest period, it was the task of Kamuzu to carry out the negotiations with the officials in Zomba and he was the star speaker at the week-end meetings of the Party. On Mondays to Fridays, however, he had tried very hard to continue as a medical practitioner while Chip, Dunduzu and Kanyama ran the routine work of the Party. There seemed to have been a change made, however, when the Government made the arrests. Although the leadership, as we have seen, had had no idea of the scale of the arrests that were going to be made, they had appeared to have made a clear decision. Every thing was to be focussed on Kamuzu and Kamuzu alone. The leadership of Congress now focussed on Kamuzu and the others had very much retreated into the background. There was no great publicity about the others in prison, everything now focussed on Kamuzu. This was not surprising among the newly awakened groups but it applied also to the well established groups of Congress also. In the writing done by Aleke in the increasing ability of the movement to provide publicity everything focussed on Kamuzu. This had been agreed by the leadership before the initial arrests.

The application for the recognition of a new political party was made before the end of August and permission for the formation of a new political party was granted at the end of September. In many ways this was surprising given the initial widespread arrests and the powerful initial crushing of all political resistance in the country. In other regards it was not so surprising because the Government had arrived at a situation when it was not clear what it could do next. The situation in Nyasaland had become a stand-off.

As the detainees were released they built up unofficial local organisations and waited for Kamuzu's release. When Orton accepted the temporary leadership of the new Party it was clear that Kamuzu was going to be released at some point. It did not change anything, it was a way of organising things while it was decided whether Macleod would have his way in the two Central African provincial territories as well as his already victorious progress through Kenya, Uganda and Tanganyika.

The national office-bearers were all based in the south but were drawn from all three provinces. The principal office-bearers were Orton Chirwa as President-General, Aleke Banda as Secretary-General and Atate Kamwendo as Treasurer-General.

In December the party was able to begin production of its own publication *Malawi News*; this was printed fortnightly at first, then weekly. Aleke Banda remained the editor and so controlled the flow of information and opinion going out to the branches. This was all centred on Kamuzu as the Messiah figure who would lead and guide the future of Malawi. Aleke was a newcomer and in no position to alter the propaganda, but no change had been planned in any case. This was the line that had been decided upon on the eve of the arrests. The line being hammered home was that Kamuzu would lead the people into the new day.

On a more sophisticated level from October 1959, two Europeans, Jimmy Skinner and Peter Mackay had begun a monthly journal called *Tsopano*. This journal was well produced and managed to maintain monthly publication while publishing material critical of the Government and sympathetic to Congress. This journal played an important part in developing a more sophisticated train of thought over the next eighteen months and in developing the thinking of the comparatively small group of educated Malawians who existed at that time.

What is important to notice about the new situation of the country, however, is that the party had come alive not only in the areas where the Nyasaland African Congress had had strength but also in areas that had had been very meagrely represented in the nationalist movement before the Emergency. So many people had been awakened by the behaviour of the Security Forces during the 'pacification process'; people had been made to feel as if they were in a newly conquered country. Lilongwe and Ntcheu had really been the only truly active Congress areas in the Central Region before the Emergency. Things were different by the middle months of 1959 and when the MCP was allowed to form branches they sprang up all over the Central Region.

This was a significant new phenomenon in the make-up of Malawi society and the make-up of Malawi politics. In the post-pacification period there came into being a large new element in Malawi politics, it was a political awakening among the Chewa people and it was entirely associated with the return of Kamuzu. The situation was paralleled in the Lower Shire. Again we have an awakening of people to political activity that had little or no previous political experience, their understanding of the leadership of the party centred entirely on Kamuzu. To the Chewa of the Central Region and the Nyanja of the Lower Shire, the young men like Masauko Chipembere and Dunduzu Chisiza, who saw themselves as key figures in the Party, and so they had been, were hardly known. The focus of the *Malawi News* on Kamuzu and him alone did nothing to dispel the picture of Kamuzu as sole leader.

The Appointment of Iain Macleod as Colonial Secretary

Meanwhile back in the United Kingdom Macmillan and his Conservative Party won a decisive victory at the General Election of October 1959. What was a significant new factor in the victory was that it brought into the House of Commons a new influx of members who looked to Macmillan as their leader and whose clear support gave him a new confidence.

Macmillan appears to have decided immediately to deal with Africa. He would visit the continent himself for the first time but more importantly, he decided to appoint a new Secretary of State for the Colonies. The new Secretary would initiate a completely new policy; the contrast with the policy of the pre-election Conservative Government was astonishing. The new Secretary of State for the Colonies would begin a policy more like the result of the victory of another party. Macmillan began this new initiative immediately.

In the very first week, immediately after his massive electoral victory, Macmillan summoned Iain Macleod to a private meeting at No. 10. The two men met alone and Macmillan gave Macleod the job he had been hoping to get, Colonial Secretary. Macleod's biographer sums up his build up of excitement at that time:

> Macleod's imagination was fired by the drama that was unfolding in Africa. This was the raw politics that excited him: the realities were stark, the differences of interest were deep, and the conflicting ideals were passionately held. Britain, like other democratic European powers, had neither the will nor the resources to maintain colonial rule by force. But progress towards majority rule, unless skilfully managed, brought a serious risk of becoming embroiled in civil and racial war. Macleod's liberal convictions left him in little doubt as to how a Conservative Government should discharge its duties. Here was a great historic challenge and he had the confidence to seek the responsibility for meeting it. Africa had become the focus of his ambition and had won his heart.[274]

Much has been made of the fact that Macleod had never been in Africa. However, he had a brother with whom he was close who had lived in Kenya for most of his adult life. Significantly Macleod impressed David Astor with the detailed knowledge of the current situation in East Africa which he had built up in the months before his appointment. Macleod was ready and well prepared.

Clearly Macmillan and his principal aide, Rab Butler, had been thinking carefully about this and had full confidence in Macleod. He was not given special instruction but was left to get on with it. His task was understood to be bringing an end to British rule in Africa. The one area in question was Nyasaland/Malawi and Northern Rhodesia. Macleod felt that they were in the same category as Kenya or Tanganyika. It was a matter of his biding his time but Home still had other ideas. The Monckton Commission also had to report before any final decision was made.

Macleod soon gained the support of all the senior officials in the office dealing with the East African territories. The key moment came for the senior officials when Macleod called them to his office and asked them what

---

they hoped to get out of the proposed conference on Kenya? The three key officials, Sir Hilton Poynton, Sir Leslie Monson and 'Max' Weber met the question originally by silence then Weber said that it was time for a breakthrough to African majority rule. Macleod nodded his head and a revolutionary change in British African policy had taken place.

For many this was most clearly symbolised when Macleod made clear that white settler leaders had no special role to play in any judgement he made about the situation. Under Lyttelton and Lennox-Boyd right up to the beginning of 1959 the settlers had always been treated as experts to be consulted first. From his arrival Macleod made it clear that those days were over and he had no intention of giving preference to the views of the minority over those of the majority.

Kenya, Uganda, Tanganyika and Zanzibar were all to be dealt with by the new Secretary of State at this time. He saw them as having somewhat different problems but all were put on the road to self-government at the same time. This was particularly a dramatic change for Kenya which had been ruled through emergency regulations since 1952.

Macleod with his first paper to the Cabinet on 10th November proposed lifting the emergency regulations governing Kenya. He also decided that the release of a majority of detainees should take place while he also brought in new regulations to ensure maintenance of law and order. From then on everything was organised on the basis of efficiently and effectively leading the British East African territories towards self-government as rapidly as possible.

Macleod was clear that he had to start his preparation of planning for the future of Nyasaland and Northern Rhodesia. Within a few days of his appointment he had a private talk with Sir Patrick Devlin. Although he had found Devlin's Report somewhat overwritten, he also found the Report to be true. Indeed he understood the opposition of the people of the Protectorate to political relations with Southern Rhodesia to be bitter and almost universal. He noted, for example, that Africans loyal to the Government still had no time for the Central Africa Federation and any kind of Nyasaland' membership of it.

Although the investigation of the whole situation by the Monckton Commission had to take place and Monckton make his report before Macleod's plans could be implemented, he believed his ideas would be allowed precedence over whatever Monckton came up with. Macleod was quite clear that as far as he was concerned first and foremost the future Nyasaland lay with Dr Banda. He was equally adamant that the young men who had brought Kamuzu back to the country were not part of this plan

Indeed they were to be kept out of affairs for as long as possible. Macleod had been clear that the future of Malawi lay with Kamuzu almost as soon as he was appointed to his new office.[275] He briefed Macmillan secretly on this at the start of his planning for Nyasaland and the Prime Minister had not objected.

It is not clear, however, where Macleod got this firm set of ideas that wrote off Chipembere, Chisiza and company and gave him so much confidence in Kamuzu. Clearly while the three, Kamuzu, Chip and Du were together in the European wing of the prison at Gwelo they were seen as a team by Foot and by Macmillan. Banda was treated as the leader and senior member but Chip and Du were clearly part of the team as can be seen in the part they play during Foot's visit. Foot clearly sees them as part of the organisation and close to Kamuzu. In Macleod's mind things are quite different and where this idea comes from is not made clear by him in any of his writing.

What has to be recognised, and Macleod did recognise the situation, is that British East Africa had been well administered but it had not been prepared at all for self-government. A situation was being created where probably the best administration was going to pull out of Africa in a period of about three years. Very little could be done in the various territories to develop and train members of the administration.

Macleod did have a major problem in that he could not proceed with the speed in the northern territories that he would have liked. It had already been decided before the General Election that the Monckton Commission was to visit the three territories and advise upon the future of the Federation. Macleod had to sit back and wait for Monckton and his team to carry out their work before he could begin his. Clearly, however, as far as Macleod was concerned Monckton's review was an exercise that had to be undertaken but it was out of date before it had begun as far as he was concerned. He already knew what his policy was to be in each of the two territories for which he was responsible as Colonial Secretary.

However, Macmillan was also left with a most frustrating task which was to make something of the Monckton Commission which was left over from the previous situation. Macmillan was still trying to make the Commission a balanced one by the inclusion of Labour Party members. On 4th December it was made clear finally that there was to be no Labour Party participation in the Monckton Commission. There then followed a strange episode in Macmillan's behaviour. It became clear that it was possible to persuade Sir Hartley Shawcross, an ex-Labour Cabinet Minister, to serve on the Monckton Commission so long as Shawcross was assured, and he was so assured

Chapter 9. *African Omlette*. p. 188.

privately by Macmillan, that secession by one or other of the two northern territories was not ruled out as a possible recommendation to be made by the Commission.

Why Macmillan made this effort to include a has-been Labour ex-Cabinet Minister on the Commission remains a puzzle. It did not make the Commission bi-partisan in any real sense and it involved deliberately misleading Welensky. Also it still did not allow the Monckton Commission to begin its work, which had to be discussed between Welensky and Macmillan when the latter met with Welensky on his African visit.

Macmillan's Visit to Africa

Macmillan's African Odyssey began with visits to Ghana and Nigeria which were successful enough but were not headline material until he gave a press conference on 13th January 1960 in Lagos. In answer to a question about the future of the Federation and the place of the two northern territories in it Macmillan said

> Before the British Government's ultimate responsibility over Nyasaland and Northern Rhodesia is removed, the people of the two Territories will be given an opportunity to decide on whether the Federation is beneficial to them. This will be an expression of opinion that is genuinely of the people.[276]

Macmillan's principal biographer Alistair Horne refers to this as an unguarded remark but it does not read like one and it was not reported as such by the *Manchester Guardian*, the *Financial Times*, and the *News Chronicle*.

However, when he arrived in the Federation Macmillan insisted to Welensky that he had been misreported and continued in his usual suave and confident style during his visit to all three territories and all four governments of the area. His astonishing ability to talk round hostile audiences was shown in Southern Rhodesia where he soon had initially hostile white audiences applauding him enthusiastically.

The Prime Minister then began his historic visit to the Union of South Africa where he would make perhaps his most famous speech - that delivered in the South African Parliament on the 3rd February 1960. Whether Macmillan' biographer, Alistair Horne is correct in saying that this brilliant address was deliberately and consciously addressed as much to Welensky and Whitehead as to Verwoerd is difficult to prove, but clearly much of what Macmilla said that day in Cape Town applied as much to the Rhodesias as to Sou Africa. The views of Welensky and Whitehead on African progress withi

---

[276] Ibid. p. 171.

the Federation did not square with Macmillan's clear statements in his Cape Town speech about what had became British policy in Africa.

> As fellow members of the Commonwealth it is our earnest desire to give South Africa our support and encouragement. but ... there are some aspects of your policies which make it impossible for us to do this without being false to our own deep convictions about the political destinies of free men to which in our own territories we are trying to give effect.[?]

Perhaps even more important for the Federation was the long term impact on Macmillan of a conversation the Prime Minister had with the Governor-General of Nigeria. Sir James Robertson, a fellow Scot and veteran of the Colonial Service in Africa. This was a conversation which Macmillan was to repeat on a number of different occasions as if it had made a definite breakthrough in his thinking on the problems of Africa.

> After some meeting of the so-called cabinet. or council. I said. "Are these fit for self-government?" and he said. "No. of course not." I said. "When will they be ready?" He said. "Twenty years. twenty-five years." Then I said "What do you recommend me to do?" HE said "I recommend you give it to them at once." I said. "Why. that seems strange." "Well". he said. "if they were twenty years well spent. if they were learning administration. if they were getting experience. I would say wait. but what will happen? All the most intelligent people. all the ones I have been training will all become rebels. I shall have to put them all in prison. There will be violence. bitterness and hatred. They won't spend the twenty years learning. We shall simply have us twenty years of repression and therefore in my view they'd be better start learning [to rule themselves] at once." I thought it was very sensible.[?8]

It is very difficult to know what Macmillan was up to at this point. He increasingly trusted Alec Douglas-Home who clearly still had his ear. However Macmillan had appointed Iain Macleod as Colonial Secretary who clearly understood his role was to move ahead as rapidly as possible in divesting Britain of its responsibilities in Africa. This was a task Macleod embarked upon immediately on appointment without seeking specific instructions. As he was to say in an interview in *The Spectator* of 17 January. 1964:

> It has been said that after I became Colonial Secretary. there was a deliberate speeding-up of the movement towards independence. I agree. There was. And in my view any other policy would have led to terrible bloodshed in Africa.

indeed it is clear that Macleod understood his job as fulfilling the task in Africa along the understanding of what needed to be done expressed so clearly to Macmillan by Sir James Robertson. Macleod was clear about the task ahead but whether it applied to either of the two Northern territories of the Federation as it did to Kenya. Uganda and Tanganyika. it would appear

---

[?] Horne. *Macmillan 1957-1986*. p. 196.
[8] Ibid. p. 190.

Macmillan had not yet decided. So Macmillan was allowing two members of his Government, Home and Macleod, to operate on somewhat different understandings of the future of the Federation. Home was allowed to go on presuming that something was going to be developed out of the Federation while Macleod believed he would be allowed to give his two northern territories the same freedom that the East African territories had received.

While Macmillan was in the Federation, Dingle Foot Q.C. was given permission by the Federal authorities to visit Banda in Gwelo prison on the 23rd and 24th of January. During the very cordial visit Foot told Banda that Monckton and Macleod wished him to be released and to give evidence to the Monckton Commission. Foot was able to have a wide-ranging discussion with Banda and was also allowed to bring Chipembere and Dunduzu Chisiza into the discussions on both days. They were finally able to agree on a memorandum which could be given to Macmillan, Macleod, and Monckton and, after rejecting some suggested senior British figures, it was agreed that David Astor could have a copy of the agreement but was not to use the text for straight publication. The Federal prison authorities were making no effort to neither take any record of this visit nor interfere with it in any way.

The British South African Police behaved quite differently however. They had set up recording equipment on their own authority and had had the full text of the meetings on Welensky's desk forty-eight hours later. Welensky knew everything that had been said and also knew that Macmillan planned to have Foot meet him in Zomba and let him have Kamuzu's letter. For the rest of the visit Welensky and Macmillan managed to fail to have effective talk or contact with each other.

Towards the Release of Dr Banda

After Macmillan's return to Britain negotiations began about the release of Dr Banda. These were complicated, and involved the Federal Government, the Southern Rhodesian Government, and the Nyasaland Administration all of whom were opposed to Banda operating as a free man in Nyasaland. As a result of the negotiations, led by Home, Macmillan had decided to delay the release of Banda, and on the morning of 23rd February he announced this to the Cabinet. There is no doubt that this decision was seen as a victory for Welensky and that it was him exercising a veto on British policy. How far the difference was also a product of Macmillan's level of uncertainty between the firm Colonial Office understanding about the future of Nyasaland at least and the rather different Commonwealth Office understanding of the future is something that is not made clear, though the notes between Macmillan and Home point in that direction.

In any case, at the end of the cabinet meeting Macleod dropped his bombshell. Macleod pointed out that he could not accept this decision and would have to resign. Writers like Horne insist that this all came as a surprise and imply that it stemmed from Macleod's personality and his perhaps having made unwise promises to Banda already. It was in fact rather a very clear effort by Macleod to insist on what he believed to be his authority which had been usurped. It was also a deliberate effort by Macleod to prevent Macmillan attempting to stay friends with both sides which Macleod believe was an impossible manoeuvre at that time.

It had its effect as Macleod had hoped it would. On behalf of the Prime Minister, Home proposed to Welensky that Banda would be released, on April 1st, three weeks later than Macleod had originally planned but four days before Monckton and company were due to leave Nyasaland. This was the overriding concern of Macleod and it was conceded. He wrote personally to Home that evening congratulating him and adding 'I will always remember the understanding and the quick sympathy you gave to me in these last few difficult days. Thank you.'

Chapter 7

The Cabinet Crisis[279]

If we have to maintain the same number of police and Special Branch as the British did to govern Malawi, we will have failed and we should pack up and go back to the village. (Words of Dunduzu Chisiza to the writer, Kanjedza Detention Centre, July 1960)

In the months between Banda's return to Malawi and 'Operation Sunrise', the young leaders had little chance to get to know the new President of NAC let alone establish close relationships with him. The long period of imprisonment they all subsequently shared welded the leadership cadres together in a new way but it did not link anyone closely to Banda. Banda was imprisoned along with Chipembere and the two Chisizas in Gweru jail, while the others were elsewhere. Some were in Marandellas while the majority were held in Kanjedza, a camp where almost every male detainee other than Banda, had to spend some time before they were finally released. The three younger men did not establish warm personal relations with Banda during this sojourn together at Gweru. Far from it, for though little significance was attached to it at the time, we must note now that when Banda was released on the 1st of April 1960, Chipembere along with the Chisiza brothers was brought up to Kanjedza where all three had to endure six more weary months of detention along with others deemed by the British to be the 'hard core' of Congress. In this connection it is also important to note that Kanyama Chiume did not undergo this profoundly significant prison experience. He had been abroad on March 3, 1959 and he stayed abroad until after Banda's release when he returned to become Banda's closest aid, 'my boy Kanyama'.

The Formation of MCP and Kamuzu as 'the Saviour of the Nation'

However, before Banda's release it had been Orton Chirwa, the first of the young leadership group - the oldest of them as it happened - to be released who founded the Malawi Congress Party. He was aided in this way by a very able high school student, Aleke Banda, who had been shipped back to his parents' homeland of Malawi after a period of detention in Southern

---

[279] This chapter is based on the article 'Some Reflections on the Malawi "Cabinet Crisis 1964-65', first published in *Religion in Malawi*, 7 (1997), 3-12. We are grateful to *Religion in Malawi* for permission to republish it in this abridged and slightly altered form.

Rhodesia for his political activities there. Their most important helpers in the setting up of the new party were a number of ex-Youth Leaguers who had recently been released from Kanjedza, in particular Sam Banda and Sam Ngoma and a group of teachers led by Shadrak Khonje. In an extraordinary short time, three months in fact, the MCP had branches all over the country. On the 5th of April, 1960, Orton Chirwa handed the presidency of the MCP to Kamuzu.

There then followed a year of hectic organizing, demonstrations and agitation during which the MCP became a larger, more effective and more popular movement than the old NAC had ever been. Conservative social groupings and certain geographical localities which had resisted all the blandishments of the NAC succumbed to the MCP; notably the Lower Shire districts and many areas of the Central Province.

During that same year, it became increasingly clear that the British Government under the leadership of Harold MacMillan and Ian MacLeod was going to allow Malawi to secede from the Federation and move towards independence. As a result of this the MCP concentrated all its efforts to encourage this perceived development in British policy. Everything was subordinated to this end and nothing was to be allowed to get in the way of this opportunity.

There is no need to outline the various constitutional manoeuvres and the conferences that followed, they are well enough known and well described in the literature, in Short's *Banda* and T.D. Williams' *Malawi*. What does need to be discussed and has not been hitherto, is the relationship between the 'hard core' of the NAC left in Kanjedza and Dr Banda now leading the country towards freedom, ably assisted by Kanyama Chiume. Orton Chirwa was at this time somewhat relegated to the background.

Banda did nothing at all about gaining early release for Chipembere and the two Chisizas. Astonishingly, during these six months as the number of the 'hard core' was diminished by a policy of gradual release, these three key young leaders had to wait for their freedom to the very end. They were released only when Kanjedza was closed at the termination of the State of Emergency. Admittedly they were immediately given important posts within the administration of the MCP, Chipembere was appointed Treasurer-General, Dunduzu Chisiza, Secretary-General and his elder brother Yatuta became Administrative Secretary. These were positions of authority, but they involved heavy work-loads which tied the men to the Party HQ in Blantyre. Whether this was intentional or not is an interesting question, what is important is that the work-load of these offices got in the way of their re-building the grass-roots political fiefdoms which they had enjoyed before March 1959.

What has not been appreciated in the literature is that they returned to help administer a party that was a new political institution. What had taken place was not simply a change of name. The MCP, by the time Chipembere came out of Kanjedza, was no longer the old Congress brought back to life, which is what Orton and the Youth Leaguers had created. It had grown up round the message, brilliantly purveyed by the Publicity Secretary, Kanyama Chiume, that Kamuzu was the one and only leader, who would destroy Federation and set the people free. Kanyama played brilliantly the role of the loyal acolyte to Kamuzu as Saviour of the Nation, and the whole country was singing the many new songs, all composed by Chiume, all focusing on Banda, such as *Zonse zimene za Kamuzu Banda*.

During the six weary months of waiting in Kanjedza, Chipembere and the two Chisizas were already growing uneasy about the new situation and the nature of the Party. During the cold season of 1960, I spent one afternoon a week with them in Kanjedza in my capacity as Chaplain. During these visits we talked about the future of Malawi and of Africa and discussed the problem areas in economics and religion and culture as well as politics, narrowly defined. It was in these very general discussions that their uneasiness emerged. They readily admitted that the propaganda line being carried out so persuasively and effectively by Chiume, hailing Dr Banda as the Saviour of the Nation, was a development of that initiated by them in preparation for his return, but they were somewhat uneasy at what they heard of its development. They used also to joke that there would be big problems if H.K.B. came to believe it. They were seriously unhappy, however, at his acting as though the Party was an agency of his personal authority. All three talked with me at different times about the traditional understanding of authority. They were each most insistent that traditionally, chiefs, however strong or popular, had to articulate popular feeling and although chiefs sought to guide such feeling they could do this successfully only through consultation. A chief always acted with his elders who all had the right to speak and be consulted. Indeed, in judicial matters cases had to be heard in public and everyone concerned had the right to speak. The term *mlandu* describes this understanding of authority and its concept in marked contrast to what they heard of Banda's increasingly autocratic style. It is also clearly a concept in direct contrast with Banda's later insistence on autocratic rule being the 'African way'; a refrain too often echoed by European 'liberals' and 'experts'. Some of this conflict is later reflected in Dunduzu's piece 'Africa-What Lies Ahead?'

However, it would be wrong to understand their attitude while they waited impatiently for their release, as one of hostility to Banda. Rather it was a mixture of sheer frustration and a vague but real uneasiness about what they heard was going on outside.

After their release there was so much to do and such high hopes of defeating the hated Federation and of gaining independence for Malawi, it was not the time to make waves or do anything that might even appear to threaten unity. The British appeared to deem unity a necessity if they were to continue to recognise the MCP as the body that represented the wishes of the Malawi people. However, there was one gesture that, with the advantage of hindsight, can be seen as expressing this uneasiness about what had been going on during the months of detention they had had to. endure after Banda's release. This was a series of very fiery speeches delivered by Chipembere in many parts of the country in the first weeks after his release. These speeches, which focussed a great deal of attention upon Chipembere, were seen by the British authorities as extremely dangerous, threatening public order in this very delicate political situation. Then and since, observers have seen these speeches as an unfortunate error in judgement on Chipembere's part. Masauko Chipembere was not the unbalanced hot-head that this judgement would deem him to have been. What observers have failed to notice was that these speeches transferred the spotlight from Kamuzu Banda to Chipembere. It was Chipembere's determination to regain both the attention of the African public and his role as a key popular leader that led him to ignore how the British would react to his speeches. React they did with a vengeance. 'Chip' was arrested, charged and found guilty of sedition and imprisoned in January 1961. By this action, a potential thorn in Dr Banda's side was removed without Banda having to respond in any way at all to Chipembere's speeches.

After the massive election victory at the polls for the MCP and its supporters in the elections of August, 1961, the signals from Whitehall were unmistakable. Malawi was going to be allowed to secede from the Federation and could then move steadily towards independence so long as nothing untoward occurred. Despite this, Dr Banda did nothing about gaining some kind of remission of sentence so as to allow Chipembere to regain his freedom and re-enter the service of the Party. This was so despite the fact that the new Governor, Sir Glyn Jones, had made it clear that he was willing at least to discuss an early release. Although both Short and Williams have posited a deep division between Chipembere and the Chisizas, it was Dunduzu Chisiza, who, in the Legislative Council, made an impassioned plea on Chipembere's behalf. On November 29th that year, Dunduzu deplored Chipembere's continued imprisonment and his absence from the Council where the Nation needed him. 'Du' was unmistakably, though indirectly, criticising Banda, not the British. The Speaker ruled that he must desist from this topic and Dr Banda sat silent.

At that time I believed that the uneasiness with Dr Banda was more than that, a vague unhappiness that had no precise focus other than the contrast of Kamuzu's style with the tradition of *mlandu*. It also appeared to be restricted to a comparatively small number of people. There was however one serious clash between the Chisizas and Banda in this period. It has never been made public but was of great long-term importance for the future of the whole of Central and East Africa. Both Chisizas had close connections with Kenneth Kaunda the leader of UNIP in Northern Rhodesia while Yatuta Chisiza was a close friend of Julius Nyerere of the future Tanzania. The Chisizas became involved in confidential negotiations with both men about a possible future federation of the territories which were to become Zambia, Malawi and Tanzania. Dunduzu explained to me that he believed such negotiations must be completed before independence was achieved, for once three separate states were established, there would soon be too many vested interests in the way of any kind of union. The Chisizas, Kaunda and Nyerere felt that their three territories could develop better together than separately. The Chisizas and Kaunda believed that their trade links which were all directed southwards through Southern Rhodesia and South Africa had to be reoriented to Dar-es-Salaam (Mozambique was not an option for that kind of development then). Otherwise independence would then be profoundly limited by economic dependence on the south. A link which later emerged as the Tan-Zam Railway was already being discussed. With a firm agreement from Kaunda and Nyerere that they were willing to enter into formal negotiations, the Chisizas approached Banda with the idea. He refused adamantly to have anything to do with it. Dunduzu and Yatuta and the few friends that knew of the scheme could do nothing in public about this, because it involved the leaders of two other territories who did not want such a rebuff made public and because of the need for public unity in the drive towards secession and independence. Dunduzu consoled himself with the hope that it might be tried again after independence but I was unable to judge how far he really believed this. In public Banda continued to talk of wider African groupings as Philip Short points out. The failure of the confidential and much more precise discussions referred to above perhaps explains Banda's later apparent volte-face on this issue which, understandably, Short finds puzzling.

However, no one was going to raise this issue nor indulge in public disagreement with Kamuzu on any other issue. Everyone was now deeply committed to the campaign to gain secession from the Federation with British help and then to move on peacefully to independence. When

Chipembere was released from prison in January 1963 he immediately took over the seat which his father held in the House and without any recriminations threw himself with characteristic energy into the task at hand.

Growing Tensions within the MCP

David Williams and Philip Short, each in different ways and from different perspectives, have effectively described the events of 1962 and 1963 which led up to the achievement of independence by Malawi on 6 July 1964. They also chart in detail the gradual political emasculation of Banda's Cabinet colleagues, his 'boys' as he habitually referred to them. They quote copiously from the many speeches in which Banda reduced these men, who had revived the old NAC into the powerful party whose Presidency they had given to him, to the level of personal assistants to the great leader.

Williams and Short also described the events leading up to the debates in the new Malawi Parliament of the 8th and 9th September, 1964 by which time the majority of the members of the Cabinet had either resigned or been dismissed. I do not intend to rehearse that story but to discuss the so-called Cabinet Crisis in the light of the events of which Williams and Short had no knowledge but which necessitate a re-appraisal of what occurred.

Along with most other observers, Short and Williams accept that there was a growing dissatisfaction with the place granted to them by Banda on the part of the rest of his Cabinet. This unhappiness became increasingly acute, late in 1963, when Banda clearly expressed his determination to have close and amicable relations with the Portuguese in Mozambique and the white regimes south of the Zambezi. When Banda appeared quite unwilling, throughout the first months of 1964, to pay any attention to the representations on this issue and that of his public denigration of his colleagues, the stage was set for a confrontation. This took place in August and September of 1964.

This conflict has been seen by observers as coming rather late in the day and manifesting itself suddenly and unexpectedly. Short and Williams both emphasize that Banda was taken aback by the open opposition shown him at the Cabinet meeting of the morning of 16 August 1964.

Banda certainly was surprised that morning but his surprise must not be taken as confirmation that the division was one which developed only in 1964, nor as the first confrontation between Banda and some of his younger colleagues. Chipembere's fiery speeches around the country which led to his arrest and Dunduzu's passionate appeals for his release from prison in the first session of the new Legislative Council in 1961 we have already noted. We have also noted the disagreement over an alternative federation. These were not open confrontations with Banda but they did show a division between Banda on the one hand and the Chisizas and Chipembere on the other. I want to suggest now that these were manifestations of real, long term differences which grew until they burst into flames in August 1964.

Before developing this further, the role of Kanyama Chiume has to be considered. He was a key figure in the events of August and September 1964. However, what has not been recognised is that he took no part in the opposition to Banda until then, that is August 1964. Although he was one of the inspired group of 'young men' who revitalised Congress in the fifties, the Emergency of March 1959, marked a parting of the ways between him and the rest of the original leadership group.

As we have noted already, it was among the 'hard core' who had to sit it out in Kanjedza to the bitter end, that the first uneasiness arose about the Banda cult so brilliantly orchestrated by Chiume. When the last batch of detainees, including both Chisizas and Chipembere, left Kanjedza there was already a gulf, at that time not yet unbridgeable, between them and Chiume. He had not undergone the experience of imprisonment, and in addition during the last six months of their time 'inside' he had been the key figure beside Banda in the building up of the Party and the Banda as Saviour campaign. He was already 'my boy Kanyama', the model performer of the role Banda was going to expect them all to accept. Whatever Chiume's original motivation for this was, when the time came for choosing candidates for the elections of August 1961, he had no alternative but to stick to the role of Kamuzu's 'boy' for the people of the Northern Province had rejected him.

The District Committee of the Malawi Congress Party for Rumphi District, the constituency for which Banda had sent the name of Chiume as his nomination, refused to accept it. The committee was made up entirely of 'prison graduates' and they were adamant that they and the people of the area would not have Chiume. They endured two bitter face to face confrontations with Banda before they finally backed down and accepted the nomination. I talked to them twice when they had come south to insist that Banda withdrew his nomination of Kanyama as their candidate. This very important contretemps is not reported anywhere in the literature on Malawi. Banda did make mention of his having to impose Chiume on the people of Rumphi much later, in September or October 1964. He did this at a time when he was attempting to show that the dismissed cabinet members were unrepresentative of the people of Malawi, each and every one.

Soon after the election and the creation of an Executive Council, still nominally headed by the Governor, but run on a day to day basis by Dr Banda as Chief Minister, Kanyama Chiume's political role and the growing tension between the 'young men' and Kamuzu came together. His conduct a

212

'my boy Kanyama' was the occasion of the first semi-public clash between Banda and the other leaders of the MCP. This major confrontation took place in July 1962 NOT in August 1964. Sometime that month, Dunduzu Chisiza, Mikeka Mkandawire and Colin Cameron demanded a private interview with Dr Banda who agreed that the meeting should take place in the presence of Sir Glyn Jones, who, constitutionally, still headed the administration. The three made a formal request that Banda should restrain Chiume, who, in various speeches on public occasions was commenting on issues other than those of his own portfolio and was 'putting down' the other leaders of the Party and the other members of the administration. This was, in fact, a way of challenging Dr Banda's style of leadership while leaving him a way out without loss of face. However, the discussion rapidly became a direct clash between Banda and Dunduzu Chisiza. Initially, Banda used his classic gambit of throwing an apparently uncontrollable fit of rage at being so challenged. When this did not succeed in deflecting Chisiza, Banda calmed down and the discussion appeared to end happily enough. However, about two weeks later, Banda and Chisiza met again, this time alone. At this meeting Dunduzu expressed himself without reservation or antipathy to Dr Banda's whole style of leadership. He went so far as to say that if things did not change for the better, he would wait until Malawi had gained her full independence and then resign from the Party and go into active opposition. He served notice that he would stay outwardly loyal to Banda's leadership for the sake of the nation and independence, but with independence achieved he would then act, unless there had been real change in the interim.

Mkandawire, Cameron and Chisiza had explained their intentions to the other leading figures in the Party leadership other than Chiume, before they went to see Banda; Dunduzu did not discuss the second meeting, as far as I am aware, with anyone save his brother Yatuta.

The Triumph and Tragedy of Dunduzu Chisiza

Outwardly all seemed well until July 1962, when the International Economic Symposium, a massive gathering of academic economists and development specialists from all over the world, was held in Malawi. This was arranged and directed by Dunduzu Chisiza. That little Malawi could have hosted such a gathering was a tribute to the respect in which Dunduzu Chisiza was held, particularly by leading specialists in the economic development field like W.W. Rostow. (Rostow and Dunduzu had corresponded with each other while Du was in Kanjedza.)

At the symposium Chisiza's keynote speech is of the utmost significance. In it Chisiza expressed a philosophy of government and society which had its roots in both modern social democracy and the traditions of *mlandu*. This was profoundly at variance with ideas consistently expressed by Banda and echoed by Chiume. In addition, Banda's coolness towards the symposium was there for all to see. One had to assume that this was because the international event was Chisiza's and represented the latter's prestige in significant circles in the outside world.

By September, within a few weeks of this triumph, Dunduzu Chisiza was dead. He died when his car apparently missed the bridge which spans the Namadzi River on the main Blantyre to Zomba road. At the first meeting of the Legislative Council after this tragic event, his brother. Yatuta felt constrained to deny that there was any truth in the rumours that 'Du' had been disloyal in any way to Dr Banda. It is very significant that he chose to describe as disloyalty, reports in the foreign media about some differences of opinion between Banda and his brother occasioned by international media coverage of the Symposium. At the time, most people were so obsessed with the final stages of getting rid of Federation and gaining independence as well as being stunned by Dunduzu's death, that they did not pay any attention to the style of Yatuta's speech on that occasion. With hindsight it was one of the markers of the change whereby loyalty was no longer measured in terms of dedication to an ideal or to Malawi, but in terms of obedience to H. Kamuzu Banda.

In May 1963, I returned to my job as a rural pastor in the Balaka-Ntcheu area. I had been out of the country at the time of my friend's death. I had been aware of differences of opinion between him and Banda over relations with Zambia and Tanzania but at that time I did not know of his two confrontations with Banda. However, I was brought to a realisation that things were not well through my contacts with the people of my parish.

One Sunday afternoon, while sharing a meal with a group of elders, someone in the group referred to Dunduzu's death using the word '*anaphedwa*' which carries the meaning of being killed by someone. When I, rather surprised, asked "*anaphedwa ndi ndani?*" (killed by whom?) there was an embarrassed silence which brought to an end a number of other conversations going on among the members of the group. Someone, rather embarrassed, then muttered "*anaphedwa ndi mfiti*" (killed by a sorcerer), in reply to the further question, 'what sorcerer?' he went on, "*mfiti mkulu uja*" (that great sorcerer over there). There was no doubt as to whom he meant and so I quickly changed the conversation to a pressing problem in the parish, to everyone's manifest relief. Although I tried to shrug off the incident, a number of other similar encounters made it clear to me that the people of my area saw Dunduzu and Banda as having been enemies, or more precisely, they saw Dr Banda as having been Chisiza's enemy.

This was at odds with the views of most political observers, African and European, who, while recognizing that differences of opinion had existed between the two men, did not perceive any deep rift. I also could not accept it. Although I was deeply disturbed by the perception of Banda's attitude towards Dunduzu that these sorcery stories in the villages represented. Sorcery (*ufiti*) in the traditional thought of southern African peoples represents the power of personal hatred to destroy the object of the hatred, either directly or by means of events which Europeans would call chance.

It was only later, after Colin Cameron had resigned from the Malawi Cabinet on the eve of the Cabinet crisis, that I heard from him of the meeting where he had accompanied Dunduzu and Mikeka Mkandawire to see Banda, and also from Yatuta Chisiza about the meeting, hitherto secret, between his brother and Banda that had followed. Village people, however they came to the understanding of affairs, had a more accurate perception of relationships between the leading figures on the Malawi political stage than contemporary academic and journalistic commentators.

The rift, it is clear, did go far back, but this makes it all the more pertinent to ask why the other ministers and their close associates did not do more back then in 1962 about their increasing discomfort with both Kamuzu's style of leadership and with the content of his foreign policy. With hindsight we can now see signs of trouble brewing but at the time they were disregarded. At that time we cast these suspicions aside because they were too disturbing to contemplate. We cast them aside because there were so many immediate and urgent concerns which seemed of overwhelming importance. Would Nyasaland be allowed to secede from the Federation whatever the Federal government said? What would Welensky and his cabinet do? If Nyasaland did secede, how soon and on what terms would independence be gained? Any sign of division within the MCP could jeopardize everything. Whether that was true or not, it was what was believed at the time. It is also important to recall the extraordinary atmosphere of the time. Everybody in the Party and those in sympathy with it were on an increasing 'high'. Everything was going so well, the vast majority of the people were united and enthusiastic in support of the Congress, areas and groups that had stayed outside the old NAC were producing mass support for the MCP, the 'Wind of Change' was blowing over Africa sweeping Malawi before it. It may appear naive and foolish now but in 1963 and the first half of 1964, the atmosphere was such that to sit back and coolly appraise the Party critically would have felt like a betrayal. Everyone seemed to be saying "Yes, there are some problems, but they are small and we'll iron them out after independence," or "The 'old man' does sometimes go over the top, but that can be sorted out later".

People did have very real worries at that time, but they were to do with what Britain, Portugal, Rhodesia or South Africa might do. Would the British stick the course in the face of the hostility of the white powers of southern Africa? It is easy today to forget that in 1964 these regimes were overwhelmingly strong militarily and they also had a great deal of political 'muscle'. Would they really stand by and let Malawi become an independent black nationalistic state? This would not only mean the end of the Federation, it would also entail a massive increase in the miles of free black territory on the Mozambique border, and with Northern Rhodesia/Zambia sure to follow, coalition of these southern powers could persuade Britain to change policy or even act on their own, if they could find some pretext or other to give some cloak of legitimacy to their actions? These were the fears that were in people's minds despite the euphoria.

Kamuzu Strengthens his Grip

So it was that the leadership group, Chipembere, Y. Chisiza, Orton Chirwa, Augustine Bwanausi, Rose Chibambo, Willie Chokani and their associates, heavily involved in the exhausting task of negotiating the disentangling of the Protectorate from the structure of Federation as well as the necessary moves towards independence, were in no mood to raise other difficulties. Yes, they were annoyed by the increasingly autocratic style of Dr Banda's utterances and Chiume's 'Banda as Saviour' propaganda. They told themselves that this was comparatively minor, it certainly could be dealt with later. Any hint of division within the Party that could be blown up as unrest, a threat to life and property, would be just the excuse Salisbury and Lourenço Marques wanted to say to the world that their interference was necessary to restore law and order. The experience of the Belgian Congo was fresh in everyone's mind.

The so-called 'young men' were completely wrong in their reading of the situation. They believed that what was at issue was some eccentricities of style on the part of Dr Banda which they could deal with after independence was achieved. They and their close associates, including the present writer, did not perceive that Banda's increasingly autocratic style reflected his actual accumulation of massive personal power. By the time of the independence celebrations, Banda's personal authority in the Malawi Congress Party was such that they could not match it, either individually or collectively.

From the time of their belated release from Kanjedza, the 'young men' who were to clash with Banda, had been totally absorbed, initially in party but primarily in governmental administration. This was heavily time consuming as the Protectorate moved through the various stages of constitutional change, to secession from the hated Federation and finally to independence

They simply had not the time, nor did they see the need, to rebuild a strong and organised personal following. The only one to attempt it, Chipembere, ended up in jail for his pains.

Meanwhile Dr Banda continued to build on the foundations firmly laid during his six months start over them. He continued to build a personal control within the Party that no one had ever had before. His prestige and authority was built up in a campaign across the country, brilliantly executed by Kanyama Chiume. Indeed, without the latter's drive and tireless dedication to the task it is unlikely that it could have achieved such success. The key central offices in the Party were now in the hands of two of Kamuzu's own men, Albert Muwalo and Aleke Banda. These men had no personal following, no territorial fief in the country. They held power because of Banda's patronage, and only because throughout 1963 the organisation of the Party more and more came into the hands of people who owed a great deal to Banda and were not associates of Chipembere, Orton Chirwa or the Chisizas. It was very significant that many of his men were from the generation that came between Banda and the 'young men'. People like Qabaniso Chibambo and Richard Chidzanja who were appointed by Banda to be Party bosses of the Northern and Central Provinces respectively. They were of the generation that had been skipped over in the fifties. They felt they had lost out. They were now given their place in the sun by Kamuzu Banda.

The appointment of Chidzanja is an appropriate reminder that the new MCP was reaching and gaining the loyalty of segments of the population that had resisted the attractions of the old NAC. Other than in Ntcheu District and Lilongwe town, the NANC had not obtained massive support in the Central Region. Its support had always been in the Northern Region and in the Southern Region other than in the Lower Shire districts. Now these districts of the Central and Southern Regions had also come to give massive support to the MCP but above all to Kamuzu as the one who could lead the people to the new day. This was a new element in nationalistic politics, the entry of people who had hitherto resisted the NAC as just another facet of the modern world they did not like. As recently as July 1959, I had been told by a group of village elders in the Lower Shire '*sitifuna matchalitchi, sitifuna masukulu, sitifuna kongeresi, tingofuna mtendere, basi*' (We don't want churches, we don't want schools, we don't want Congress, we just want peace.) There was no doubt that these conservative groups were reached by a quite new style of appeal initiated by Banda and Chiume while the other leaders languished in detention. This emphasized traditional institutions like the Nyau, the ancient male secret society of the Nyanja speaking peoples. This society had been eliminated in Ntcheu district and in the Southern Province other than the Lower Shire through a combination of the churches, NAC, the Yao chiefs in

217

the Shire Highlands and the Ngoni paramountcy in Ntcheu. Indeed the very groups who created the old Native Associations which then became the NAC were the very groups who opposed Nyau. The great Inkosi Gomani, hero of the fight against the inception of Federation, had vigilantly stamped on any attempt to resurrect Nyau in Ntcheu. He did this as a Ngoni, a Christian and a Congress man.

Dr Banda had also created another string to his bow, a modern one. This was the national youth movement, the Young Pioneers, launched in August 1963. It took the place of the old Congress Youth League, the organisation from which the 'young men' had sprung. The new organisation was quite different. It was not an organisation of young radicals and intellectuals aiming to ginger up the Party, which was the old Youth League tradition, rooted in the pattern of the Youth League of the ANC of South Africa. The new organisation, the Young Pioneers, was a uniformed organisation made up primarily of young people who had failed to climb the educational ladder. Many were taken on as full-time members of the Pioneers and were paid, fed and clothed as the key cadres who then organised the rest. This organisation was firmly grounded in the Banda, Saviour of the Nation ideology, and was under the control of the central Party machine led by Albert Muwalo. This gave Dr Banda a political tool which had not been available to any previous figure in Malawi politics.

People did not put all these pieces together in their minds in 1963. Indeed Chipembere, Yatuta Chisiza and the others tended to be somewhat amused at Dr Banda's pro-Nyau speeches and his harping on about Chewa tradition; they found them almost quaint. They firmly believed that his autocratic style and the increase in the number of his references to them as 'his boys', could all be dealt with after independence. However, in the weeks of the run-up to the independence celebrations, the ministers began to express openly to friends, their uneasiness about Banda's leadership. They showed that they felt threatened in a way that they had not before. I was made aware of this in a series of conversations with Colin Cameron, Orton Chirwa, Chip and Yatuta at that time. What they all talked of was vague, but always included phrases like 'difficult times ahead', 'grave difficulties to overcome' and it was clear that they were not talking about the situation of the economy nor of international relations. Although they were clear that the style of Banda's leadership was central to all this, none were very precise, nor went into any detail about what they meant.

From Independence to Cabinet Crisis

After Independence Day the situation developed rapidly into one of crisis. On the 26th July 1964, Banda arrived back at Chileka Airport from th

Organisation of African Unity meeting which had been held in Cairo. In a speech to the massive crowd gathered to meet him, and with all the cabinet on the platform beside him, Banda humiliated them in an extraordinary and public way. He told the assembled multitude that the nation's future was in their hands, that they alone could save it from the machinations of the traitors who threatened it. He exhorted the people to be vigilant in seeking out such traitors be they men or women, and to denounce them unhesitatingly so that they could be dealt with. He went on to urge the people in no uncertain terms to scrutinize carefully everything that the members of the cabinet did or said for any sign of treason. In the context of his speech treason meant any criticism of or disagreement with Banda's policies who, after all, had alone 'broken their stupid Federation'.

Short, on the basis of discussions with Chiume, holds that this outburst was provoked by a quarrel that had taken place in Cairo between him and Banda. Such a quarrel with 'my boy Kanyama' would clearly have upset Banda. However, this speech at Chileka was only different in degree not in essentials from many that he had been making in the previous months. The other ministers saw the speech as yet another attack on them and having nothing to do with Chiume whom most still saw as Kamuzu's 'boy'. This was so clear when the delegation of cabinet members who went to confront Kamuzu about his campaign of denigration, deliberately chose to go only after Chiume had left the country on an overseas trip. Colin Cameron did not go with them as he had come to feel by this time that his presence would only complicate the issue. Indeed it seemed to me (I cannot remember whether Colin said anything explicit or not at that time) that he had decided that a critical point for the future of the government had been reached and that it would be best dealt with by his Malawi colleagues if he, the sole European, was no longer in the cabinet. So at the cabinet meeting of 4 August, he resigned. He chose to resign over a very significant issue, the re-instatement by the new Malawi government of the British colonial powers of Preventive Detention without trial.

Later on the 4th, I spoke with Colin Cameron at his house together with Orton Chirwa and Yatuta Chisiza. The latter two had come there after the end of the cabinet meeting. What was significant in their description of what went on after Colin had left the Cabinet meeting was the role Chiume had played in it. Chiume alone had welcomed the legislation enthusiastically and derided Cameron's scruples which had led to his resignation. Both Chirwa and Chisiza reluctantly agreed with Cameron when he forcefully pointed out that since there was no real opposition at the time to the MCP in Malawi the new legislation could only be aimed at them if they stepped out of line.

Events now rushed ahead with bewildering rapidity. Banda appointed a prominent Portuguese businessman and right-wing politician, Jorge Jardim, as honourary Malawi consul at Beira. There could have been no more unambiguous assertion of his policy of friendship and cooperation with the Portuguese, a policy Chirwa, Chipembere, Chisiza and most of the others had already spoken out against, publicly as well as in the Cabinet. There then followed Chiume's visit to Dar-es-Salaam to discuss the possibility of aid with the ambassador of the People's Republic of China. The Chinese declared their willingness to set up an aid deal if Banda was willing in return to give up his 'two Chinas' policy.

Banda's refusal to countenance this is seen by Short as 'the pretext for which Bwanausi, Chisiza and Chiume had been looking'. This is an extraordinary interpretation of the relationships between the members of the Cabinet, as I have suggested. Short's version presumably comes from Chiume, but Chisiza and Chiume were never close and in exile in Tanzania were to become bitter enemies. Even more strange was that this moment they were said to have chosen was the time when Chipembere was out of the country. Short says this was because the triumvirate of Bwanausi, Chisiza and Chiume wanted a government that excluded Chipembere and would be led by Orton Chirwa. This is an extraordinarily strange suggestion. Bwanausi was a friend of Chipembere's, Yatuta was no friend of Chiume's, neither was Orton and in any case as soon as Banda acted against them which appeared to come as a surprise, they sent for Chipembere to come home immediately.

What actually happened after Banda's refusal to have anything to do with Kanyama's China policy is not very clear. One thing is certain, Kanyama now changed sides with a vengeance. Now only days after being Banda's most trusted and subservient servant, Chiume began to attack him in public with a vitriolic tone that had not been used by the others in their increasing criticism of Kamuzu. This is the nub of Banda's profound shock at the attack on him in the cabinet meeting of 16 August. He was profoundly shocked because a new virulent opposition had appeared led by 'his boy Kanyama'.

In many ways Kanyama, with his extraordinary energy and eloquence was suddenly taking over. He was trying to get rid of Banda completely and immediately. In many long talks with Yatuta Chisiza, Orton Chirwa, Bwanausi and 'Chip', I had got the impression that they were being overtaken by events rather than initiating them. Before 16 August they saw themselves as getting ready to try to force Banda to modify some of his policies and above all modify his insulting and humiliating treatment of them and his interference in their ministries. His inability to make any concession and even concede they had any case at all, left them at a loss as to what to next. The nearest thing to a plan that they had before 16 August was the suggestion that when a republican constitution was created, as was planned for the future, it would include a very honourable but essentially non-Executive Presidency which Banda would be forced into. The country would then be run by a cabinet led by a Prime Minister. The one immediate change they all agreed was essential was the ending of the 'Kamuzu as Saviour' type of adulation and a restoration of their dignity and authority as cabinet ministers. This was before the meeting of 16 August and Chiume's bid to take over the whole operation.

In fact it was Banda who now struck. It has been widely reported that after the 16 August meeting, Banda had been so depressed that he had wanted to resign and had only been dissuaded from doing so with great difficulty by Sir Glyn Jones, the Governor-General. Whether this was so or not, it was an aggressive not a defeatist Banda who now set about destroying opposition to him. He called an emergency session of Parliament for 8 September and dismissed from office, Bwanausi, Chirwa, Chiume and Rose Chibambo. Yatuta Chisiza and Willie Chokani resigned immediately in sympathy with their colleagues.

Chipembere now flew back from Canada on receipt of a cable from Chiume. He arrived in Zomba on the evening of the 8th too late for the meeting of Parliament. He sent his resignation to Banda that evening. This left only John Tembo, hitherto a fringe member of the young graduates' group, as the only one left in office.

What will never be clear perhaps, is how far Banda really believed that he could dismiss Bwanausi, Chirwa, Chiume and Rose Chibambo and still work with Chokani, Chisiza and Chipembere. Whatever he thought would happen, it did not work and the leadership stuck together but now the group included their hitherto opponent, Kanyama Chiume.

In Zomba during the two days of the special session of Parliament, 8-9 September 1964, there were some extraordinary scenes. Huge crowds gathered in streets near the Parliament building, many of them civil servants who left the government offices nearly empty. The ex-ministers were cheered to the echo every time they appeared, while the Prime Minister, the Ngwazi, H. Kamuzu Banda, for the first time ever, was booed and jeered at by a Malawi crowd. What must have been particularly galling was that the crowds chose to use the old anti-Federation chant against him. So they shouted instead of 'Welensky-zi, Welensky-zi', the astonishing cry of 'Banda-zi, Banda-zi'. In Blantyre, the other main urban centre in those days, the vast majority of the people also seemed to support the ex-ministers.

The Triumph of Kamuzu Banda

However, catastrophically for them, the ex-ministers did little or nothing to organize their support in the Southern Region and Ntcheu where their strength lay (not in the two Lower Shire districts, where the ministers had little direct support); nor did they contact the key party cadres in the Northern Region, their other area of popularity; (except, that is, for Chiume, who, though a Northerner, was very unpopular there). Instead it was the Party machine on Banda's orders that went into action. The Young Pioneers were the spearhead of this action but there were other groups organised by the party which took drastic direct action. A reign of terror was created throughout the country in which many lost their lives, many were beaten and many fled into exile. At the time I was assured by various informants, including some who were deeply involved, that Albert Muwalo was the executive head of this whole campaign.

All the ministers (except Chipembere) and many of their relations and friends left the country. Apart from Chip's later abortive attempt at a coup d'état, the ministers were defeated and Kamuzu Banda had triumphed. A number of fundamental issues need to be underlined.

First, the ministers had made no preparations at all to overthrow Banda, so they were very exposed politically when he decided to strike. Second, Chiume, for reasons that will perhaps never be explained satisfactorily, precipitated the crisis by changing sides between the 4th and 16th of August and bringing a new violently anti-Banda note to the conflict that was developing, this at the most inopportune moment when Chipembere was out of the country. It was Kanyama's actions that made it a 'Banda must go' situation when what they had been doing until mid-August was to attempt not to remove the 'old man' but, as it were, only to clip his wings. Third, the impact of Chiume's change of sides on the Northern Region was fatal for the cause of the ministers once the crisis had erupted. As many Northerners told me later, the people of the North were sympathetic to the ministers' position but, no one in the North was willing to do anything to support activity that apparently was being led by Chiume for whom there was widespread and deep dislike, amounting in some places to hatred. So Chiume's abrupt change of tack guaranteed that the one Region that could have been the ministers' entirely, simply did nothing at all in the crisis. They were later to pay heavily for this mistake as Banda's anti-Northerner policies over twenty years was to prove.

In the months following the critical days of September 1964, an interesting picture emerges. The areas where the Party had to be most thoroughly purged and where the most people were detained, many of them veterans of the '49-51' struggle as well as of 1959, were in the Northern Region, the

Ntcheu district of the Central Region and the densely populated districts of Blantyre/Limbe, Chiradzulu, Zomba and Thyolo in the Southern Region. These were precisely the strongholds of the old Nyasaland African Congress. The Central Region except for Ntcheu and Lilongwe town and the Lower Shire districts of the Southern Region, had resisted the old Congress and had only been brought into mainstream political life by the new MCP of the 'Kamuzu as Saviour' ideology.

From April 1960, Banda had played on the conservative feelings of these areas and of conservatives elsewhere in the country. A particularly important element in this campaign was his consistent praise of Nyau. In the past the people who had rejected Nyau were precisely those who formed the old Nyasaland African Congress. As I noted before, Chip, Orton, Chisiza and the others had been amused by his Nyau speeches which they had tended to see as quaintly eccentric and not the danger they were. This danger became so clear in the House on 8 and 9 September when Central Region members like Richard Chidzanja went on about 'we the Nyau, we the Chewa' being behind Kamuzu all the way. Chidzanja, in particular, complained bitterly about how the educated smart young people of the North and of Blantyre had snapped up everything for themselves despising and ignoring the Chewa. I became personally aware as the pastor of the CCAP in Ntcheu, of another aspect of the Nyau/Chewa position when the Party in the Central Region began busing in Nyau dancers to go through villages at night, villages where the Nyau had long been suppressed and where there was support for the ex-ministers. At the same time an outburst of witch-hunting took place under Party auspices in this area and again it was supporters of the ex-ministers who were consistently found guilty.

From the time Banda took over the new MCP with so many old-style Congress militants still in Kanjedza, he created something new, not the NAC redivivus. The new Party reached geographical areas the old party had barely penetrated and gained the loyalty of social groups who had often in the past been suspicious of the NAC. All the while this party was playing incessantly, the 'Banda the Saviour' tune composed and orchestrated very effectively by Chiume. When you add to this his bringing to power many of the generation that had been bypassed by the 'young men' and his powerful new para-military organisation, the Young Pioneers, it is clear, with hindsight, that the kind of reformist, palace revolution the ministers were attempting without much clear planning, was doomed from the first. Now, with the dismissal and resignation of the young ministers, the last obstacles on the road to dictatorship had been removed.

A Personal Postscript

Between September 1964 and April 1965, Andrew Ross was in contact with Masauko Chipembere who was hiding in the hills near Mangochi. The following account tells how he acted as a go-between, helping to keep contact between the British and American representatives in Malawi and Chipembere until the ex-minister was smuggled out of the country in April 1965. Under threat of arrest Andrew Ross and his family left Malawi the following month - May 1965. The account which follows is based on an interview he gave to the Edinburgh University History Graduates' Association,[280] following his return to Malawi in 1997 and ends with some reflections on how Malawi looked to him, returning after an absence of more than thirty years. This interview, and Colin Baker's account of Chipembere's evacuation from Malawi in his 2008 book, Chipembere: the Missing Years[281], together provide the most detailed descriptions of Chipembere's escape. Unfortunately, Andrew was able neither to read Baker's account, nor to provide an up-dated version of his own story before he died. [Editor's Note].

Repression and Resistance

The former ministers had not prepared for this kind of overthrow. Most of them left the country. The exception was Masauko Chipembere, who went up into the high mountains, very near the border with the Portuguese colony of Mozambique, the only tiny bit of Malawi to the east of Lake Malawi. It is very inaccessible, difficult, high, densely forested mountains. Chipembere held some public meetings as he retreated to the mountains, one in the village where my house was, where I was living as pastor to a group of congregations. I saw him at that point before he retreated into the hills where the police and army cut him off. I had resigned from the two quangos of which I was chairman.[282] I hoped that I could just sit quietly in my parish. I was heart-sick about what had happened, but I felt I had done all I could, that there was nothing else I could do.

---

[280] Andrew Ross, 'A Return to Malawi' in *Edinburgh University History Graduates Association Newsletter*, (30), October 1998, 12-20.

[281] Colin Baker, 'Evacuation from Malawi, April 1965' in *Chipembere: the Missing Years*, 134-147, Zomba, Kachere, 2008.

[282] Andrew Ross was chairman of the National Tenders Board and the Lands Tribunal.

Leaving Malawi

We were told later, when Jonathan Sangaya stopped in Scotland en route to Canada and came to see us, that as the plane was a dot on the horizon, police cars had arrived with sirens blaring. He had then gone to Banda immediately and told him that he had dismissed me for being involved in politics. The Prime Minister had then said, 'No, don't say that. Say he is unwell and had to go home.' Sangaya said, 'The President knew that I knew that he knew about the whole thing.' But he could not go on saying that Chipembere's was an insane racist plot, that whites were going to have their throats cut in their beds, and then also say that a white Presbyterian minister was one of his associates. I did not fit the image Banda was painting, so he was quite happy for me to go, and no action to be taken. He did remember me because from time to time in speeches he would list the dangerous animals that he had rid Malawi of, and I had the honour of being in the list for about the next five years. After that I was more or less forgotten by him. He did tell the Malawian team to the 1970 Commonwealth Games, which were held in Edinburgh with Pollock Halls[283] as the games village, that they were forbidden to see me. In the Presidential Palace, before they came over, he spoke to them about being good representatives of their country and warned them about Grant House - he knew I was warden! - because there was a dangerous hyena there, even the saliva of which would poison, and they were not to go near the place. They told me this when they came to see me. Sometimes people would be frightened to visit me, and we'd speak on the phone. Others would visit. I kept in touch with the exiles down the years until there was the marvellous opportunity of going back again in 1997.

Final Thoughts Thirty Years On

Malawi is a startlingly beautiful country. During my thirty years of absence, when I had been in other places in Africa, like South Africa or Kenya, which are beautiful, I had begun to wonder if my memory was distorting my recollections. But no: Malawi is one of the most breath-takingly beautiful places in the world. And the people are friendly and charming still. But there have been a number of changes that are profoundly depressing. It is not the poverty, for Malawi was always poor, though I do not mean to write off the appalling level of poverty some have to suffer. What has changed is that the spirit of the Malawi people has not been broken, but has been dampened. There is no doubt that it was little Malawi - though Southern Rhodesia was four times bigger, Northern Rhodesia seven times bigger - that overthrew

---

[283] Pollock Halls were the student residences of the University of Edinburgh. At that time Andrew Ross was warden of one of the Halls there.

225

Federation. It was the people of Malawi or Nyasaland who never gave up the fight. Nyasas had enormous dynamism. Once they got involved in the modern world, from the 1890s onwards, it was Nyasas who were aggressive, dynamic, refusing to be told what to do - really a people with tremendous energy and drive, and also a tremendous sense of communal support for each other. The effect of thirty years of the Banda tyranny has been to dampen this. Sometimes before Nyasas would take initiatives that were not appropriate. Now they will not take them at all until they are sure it is OK.

The Young Pioneers used to impose duties on village people. These were really duties that people did anyway. But the Young Pioneers would rush around saying, '*This* is the day the path clearing between villages must be done.' '*This* is day when something or other has to be done.' Left alone the village people would have chosen the day themselves. Instead they had thirty years of being told *this* is the day. Now that there are democratic elections, a free society, and the Pioneers are no longer there to bully them, what is extraordinary is that the people have stopped doing the communal tasks. A friend of mine went home to his own area of Katabe and was astonished that the traditional paths between villages had become completely overgrown. When he asked, 'Why aren't we clearing the paths?,' the reply was, 'Ah well, the Pioneers made us do it. To hell with it. We are not going to do it now.' Thirty years of having something imposed has damaged a very important communal discipline. Now the villages have paths to the main road but not each other. It is bizarre. Banda kept on talking about maintaining African traditions, but certain traditional duties have been set aside as something Banda imposed.

More frightening than that, because traditions can be recovered, is the business of how to change somebody, say in their forties, who for the last twenty years as a schoolteacher or civil servant has always had to be careful never to do anything that might be wrong, never to take a chance, never to stick out his neck, never to take responsibility. I am not blaming them, because if you had stuck out your neck, you might have ended up in a detention centre, where you might die, or you might just be killed, not perhaps there on the spot, but eliminated because you had annoyed the party. People in their forties and fifties have had their professional lives shaped by being careful, by not making a move. How to get rid of these attitudes is a massive problem.

As in most of Southern Africa the rate of church growth over the last thirty years has been absolutely phenomenal. An area where two of us ran two parishes had about 25 churches. Now the same area is a presbytery with 15 ministers and 200 churches. It was the combination of the Catholic and Presbyterian churches uniting that broke Banda's power in the end. There were only three institutions that were genuinely powerful in Malawi under Banda. One was the Malawi Congress Party run by him; the others were the Catholic and Protestant Churches. About 70 per cent of people in Malawi are either Catholic or Presbyterian. There is a small, quite significant and lively Muslim community and many other small Protestant denominations. There is also traditionalism or traditional religion, but it is deeply intertwined into the Christianity of Malawi, and just as deeply into Islam.

Though the massive increase in church membership is happening all across Southern Africa, there was an extra reason for it, I think, in Malawi. In the Catholic and Presbyterian churches you could be yourself. It was the one area where you had autonomy - a limited autonomy, of course - but here was an institution you ran yourself, which the party did not run. Nevertheless, though the CCAP was not so close to the Malawi Congress Party as it had been to the old Nyasaland African Congress, it was still deeply involved with it. When the party split in 1963-64, the terrible internal divisions resulted in detentions and murders. Most of the victims, and the majority of cabinet ministers who fled the country, were members of the CCAP. It was a political crisis in which the Presbyterian church took a hammering.

Under Banda it had to be the Catholic Church which took the initiative. The Catholic Church since colonial days had been nonpolitical, but in the end the Bishops, under pressure from the complaints and petitions of their people, could not stay quiet and produced a pastoral letter, which was read in every Catholic church, condemning the regime. Banda's response was to have every Bishop arrested, and to make a broadcast stating that Catholics were trying to do what they did in Northern Ireland, in an obvious attempt to bring about a Catholic-Protestant split. On the Sunday after the arrest of the Bishops there were huge attendances in every CCAP church in the country, and with a few exceptions ministers, either enthusiastically or more quietly, endorsed the Catholic action. Then emergency meetings of the Synods again endorsed the need for change.

With the collapse of the Soviet Empire and the end of the Cold War, and the Soviets and Americans no longer fighting proxy wars in Africa, as they had been doing in Mozambique and Angola, Banda was no longer seen as the great friend of the West which had been his role until then in so many ways. In fact international pressure was brought to bear on him, focussing on the imprisonment of Orton and Vera Chirwa, two internationally known lawyers. The opposition of the Catholic and Protestant churches, the only two autonomous institutions in Malawi, was vital to the ending of the Banda regime, but they could not have pulled this off on their own. International pressure also played a part in forcing Kamuzu to concede a referedum, and even after this concession had been made, people were still extremely nervous about how a referendum would go with the Pioneers still around.

Then there was an extraordinary moment. The army came out of their barracks at midnight one night and eliminated the key headquarters units in each region and district of the Pioneers, confiscated all the weapons and warned that anyone seen in a Pioneer uniform would be shot. This happened over twenty-four hours. Then, *mirabile dictu*,[284] the army returned to barracks.

Four years before this a young major, who was on a staff college course in Britain, had come to see me, because his grandfather had been one of my church elders in the Ntcheu mountains. We spoke in Nyanja. As in other African languages, one need often not articulate replies but make simply a welcoming noise, 'Yeh, yeh.' That he was saying things that were coded messages was amply borne out by events. He suggested, 'You'll be very pleased now that we have four battalions and one battalion in Mozambique fighting the bandits.' 'But,' he added, 'it is more than that, father. There's a battalion in each province as well as the one in Mozambique which we can pull back into the country if need be. And we will make sure that whatever happens in the future, the Tsotsis will not be allowed to take over.' Tsotsis is old South African slang for gangsters - Malawians have always worked in South Africa. I took it that he meant the Pioneers, but I didn't cross-examine him. It seemed to me he was bold enough in telling me this. And, of course, this is exactly what the army did do. In one night they destroyed the Pioneers. They did not kill many of them. I think there weres only about 40 people killed in fighting. They took them completely by surprise, smashed their headquarters units, their radios and control centres, and confiscated their stacks of weapons, and the political process was allowed to take place.

Although the army played a key role, unlike in many other African countries it did not stay in politics. Zomba, where I spent most of my time when I returned last year [1997], is a university and army town. The army Headquarters and training battalion are there, and in the streets you see students and soldiers (who actually get on quite amicably). It may sound crazy. I was really very proud of the soldiers: they were all extremely smart. As you've seen on film, the armies that are scary are the ones with soldiers wandering around, sloppily dressed, with their weapons. In Malawi the weapons are in the armouries, and you could cut your fingers on the creases of the uniforms of the soldiers in the streets. They are terribly British in an old-fashioned way. I remember being in a queue in a bank with two young officers in front of me, one of whom said literally to the other, 'I thought your chaps did awfully well this morning.'

---

[284] 'wonderful to relate'.

As in former Communist countries the relationship in Malawi between the supporters and opponents of the old regime is extremely complicated. The Congress Party was allowed to participate in free elections and has members in the Parliament. Two or three people have been convicted of ordinary civil crimes, but there has been no real attempt made to mount political trials. The returning exiles have been given positions of honour, such as chairman of the board of governers of the University, Vice-Chancellor of the University, ambassador to the United States, ambassador to Britain. None of them has a key cabinet role. The cabinet is made up of ministers who broke with Banda some time in the past, early enough for them not to be tainted by association, and really young people who only entered politics in the 1990s. Many able young men and women were abroad at university and only became politically active under the new system. There is freedom of political debate, and freedom to criticise publicly in the press. It is very free in that respect. There is no doubt, however, that a number of those in power do not want much investigation into a past in which they were involved. Although none of them were in the cabinet in the '90s, some only broke with Banda as late as '86 or '87.

It is difficult to know what will happen. Certainly there is no recrimination. On one particular matter, however, many do want to see a trial. Three young men, one of whom I knew very well, who was a dear friend of mine, in the early 1970s were plucked from academia to become cabinet ministers. They had had nothing to do with the events of 1964-65 and began a very moderate reformist development within the government, while being loyal to Banda. One night they were beaten to death. Publicly it was said there had been a car accident, but everyone now knows they were executed, and some of their relatives want a trial. I met the daughter of one of the ministers, my friend Dick Matenje. I had known her as a little toddler running around our garden. She is now a woman in her early forties and determined her father's murderers should be brought to book - not the actual policeman, who has already been tried and gaoled, but those who ordered it. This is unlikely to happen. In any case it relates to a one-off incident. Kenneth Ross, whose PhD I supervised and who is now a Professor at the University of Malawi, feels that a Truth and Justice Commission on the model of the South African one may be desirable, but this idea has not been taken up.

It is very difficult to come to terms with history. Soon after I returned to Britain in 1965 I wrote an article about the collapse of democracy in Malawi, which was rejected by the *Journal of Imperial and Commonwealth History* on the grounds that it was a political diatribe. I tried to persuade another journal to take it, and mentioned the fact that Chipembere had used it when giving a seminar at Harvard, but that seemed simply to be taken as confirmation that it was a political diatribe. What delighted me was that Ruth First[285] came across it and had it published in *The New Left Review*. Again, I suppose, to some that would be confirmation that it was not academic. Obviously I never pretended that I did not have a position to adopt. But what historian does not have a position to adopt? In fact many people, including historians, did not want to hear at that point what had actually happened.

---

[285] Then a radical activist in South Africa.

Time-Line: Main Events Mentioned in the Book

1875: Arrival of the Livingstonia Mission at Cape Maclear.

1876: Arrival of the Blantyre Mission.

1891: British Central African protectorate formed with Harry Johnston as Commissioner and Consul-General.

1907: The British Central African Protectorate renamed to the Nyasaland Protectorate.

1912: Issue of District Ordinance, dividing the country into districts.

1912: First Native Association – North Nyasa Native Association - founded at Karonga.

1914: West Nyasa Native Association founded at Bandawe.

1915: January: Insurrection of John Chilembwe – The 'Rising'.

1916: Report of Commission of Enquiry into the Rising.

1919: Industrial and Commercial Workers' Union organised by Clements Kadalie in South Africa.

1920s: Native Associations formed in all three regions.

1923: The Devonshire Declaration setting out the principle of 'the paramountcy of Native interests' – related to Kenya.

1924: The Church of Central Africa, Presbyterian inaugurated.

1924: Northern Rhodesia taken under authority of Colonial Office.

1925: Dr Banda arrives in the United States.

1928: The Hilton Young Commission.

1929: The Hilton Young Report.

1930: Passfield Memorandum on Native Policy in East Africa.

1935: Meeting of Blantyre Native Association and chiefs to discuss the threat of amalgamation and to petition the Colonial Secretary.

1936: Victoria Falls Conference of Southern and Northern Rhodesian settlers.

1938: Dr Banda enrolled at Edinburgh University.

1938: Reverend Thomas Maseya and Blantyre Native Association petition Bledisloe Commission for elected members to Legco.

1939: Bledisloe Commission Report – there should be no amalgamation against African wishes.

1943: October: Frederick Sangala's circular letter proposes an organisation for African interests.

1944: October: First annual conference of Nyasaland African Congress with Levi Mumba as President-General.

1944: December: Government recognises NAC as mouthpiece of all African Associations.

1944: Setting up of Central African Council to facilitate co-operation amongst the three territories.

1945 Dr Banda moves to London as family doctor.

1946: Salima conference of NAC which turns down proposal of central office to appoint a full-time secretary.

1947: September: Fourth annual conference of NAC in Zomba proposes sending delegates to London.

1948: Delegation of Congress to London to see Colonial Secretary result in discord.

1948: October: Meeting in Lusaka of leaders of settlers decides to campaign for Federation.

1949: February: Second Victoria Falls conference.

1948-56: Governor, Sir Geoffrey Colby, encourages economic development

1949: Internal dissension leads to near breakdown of Congress.

1950: February: British General Election – slim Labour majority.

1950: August: Rebirth of Congress under Sangala at Mzimba conference with Chinyama as President-General.

1950: November: Government asks Colonial Office and Central African territories to examine possibilities of closer association.

1951: January: Conference of Officials based on paper on *Comparative Survey of Native Policy.*

1951: Dr Banda and Harry Nkumbula publish pamphlet *Federation in Central Africa* based on their earlier memorandum.

1951: September: Victoria Falls conference quickly discontinued Congress refuses to attend.

1951: October: British General Election – Conservative victory.

1951: December: Doig, Mposa and Muwamba in Legco urged that authority should only be given up to people of Nyasaland.

1952-3: Continued Scottish support for Nyasaland Africans and bi-party protests against Federation.

1952: Formation of Chiefs' Union under Chief Mwase which supports Congress.

1952: April: Lancaster House Conference – The Congress delegation once in London refused to attend.

1953: January: Conference at Carlton House Terrace held in secret.

1953: April: Special NAC conference in Blantyre resolves that Congress and Chiefs oppose Federation by non-violent protest.

1953: Resistance with Chief Mwase refusing invitation to Queen's Coronation and Chief Gomani urging people to ignore forestry and agricultural regulations.

1953: August 1st: Central African Federation came into being with Federal Parliament, Nyasaland Legco, Northern Rhodesian Legco and Southern Rhodesian parliament.

1953: August-September: Disturbances at Thyolo, Nsanje, Blantyre, Zomba, Mulanje and Domasi.

1953: Dr Banda moves from London to Kumasi in Ghana.

1953: September: Sangala arrested – charge dropped in December.

1954: January: National conference of Congress – Sangala elected President and resistance measures put on hold.

1954: Manoah Chirwa and Clement Kumbikano take the two Nyasaland seats in the Federal Parliament with Congress approval.

1954-6: Continued political resistance in the North led by Flax Musopole, with more sporadic resistance in the South.

1955: Governor Colby introduces new structure of Legislative Council with five elected African members.

1956: Annual conference of Congress calles on Nyasa African Federal MPs to resign – T.D.T. Banda elected as President-General.

1956: Chipembere, Chiume, Chinyama, Kwenje and Chijosi elected to Legco.

1956-8: New Legco members able to exploit constitutional loophole with appeals to colonial government and publicity of Hansard.

1957: January: Annual conference of Congress issued strong appeal for Nyasa African Federal MPs to resign.

1957: March: Dr Banda starts planning to move back to Nyasaland.

1957: April: Sir Roy Welensky visited London and agreed that review of Federal constitution would take place in 1960.

1957:	July: Manoah Chirwa and Clement Kumbikano (the Federal MPs) expelled from Congress.
1957:	Conference of Congress formally invites Dr Banda to return.
1957:	Delegation from Congress discusses constitutional reform with new Governor, Sir Robert Armitage.
1958:	Jack Report points to economic gains from Federation – flawed analysis.
1958:	Meeting in London with Lennon Boyd – Colonial Secretary.
1958:	May: Congress delegation of Dr Banda, Chipembere, Dunduzu Chisiza and Chief Kuntaja meet Colonial Secretary in London.
1958:	June 29th: Huge crowd at Chileka airport to greet Dr Banda on his return to Malawi. He fails to arrive.
1958:	July 6th: Dr Banda finally arrives back in Malawi from Ghana.
1958:	August: conference of Congress at Nkhata Bay; Dr Banda elected as President.
1958:	September: Arrival of 500 members of Royal Rhodesian Regiment raises tension.
1958:	October 26th: Speech by Dr Banda at Blantyre market leads to 'Clock Tower incident'.
1959:	January 24th-25th: Emergency meeting of Congress; policy of non-co-operation and non-violent civil disobedience approved.
1959:	February: rioting begins to spread in the North.
1959:	February 20th: Police open fire on demonstrators at Fort Hill, wounding four.
1959:	February 24th: two people shot by police in Lilongwe.
1959:	March 3rd: State of Emergency declared: riot breaks out at Nkhata Bay; at least twenty people killed by troops. Altogether, in rioting in various parts of the country in the next few weeks, around fifty people killed by troops.
1959:	March onwards: as a result of Emergency, Nyasaland African Congress declared illegal and around one thousand five hundred people detained, including almost all the leaders of Congress.
1959:	British Government sets up Commission of Enquiry headed by Lord Devlin to look into the situation.
1959:	July: Devlin Report: justifies declaration of the State of Emergency but is also very critical of several aspects of government policy.

1959: On release from detention, Orton Chirwa becomes leader of newly formed Malawi Congress Party.

1960: February: Monckton Commission to look into future of Federation.

1960: April 1st: Release of Dr Banda from Gwelo.

1960: April 5th: Orton Chirwa hands presidency of MCP to Dr Banda.

1960: October: Monckton Commission Report.

1960: December: Federal Review Conference.

1961: January: Chipembere arrested and imprisoned for sedition.

1961: August: Massive victory for MCP in first Nyasaland elections.

1961: Death of Lawrence Makata.

1962: July: Nyasaland Economic Symposium.

1962: August: Request by Colin Cameron, Dunduzu Chisiza and Mikeka Mkandawire to Dr Banda to restrain Chiume.

1962: September 3rd: Death of Dunduzu Chisiza.

1962: November: Marlborough House conference.

1963: January: Chipembere released and takes seat in Legco.

1964: July 6th: Malawi Independence.

1964: July: Creation of Executive Council.

1964: August 4th: Colin Cameron resigns from Cabinet in protest at Banda's desire to introduce a Preventive Detention Bill.

1964: August 16th: Attack on Dr Banda in Cabinet by Chiume.

1964: August-September: 'The Cabinet Crisis': confrontation between Banda and ministers. Banda dismissed Bwanausi, Orton Chirwa, Chiume and Rose Chibambo: Yatuta Chisiza and Willie Chokani, resigned and Chipembere flew back into the country and resigned.

1964: September 8th - 9th: Emergency session of Parliament: Banda wins Vote of Confidence.

1964: September onwards: reign of terror under Muwalo and Young Pioneers. Most ex-ministers leave the country and go into exile.

1964-65: Masauko Chipembere retreats to hills beyond Mangochi, and then attempts unsuccessfully to march on Zomba to overthrow Dr Banda's government.

965: April: with the help of British and American diplomats Chipembere is smuggled out of Malawi by Special Branch officers and taken to USA.

Select Bibliography

Primary Sources

Bledisloe Report

Hilton Young Commission: *Report of the Commission on Closer Union of the Dependencies in Eastern and Central Africa* 1929 Cmd 3234

Edinburgh University Library (EUL)
Centre for the Study of Christianity in the Non-Western World Archives
Special Collections

Indiana University Bloomington
H.K. Banda Archive

National Archives (London)
Colonial Office Papers, File 525

National Archives of Malawi (NAM)
Livingstonia Papers

National Library of Scotland (NLS)
Livingstonia Papers

University of Oxford (Rhodes House Library)
Sir Glyn Jones Papers,

Zimbabwe National Archives
Cecil Rhodes Papers

Secondary Sources

Baker, Colin, *Chipembere: the Missing Years* (Zomba: Kachere, 2008)

Baker, Colin, *Development Governor* (London: Tauris, 1994)

Baker, Colin, *The Revolt of the Ministers* (London: Tauris, 2001)

Baker, Colin, *Seed of Trouble: Government Police and Land Rights in Nyasaland* (London: British Academic Press, 1993)

Baker, Colin, *State of Emergency: Crisis in Central Africa, Nyasaland 1959-1960* (London: Tauris, 1997)

Banda, H. Kamuzu and Harry Nkumbula, *Federation in Central Africa* (Harlesden, 1951)

Bandawe, L.M., *Memoirs of a Malawian* (Blantyre: CLAIM, 1971)

Cairns, H.A.C., *Prelude to Imperialism: British Reaction to Central African Society 1840-1890* (London: Routledge and Keegan Paul, 1965)

Chipembere, H.B.M., "Malawi in Crisis: 1964," *Ufahamu I* (Fall, 1960), 6-11

Chipembere, H.B.M. and R.I. Rotberg, *Hero of the Nation: Chipembere of Malawi* (Blantyre: CLAIM-Kachere, 2001)

Chiume, M.K. Kanyama, *Kwacha: An Autobiography* (Nairobi: East African Publishing House, 1975)

Franklin, Harry, *Unholy Wedlock* (London: Allen and Unwin, 1963)

Gray, Richard, *The Two Nations: Aspects of the development of race relations in the Rhodesias and Nyasaland* (London: OUP, 1960)

Griffiths, James. *Pages from Memory* (London: Dent, 1969)

Hazlewood, Arthur. *African Integration and Disintegration* (London: OUP, 1967)

Hazlewood, Arthur. *Economic Integration: The East African Experience* (New York: St Martin's Press, 1975)

Hazlewood, Arthur and P. David Henderson, *Nyasaland: the Economics of Federation* (Oxford: Blackwells, 1960)

Hetherwick, Alexander, 'Nyasaland Today and Tomorrow' *Journal of the Royal Africa Society*, 17 (1917), pp. 11-19.

Hetherwick, Alexander, *The Romance of Blantyre* (London: James Clarke, 1931)

Horne, Alistair. *Macmillan 1957-1986* vol. 2 (London: Macmillan, 1989)

Jackson, William M., *Send us Friends* (Privately published, n.d.)

Jones, Griff, *Britain and Nyasaland* (London: Allen and Unwin, 1964)

Langworthy, Harry W, *Africa for the African: the Life of Joseph Booth* (Blantyre: CLAIM-Kachere, 1996)

Lapping, Brian. *End of Empire* (New York: St. Martin's Press, 1985)

Leys, Colin and Cranford Pratt (eds.) *A New Deal in Central Africa* (London: Heinemann, 1960)

Life and Work in British Central Africa, December 1894

Lwanda, John L.C. *Kamuzu Banda of Malawi* (Bothwell, Scotland: Dudu Nsomba, 1993)

Macmillan, Harold, *Pointing the Way: 1959-1961* (London: Macmillan, 1972)

Macmillan, Harold, *Riding the Storm: 1956-1959* (London: Macmillan, 1971)

McCracken, John, 'Ambiguities of Nationalism: Flax Musopole and the Northern Factor in Malawi Politics, c. 1956-1966' *Journal of Southern African Studies*, 28.1 (2002), 67-87

McCracken, John, *Politics and Christianity in Malawi, 1875-1940* (Cambridge: CUP, 1977)

Mkandawire, Austin, *Albert Muwalo Nqumayo. His Life and Times. His Death and Legacy*, Balaka: Montfort Media, 2008.

Mkandawire, Austin, 'A Short History of the Chisiza Clan' *The Society of Malawi Journal* 58.2 (2005)

Munger, Edwin S., *President Kamuzu Banda of Malawi*, American Universities Field Staff Reports, 1960

Mwase, George Simeon, *Strike a Blow and Die* (ed.) Robert I. Rotberg, (Cambridge: Harvard University Press, 1968)

Oliver, Roland, *The Missionary Factor in East Africa* (London: Longmans, 1952)

Pachai, Bridglal, *The Early History of Malawi* (London: Longman, 1972)

Pachai, Bridglal, *Malawi: The History of the Nation* (London, 1973)

Phiri, D.D., *James Frederick Sangala* (Lilongwe: Longman, 1971).

Ross, Andrew, 'A Return to Malawi', in *Edinburgh University History Graduates' Association Newsletter* (30), October 1998, 12-20

Ross, Andrew, *Blantyre Mission and the Making of Modern Malawi*, (Blantyre, CLAIM-Kachere, 1996)

Ross, Andrew, *David Livingstone: Mission and Empire* (London: Hambledon and London, 2002)

Ross, Andrew, 'Scotland and Malawi, 1859-1964' in S.J. Brown and G. Newlands (eds.) *Scottish Christianity in the Modern World* (Edinburgh: T&T Clark, 2000), 292-94

Ross, Andrew, "Some Reflections on the Malawi Cabinet Crisis' 1964-65," *Religion in Malawi*, 8 (1997), 3-12

Rotberg, Robert I., *The Rise of Nationalism in Central Africa* (Cambridge, Mass.: Harvard University Press, 1965)

Sampson, Anthony. *Macmillan: a Study in Ambiguity* (London: Penguin, 1967)

Sanger, Clyde. *Central African Emergency* (London: Heinemann, 1960)

Shepherd, R. H.W., *Lovedale South Africa 1841-1941* (Lovedale: Lovedale Press, n.d. [1941])

Shepperson, George and Thomas Price. *Independent African* (Edinburgh: EUP, 1958)

Short, Philip, *Banda* (London: Routledge & Kegan Paul, 1974)

Stokes, E. and G. Brown (eds.), *The Zambezian Past: Studies in Central African History.* (Manchester: The University Press, 1965)

Taylor, Don, *The Rhodesian: the Life of Sir Roy Welensky* (London: Museum Press, 1955)

Thompson, T. Jack, *Touching the Heart: Xhosa Missionaries to Malawi 1876-1888,* (Pretoria: University of South Africa Press, 2000)

Watkins, Mark Hanna, *A Grammar of Chichewa: a Bantu Language of British Central Africa* (Philadelphia: Philadelphia Linguistic Society of America, 1937)

Welensky, Roy, *Welensky's 4,000 Days: The Life and Death of the Federation of Rhodesia and Nyasaland* (London: Collins, 1964)

Williams, T. David, *Malawi: The Politics of Despair* (Ithaca: Cornell University Press, 1978)

Wills, A.J., *An Introduction to the History of Central Africa* (London: OUP, 1967)

Wood, J.R.T., *The Welensky Papers: A History of the Federation of Rhodesia and Nyasaland* (Durban, 1983)

Young, Thomas Cullen, H. K. Banda et al. (eds), *Our African Way of Life* (London: United Society for Christian Literature, 1946)

Theses and Unpublished Sources

Kavaloh, B.M., 'Joseph Booth; an evaluation of his life and thought and their influence on religion and politics in British Central Africa (Malawi) and in South Africa' (PhD thesis, University of Edinburgh, 1991)

Leys, Colin. 'The Making of the Federation', Conference paper delivered at Rhodes House, Oxford, 17 April, 1959

Tangri, Roger Keith. 'The development of modern African politics and the emergence of a nationalist movement in colonial Malawi, 1891-1958' (PhD University of Edinburgh, 1970

Index

A

Aberdeen 15, 192
Accra 130, 132, 138, 166f
Acland, Sir Richard 71
Africa Bureau 73
African Affairs Board 61, 85f, 100, 137
African American Christianity 25
African Delegations 60f, 104
African Interests 43, 46, 49, 53, 65, 70,
    85f, 137, 232
African Lakes Company of Glasgow 14,
    123
African Linguistics 117
African Methodist Episcopal Church 116
African National Congress 33
African Nationalism 62, 144, 183
African Opinion 30, 40, 43, 67, 70, 72,
    86, 183
Africanus 31
Aggrey Memorial College 93f
Aggrey, Dr James Kwegyir 116f
Agricultural Rule 163
Agriculture, Ministry of 103
Ajawa 24
Alliance High School 89
Amandebele 19, 93, 167, 246
Amang'anja 21
Amazulu 13
Amery, Julian 180
Anglican Missions 28, 32
Annual Conference of Congress 84, 95,
    108, 233
Annual Report on Nyasaland (Colonial
    Office)
Apartheid 62, 116, 183
Apocalyptic Christian Movement 25
Armitage, Sir Robert 82, 106-108, 139,
    143, 149, 167, 169f, 175, 179, 190,
    192, 234
Ashanti Kingdom 131
Asian 35, 87, 104, 161, 172f, 175, 179f
Asikari 24, 45

B

Astor, David 199, 204
Attlee, Clement 71
Attorney General (Malawi) 111

B

Baillie, Very Rev Dr John 70
Baker, Colin 18, 50, 61, 80, 82, 87, 109,
    153f, 158, 162, 167-169, 171, 175,
    177, 185-190, 224, 236
Balfour, Lord of Burleigh 15
Ballinger, Margaret 45
Banda, Aleke 195ff, 206, 217
Banda, Dr H. Kamuzu 10, 12, 31, 38, 42,
    48, 54, 62ff, 66f, 70, 77f, 81, 85f, 89f,
    97f, 103, 105f, 109-142, 147-177,
    180, 188, 191, 200-238
Banda, Sam 207
Banda, T.D.T. 97f, 104-106, 108, 133-
    135, 158f, 233
Bandawe 22, 231
Bandawe, Lewis 30, 236
Baptists 25, 27, 119
Barnes, Correll 190
Barotseland 36
Baxter, C.R. 59
Baxter, G.H. (Commonwealth Relations
    Office) 55
Beira 24, 220
Belgian Congo 36, 216
Bismarck, Joseph 19, 22, 28
Blantyre 21, 23, 27, 31, 39f, 40, 43, 54,
    64, 68, 73, 78f, 85, 93, 98, 148, 150,
    152, 156f, 161-165, 172, 174, 182,
    194, 207, 221, 223, 233
Blantyre Church 30
Blantyre Clock Tower 106-108, 170, 234
Blantyre Conference 73, 159
Blantyre Market 93, 234
Blantyre Mission 6, 11, 14, 16-1823, 26,
    29, 32, 43, 46, 118, 120, 134, 137,
    195, 231, 237
Blantyre Mission Council 40, 85
Blantyre Native Association
Blantyre Presbytery 29f, 40, 43

247